A Closer Look At Catholicism

A Guide For Protestants

A Closer Look At Catholicism

Bob Moran, CSP

WORD BOOKS
PUBLISHER
WACO, TEXAS

A DIVISION OF
WORD, INCORPORATED

A CLOSER LOOK AT CATHOLICISM:
A Guide for Protestants

Copyright © 1986 by Bob Moran. All rights reserved.
No portion of this book may be reproduced in any form, except for brief quotations in reviews, without written permission from the publisher.

The views and beliefs expressed by the author in this book are not necessarily those of the publisher.

Scripture texts used in this work are taken from the *New American Bible*, copyright © 1970, by the Confraternity of Christian Doctrine, Washington, D.C., and are used by permission of copyright owner. All rights reserved.

Library of Congress Cataloging in Publication Data:

Moran, Bob, 1931–
A closer look at Catholicism.

1. Catholic Church—Apologetic works. 2. Moran, Bob, 1931– . I. Title.
BX1752.M67 1986 230′.2 86–7833
ISBN 0–8499–0514–1

67898 BKC 987654321

Printed in the United States of America

Dedicated to a host of men and women, starting with my parents, through the Sisters of St. Joseph, the Jesuit Fathers, the Sisters of St. Dominic, the Paulist Fathers, and many others who handed on to me what I consider the faith once delivered to the saints.

ACKNOWLEDGEMENTS

This book was made possible by the assistance of many. I wish to thank:

The Missionary Society of St. Paul the Apostle, known popularly as the Paulist Fathers, who provided me with a sabbatical year in which I could explore evangelical Protestantism.

The Institute for the Study of American Evangelicals, which invited me to participate in its first major conference, "Evangelical Christianity and Modern America, 1930–1980," organized by Dr. Mark Noll, Dr. Nathan Hatch, and Joel Carpenter of the Billy Graham Center in Wheaton, Illinois.

The president, faculty, staff, and students of Wheaton College in Wheaton, Illinois, for their warm welcome, friendship, and help during my sabbatical year with them.

Dr. Robert Webber of Wheaton College, the first enthusiast for this book, Mr. Floyd Thatcher of Word, Inc., a helpful sideline coach, and Sheri Livingston of Word, Inc., a most careful editor.

CONTENTS

1

A Closer Look at

A PERSONAL JOURNEY

As I entered the white frame church at street level, I mounted steps with the other wedding guests to a second-floor sanctuary. We found our seats among the rows of wooden pews stretching the length of the church. At the front, a long platform supported a miniscule communion table was overshadowed by a huge lectern. Afternoon sunshine warmed us through milk glass windows as we listened to a Protestant pastor lead the radiant young couple through Scripture readings, prayers, and exchange of vows. The bride's brother, also a minister, then pronounced a blessing on the newlyweds. I was a friend of the groom and I should have felt joy for him, but instead I kept experiencing deep pangs of sadness.

The organ sounded the last notes of the postlude, and I followed other wedding guests down the stairs from the sanctuary to a first floor hall where the reception was beginning. Good wishes, pleasant chatting, and friendly conversation filled the air as two sets of families and friends deepened their acquaintances. Feeling ill at ease, I sipped fruit punch and waited for two key events: a chance to congratulate the couple, and satisfaction of my sweet tooth with wedding cake. From the solemn, seemingly didactic ceremony upstairs we had moved to what appeared to be an equally sober celebration downstairs. Discomfort continued to nibble at the edges of my self-possession.

Standing away from the small groups of guests, I had a chance to think about the reasons for my being there. The young groom had been raised a Catholic and had attended campus masses over which I presided. But in his first years of college he had become interested in an evangelical Protestant group on campus. One of the leaders of that group had helped this radiant groom accept Christ. And it wasn't long afterward that he stopped attending Catholic services. He had, in effect, ceased to be a Catholic. And while browsing through a nearby Good News Bookstore one day, he met the love of his life. He and I had many conversations and remained friends, so when the time came for the wedding, he sent me an invitation. The former bookstore saleslady was the young woman in the white veil, now being hugged by her father at the reception.

Fingering my glass of fruit punch, I took a quick look across the reception hall at the groom's parents. The Shanahans were from eastern Massachusetts, Irish-American, and culturally Catholic. Their Irish ancestry was evident in the face of each member of the large family. And so it was that Father Moran and the Shanahans were sipping non-alcoholic beverages in a Protestant church hall on the occasion of their son Terry's wedding.

As far as I could judge, the Shanahans were smiling and chatting like everyone else. But I wondered how they really felt. Wouldn't they have been more at ease if we were in St. Lawrence's parish hall, drinking something a little more potent, eating a huge meal, and enjoying the band?

Terry, my former parishioner, was resplendent in his groom's attire, his boyish face a little flushed, every hair in place. He moved through the room greeting friends, smiling broadly. I really was happy for him, but another part of me felt a keen sense of loss. I, a Catholic chaplain at a prominent university, had "lost" a member of the flock. A Protestant group had raided my sheepfold, inducing a change by preaching what seemed to me to be a weaker form of Christianity. Yet I had to ask myself, "Which is better, that Terry be a 'nominal Catholic' or a vigorous, fully committed Protestant?" His new conviction was perhaps better than the previous "culture Catholicism."

My chance to congratulate the couple and share in the cake came in due course. When the reception broke up, I drove back to the university campus with some of Terry's fraternity buddies. One of them asked me how I felt about the wedding, but I didn't know how to express my sense of loss. I did what I do better. I gave a short lecture about Protestant-Catholic theological differences which he had just experienced, particularly as evidenced in the architecture of the church which Terry and his bride had chosen for the wedding.

Neither Terry nor these young men had had my experience of Catholicism. They were bright young collegians, evangelical Protestants. They had embraced what I felt was too naïve a form of Christianity, a kind of simple catechism. In my thinking, they had leapfrogged ancient debates about the formation of Scripture and its authority, the history of the Church, and alternate views of grace, works, and salvation.

On the other hand, I viewed Catholicism as a richly appointed banquet with lots of courses and plenty of substantial food. To me, the Christianity which had appealed so powerfully to Terry and his earnest fraternity friends seemed like a quick lunch at a drive-in. It nourished at a basic level for a while, but appeared to lack depth, breadth, and an awareness of history. Was I a *snob?* Perhaps, but for you to understand my view, let me explain more about my own history and faith.

Unlike the groom, I had never encountered an alternate view of either religion or Christianity which could hold a candle to Catholicism. Mom and Dad were believers, regular churchgoers, but not intensely so. Baptized as an infant, I was later enrolled in a parochial elementary school where I received instruction for First Confession and First Holy Communion. Confirmation as a "soldier of Christ" came later.

I was prepared for each of these sacraments, excepting baptism, by nuns of two different religious orders. These devout women were at the time the backbone of American Catholic education, health care, orphanages, and homes for the elderly. While they all wore those somewhat forbidding habits—long black dresses, heads confined by stiff white frames—they were as varied as they could be.

Sister Sigismund, short and as stern as her name, had a reputation for discipline. When sixth graders complained of her rulings, she would stand firm and repeat her motto, "No Cross, No Crown!" By contrast, Sister Virginetta was a pushover. Tall and thin with glasses perched on her nose, she presided over the fifth grade. Once after she had corrected my behavior, I replied with a smart-aleck answer. This, to my utter astonishment, reduced her to tears.

Varied in temperament and ability, these were valiant women who supervised our advance in knowledge, both spiritual and temporal. Class began as we stood at our desks, hand over the heart, to recite the Pledge of Allegiance to the flag. Next came the prayer "Morning Offering," a dedication of our whole day to God. These women taught us to multiply and divide, to spell and write. They monitored the lunch room to prevent food fights and told us about the exploits of saints and missionaries who had given their lives for Christ. They helped us memorize catechism responses, a summary of Christian principles and teachings that we learned in the form of questions and answers in preparation for our initiation into the Church.

Monsignor Farrell, our somewhat distant yet benevolent pastor, showed up in classrooms from time to time wearing his cassock and monsignorial trimmings. While he had the formal responsibility for passing on the faith, it was the nuns who bore the burden of catechism teaching and character training. They were the ones who led us from the school in orderly lines to the church where we confessed our sins on a monthly basis, "whether we needed it or not." We were also expected to appear every Sunday at St. Jerome's, the parish church, for the children's mass. There the nuns led us to assigned front benches. Under their watchful eyes we learned to make a precise "sign of the cross" and fully reverent genuflections in the presence of the Lord, bending our right knee at certain times in the service or at certain places inside the church. This body language was to show our reverence to the Lord and his house. If we were too giggly, combative, or talkative in church, we would feel their firm pinch or warning touch.

With them my schoolmates and I watched the unfolding of the rich array of the Church's liturgical year. Quarterly fast days punctuated the cycle of Advent Expectancy, Christmas brilliance around the Crib, Epiphany's Kings, January doldrums, and then Lenten hangings and ashes. From the nuns we learned that St. Jerome translated our Catholic Bible and was a saint despite the fact that he had a terrible temper all his life. From them we found out why we didn't eat meat or meat gravies on Fridays and what Lenten "mortification" was.

Lent is an ancient Christian season of extra devotion to penitence, fasting, giving to charity, and prayer. It consists of the forty days between Ash Wednesday and Holy Thursday just before Easter. The sisters conducted us once a week during school hours to the church for special Lenten services. Delighted to be out of the classroom, we went in our orderly lines to pews at the rear of the church to observe the Stations of the Cross. Since we couldn't walk the actual Via Dolorosa of Jerusalem in person, we walked it vicariously in our parish church. Preceded by a cross-bearer and flanked by acolytes, the priest prayed and reflected at each of the fourteen Stations on Jesus' road to death. As the priest moved around the church to each of the Stations, we could see projected on a screen at the front of the sanctuary a colored slide portraying Jesus at each stage of his walk to Calvary. Youthful piety was focused on the images of Jesus, the crowds, cruel soldiers, his mournful mother, and the cross.

By the time Easter came, we were ready to return, not to our youthful sins, but to the pleasures we had temporarily abandoned—ice cream, coconut bars, or movies. At church there was rich music, clouds of incense, colorful vestments, banks of lilies, and St. Jerome's parish choir putting forth its best. When Chicago's spring weather cooperated with sunshine and daffodils, no one in his right mind could doubt that Jesus had risen to new life.

Mom and Dad, by entrusting my education to Catholic schools, were freed of the responsibility of being the formal teachers of my faith. Still their example, our family observance of Christian fasts and feasts, and evening prayer before dinner reinforced the texture of Christianity. For the head and heart there were inspirational Bible stories—the heroism of David, the courage of Judith, the wisdom of Solomon. In short, I grew up with quite a rich religious environment.

Memorized catechism responses were only the skeleton of our belief. St. Jerome's gilded pictures, pealing organ, and hard marble meeting our knees gave flesh to our convictions. After each communion worthily received or each confession honestly made in the darkened box, I felt the closeness and love of God. Patron saints were in the stands of heaven cheering us on, and guardian angels kept us out of traffic accidents on the way to school.

After I graduated from elementary grades, my parents sent me to a Catholic high school—Chicago's Loyola Academy. During my freshman year I already began to feel the pressure of the adult world. Some of us whose parents wanted us to pursue a higher education enrolled in the "collegiate track" while others took more practical courses. Whichever route one chose, black-robed Jesuit priests and brothers patrolled the school, looking out for discipline and academic excellence.

Some of the Jesuits were witty, some of them were stern, but they all believed as deeply in the value of memorization as they believed in Jesus. Our parochial school nuns had drilled us in arithmetic, spelling, and catechism questions and answers. But the Jesuits drove us to greater heights in the mastery of Latin case endings and Greek verbs.

Parochial school catechism classes gave way to "religion courses," and the Jesuits led us in daily prayer. They linked silence during study periods with God's will and directed my mind to the intellectual aspects of Christianity. From them I learned how to give a reasoned defense of my faith, and handle such questions as, "Was the world created by chance?" or "Did the Gospel writers harmonize their stories just enough to fool the world about Jesus, but not enough to cover the differences in the Gospels?"

Growing up in a Catholic subculture provided me with little contact with Protestants. What contact I did have, though, was both good and misleading. Our summer neighbors on a Wisconsin lake were devout Lutherans of the Missouri Synod. My two sisters and I knew they were different, but our main concern was having fun with their children. Swimming, fishing, berry picking, and wiener roasts kept us united. On Sundays we went our separate ways to country churches, and we knew that later in the day our neighbors' radio would be unerringly tuned to the "Lutheran Hour," where Rev. Walter Maier's message supplemented the morning church service.

When we children visited their cottage next door to ours, we drank fruit juice because cola drinks were not permitted. When their children came to our cottage, we served the forbidden soda pop, played cards (not for money), and listened to records on our hand-wound Victrola. We had the feeling that we Catholics were slightly decadent compared to Lutherans. It was only years later that I learned that not all Lutherans were opposed to cola drinks or social dancing. We maintained neighborly friendships over the years, and ecumenism consisted in careful avoidance of religious or political discussions. They were staunchly Republican and we were just as staunchly Democrats of the New Deal persuasion.

After high school graduation, despite objections from nuns who felt that atheist professors would overturn my faith, I went to a secular university. At the end of my freshman year, in the summer of 1950, the Korean War erupted. With my father's encouragement, I continued with my summer studies in Europe, an expedition which was led by my French professor from the university. His own lack of faith never dimmed the light he threw on cathedrals, the chateaux of the Loire, or the grandeur of Avignon.

I was the only practicing Catholic in the group and, during the week of free travel allowed, I joined thousands of Catholics heading for Rome. Pope Pius XII had designated 1950 as a Holy Year, a season of prayer and pilgrimage to Rome's four major basilicas. There were many tourists and pilgrims in the city, but I was able to procure a front-row spot one day in St. Peter's Basilica just prior to a general audience with the pope. From my vantage point I could admire St. Peter's stunning beauty, mosaics, vast spaces, and shafts of sunlight.

With thousands of others elbowing for position around the Bernini columns at the front of St. Peter's, I watched Pius XII borne in on the *Sede Gestatoria*, his ceremonial chair. Waves of fervent emotion and greetings arose from the jammed aisles. Thin, solemn, soberly hospitable, the pope pronounced blessings and welcome in many languages and was rewarded by cheers and applause from the groups represented there. I wondered why I felt so little emotion. Was I too Americanized, with less ethnic passion than the others? He seemed to be just another man with a great administrative burden, and I felt no personal pull or devotion.

When Pope John Paul II visited Boston thirty years later, I was once more in a crowd of people—priests and nuns, mainly—who had gathered in Boston's Cathedral to greet a pontiff. As the pope entered the Cathedral, the audience rose en masse to applaud and, as at St. Peter's, I felt more curiosity than excitement. Once again I felt oddly out of place amidst the enthusiastic priests and nuns around me. He was new in his pontificate and I was not ready to applaud him until I saw how he would govern the Church.

At the end of my summer holiday, I returned to college and hit the usual sophomore slough of indecision. What should be my major? How should I direct my life? As I pondered, the months passed, and the Korean War dragged on. We held several family conferences, and I decided that I should follow my father's advice to enlist in the Air Force. I was, in effect, buying time—trying to "get my head together."

Air Force travel broke open my world scheme even more than that summer in Europe did. While in the service, I had my first experience of living with American blacks. Predictably, my friendships and contacts were both positive and negative. Whenever it was possible, I attended church services at the Air Force chapels or in local Catholic parishes. But I was away from home, a lonely, confused soldier tossed in among many different types of young men. My emotions, particularly while I was overseas, were on long and scary roller coaster rides. Thankfully I had some good Air Force buddies who provided fellowship and encouragement during the rough periods. Although I remained confused about my life goal, a glimmer of light was beginning to appear.

While stationed in Morocco, I had a chance to listen to overseas radio broadcasts and to read foreign newspapers. I saw for the first time how differently Europeans looked at the United States and its policies. This led me to plan for a career in diplomatic service. When my four year Air Force enlistment ended, I enrolled at the Georgetown School of Foreign Service in Washington, D.C. By September of 1955 I was once again in school under the tutelage of the Jesuits.

Along with stimulating classes in international law, economics, and history, I benefited greatly from the wise counsel of Father Ed Farren, my Jesuit spiritual director. An energetic, hard-working man of deep faith, Father Farren encouraged me in habits of regular meditation and what is now called "involvement."

In those days it meant joining a team of college students teaching catechism on Saturday mornings. Trying to explain notions like "grace" or "Holy Spirit" to the rural rebels of Waldorf, Maryland, made me more appreciative than ever of the nuns who had taught me. However by mid-semester I felt that my unruly students in that parish had beaten me. I pleaded with the nun in charge to let me do something else.

She told me to hold fast, reviewed some basic skills of teaching, and replenished my supply of gold stars. These stars decorated the attendance and deportment charts displayed prominently in the classroom. Rewarding the docile and motivating the sinful, I survived the second semester. The children were rural poor, and I was deeply touched at the end of the term when one of them brought me a little bouquet of wildflowers. Somehow we had all survived and learned.

Georgetown schooling continued with courses in Russian History and Constitutional Law. As my second year unfolded, my appetite for diplomatic service waned. There were rumors that the State Department rarely gave good jobs to Catholics and the best posts in any case went to businessmen who supported the incumbent president. I was haunted by visions of being a lifelong clerk stamping passports in some dusty provincial backwater.

These disturbing thoughts led to disenchantment and raised once more the question of my life direction and goals. Stern Sister Sigismund of St. Jerome's sixth grade had once suggested aloud in front of others that I would make a fine priest, and I had bristled with indignation. On and off in my travels and studies, during moments of both action and quiet, the idea of priesthood returned. Thanks to Father Farren's spiritual direction, I was beginning to make some tiny steps in greater spiritual maturity, and since every other career gambit I had tried had disappointed me, I came to the conclusion that I should "test" my vocation.

If this move toward priesthood were also an error, I would be able to lay the haunting idea to rest once and for all. If it were not an error, my "life direction" problem would be at an end. But once having decided to test the idea, a new problem arose. Should I be a diocesan priest, working mainly in one geographical area? Should I join a religious order, probably working in different places and living in a group? If I were to join a religious order, which one should I choose? Did I want to be monkish like the Trappists?

Having observed parish priests in varying places over the years, I did not think their lifestyle would be for me. Some of them seemed quite under the thumb of their pastors or bishops, and others seemed to live lonely lives in isolated spots. I thought I would prefer a religious order committed to communal living and a shared missionary goal. I began to write for literature and set up interviews with various members of these religious orders.

While in the Air Force I had attended special services held one week in Chanute Field, Rantoul, Illinois. These had been conducted by two priests who presented Catholic faith in a dialogue form from twin pulpits in the base chapel. These priests, Paulist Fathers, had intrigued me with the novelty of their approach and left a good impression. I later met a young woman at Georgetown who had been converted to Catholicism by the Paulist Fathers; she recommended that I consider them. Their seminary was located in the Washington area, so I arranged to visit them one Sunday afternoon for dinner. I liked what I saw and heard.

Then, as now, the Paulist Fathers were a relatively small band of priests. Founded in the United States in 1858 by Isaac Hecker, a convert to Catholicism, they have tried to continue his own zeal to evangelize, to explain Catholicism to Protestants, and to renew the faith of Catholics. I liked their outward missionary thrust and their use of newer techniques in press, radio, and television. And so, in the late spring of 1957, I applied to them and was accepted.

The Paulist Fathers directed me to their novitiate program, one year of testing and orientation at Oak Ridge, New Jersey. So at the age of twenty-six, I joined seventeen other men in rural northern New Jersey where we were to spend a full year, testing our calling by living the rule of the Paulists.

In those pre-Vatican II days, candidates for religious orders were closely directed by a director or "master" of novices. By Church law and the customs of the particular religious order, this person had considerable autonomy and authority to be used for good or occasionally for ill. Our own novice master was a tall, white-haired priest, Father Frank McNab, a Canadian by birth and a veteran of Paulist work and life.

He did not claim to be a giant of the mystical life, nor did he function as a guru. Rather, he oversaw our observance of a "rule," a daily round of tightly-woven activities which included prayer, Bible reading, devotional talks, and a study of Paulist history and Constitution. There was a daily Eucharist, our sacrament of the Lord's Supper commemorating Christ's sacrifice on the cross, as well as regular manual labor and obligatory periods of recreation. We stayed within the confines of the novitiate grounds, and could not leave the grounds without permission. During most of the day we were to observe a rule of silence, and we learned to do without newspapers, radios, television, films, visits to shopping malls or local restaurants, unless accompanied by visiting parents. Visitors were not in any case encouraged.

The purpose of this geographical and psychic isolation was to channel our emotional and spiritual lives toward Christ and our brothers in the novitiate. We prayed together, worked together, ate together, and played softball together. Little by little, we became more like brothers than strangers.

One day a week, with the novice master's blessing, we were ejected from our close little pod for a day-long hike through the neighboring backroads. We packed lunches and carried jugs of coffee and cocoa on these expeditions to local lakes or wooded picnic sites. Since none of us had any pocket money, as the Paulist rule required, we could not dally at drugstores, bars, or movies.

Our solitude, interrupted by our weekly excursions, was also lightened by the monthly "day of retreat." While we were to observe even more silence on this day, it was welcome because it brought a visiting Paulist priest to give us devotional talks—sometimes a very serious speaker, at other times a comedian cleric. After weeks of confinement with our small, isolated group, we were delighted with any new face!

As the year passed, a group which had numbered eighteen at the onset began to dwindle. The sixteen of us who decided to remain continued to wrestle with our calling. As we worked, hiked, and studied, we learned to enjoy each other's company. Routine and the challenge of common life did more winnowing than the novice master's decision to ask someone to leave. Pains, laughter, and trials were interwoven with regular worship in our small chapel. Perhaps because of our isolation, or possibly because of God's graciousness, liturgical seasons brought new depth to our lives.

With fewer distraction than typical college students or working people, our daily prayers of praise were enriched by the unforgettably beautiful foliage of that New Jersey autumn and the dazzling moonlight on winter snow marked by a hare's footprints. Monotonous winter gray fitted well with Lenten fasting, and the rites of Holy Week came alive, fervent and faith-filled, as the spring's warmth unfroze both the nearby lake and some corners of the heart.

Of course, all our communal worship—from pre-dawn meditation, through mid-day examination of conscience, to night prayers before going to bed at ten o'clock—was conducted in Latin. Prayers before and after meals were also in Latin. In private prayer, I used a well-worn Latin breviary which I had found, probably discarded by someone. The breviary is by and large the Church's arrangement of one hundred and fifty psalms, to be sung or recited at various hours of the day and on specific days of the week. I learned that year to appreciate the strong-rhythmed moods of the psalms. They showed me that neither great despair nor great joy was unfit for prayer, and they helped me be myself before the Lord.

A year and a day after coming to the novitiate, the time prescribed by Church law, we who had survived received with considerable pride the Paulist habit, our religious clothing. It was a floor-length, black wrap-around gown, closed at the top by a high collar lined with a white linen cloth and at the waist by a black sash. A mark of belonging to a distinctive Catholic sub-group, it was also the customary indoor cover-all garment for the next phase of our training—six years of philosophical and theological study. As we tried on our habits, buttoning them across the shoulder, adjusting the cincture, we were excited by our future. I felt that I had grown spiritually, and that for the moment I was on the right path.

In the fall of 1958 I found myself once more in Washington, D.C.—not at Georgetown, but at the Paulist House of Studies. I was no longer the footloose college student; I was a clad-in-black seminarian at the Paulist-administered school of theology, St. Paul's

College, located a short distance from Catholic University in the northeastern sector of Washington, D.C. It was a neighborhood where many religious orders had study centers for their members, and the presence of so many seminarians in religious garb caused local residents to call it "Little Rome."

Our seminary schedule, while a continuation of the novitiate regime, did introduce us to a wider brotherhood—the upperclassmen and faculty members.

The daily rule of seminary life included visits to the chapel, Bible and devotional readings, a Eucharist, and regular prayer times (the latter in Latin). Professors challenged our minds as they tried to guide us through the riches of Thomistic philosophy, theology, Bible criticism, Church history, patristics, moral theology, Church law, homiletics, and convert-making.

Friendships and understandings which had been shaped by the common novitiate experience now had to be enlarged. Here, as in the novitiate, there was great stress on the collective or communal side of life. We arose at an early hour, shaken by the knock on the door and the Latin cry, "*Benedicamus Domino*"—Let us bless the Lord. Tradition required the sleepy seminarian to shout back, "*Deo Gratias!*"—Thanks be to God! We were to appear together, dressed in our religious habits, at scheduled times for prayer, studies, meals, and brief recreation periods. Obviously, dating girls was forbidden, as were smoking and the use of alcohol. Silence was to prevail from bedtime at ten o'clock each evening until the morning call to bless the Lord. During our weekly free times, we explored Washington's parks, museums, and historic sites. Because of our promise of poverty, we had—at least temporarily—given up the right to have our own money. Thus, any free place of interest in the city drew us.

This system, now much more relaxed, had its strengths and its weaknesses. We were led to appreciate regular devotion, exercise, and study. We learned, if not to like, to deal with silence. Here too, as in the novitiate, with the priests leading us, we enjoyed the full array of Catholic worship.

Pre-dawn darkness shadowed our efforts to meditate in the seminary chapel. On great feast days we celebrated God's love with a full display of vestments (the ecclesiastical garments used by clergy, acolytes, choir members, etc.), candles, incense, and Gregorian chants provided by the choir and congregation. Through a repetition of rites and the shifts of the liturgical year, we learned the value of rhythms of feast and fast, silence and song.

Academic work stimulated my mind, but life presented me with its share of pains and joys. Despite frequent confusion about my suitability for this life, despite customary feelings that marriage and a family would be more attractive, I continued year after year to move toward ordination. The novitiate had been the first rough filtering of the eighteen who had been accepted. The six year seminary stay—study, work, prayer, and recreation under the watchful eyes of the seminary faculty—was a second filtering device.

Each of us was expected to have a spiritual director, and as I had been fortunate to have Father Farren at Georgetown, so I was blessed to have a good Paulist director in Washington, D.C. Somewhat small in stature, thin, sickly at times, Father Ben Hunt was a Texan who taught philosophy and spirituality. He believed in teaching by the Socratic method, posing questions and guiding through one's response. He had a razor-sharp mind and a very kind heart.

It was our custom to report to our spiritual directors at least once a month, and depending on the confidence one had in his advisor, we would speak of our boredom, frustrations, sins, temptations, or anxieties of whatever kind. Although St. Paul's College was far less confining than the Oak Ridge Novitiate, we lived in a tight little island where personal relationships could both enrich and complicate close living.

Every spring, as the academic year drew to a close, the seminary rector and faculty members huddled in lengthy meetings to evaluate the seminarians under their direction. One of our local cynics called this the time of the "May Games." As these priests met and deliberated on our fate, we seminarians bit our nails, passed rumors, prayed, and tried to calm our nerves, hoping that we would not be ejected against our will. At the end of these annual deliberations, some of the graduating class went forward to ordination and some of the others were asked to leave. When decisions were made involving the departure of friends, there was sadness. Survivors rejoiced.

At the end of six years in St. Paul's College, I had not been asked to leave. I had in fact been encouraged to remain. I was not like one of my classmates who had known from a very early age that he wanted to be a priest. I did not know with great clarity what kind of priest I would be or what kind of work God would have me do as a priest. It seemed as though I was always following faint trails with bad lighting while some of my companions seemed to be far more confident, far more clear.

I envied them their certainty and wondered about my own conviction as we boarded a train one spring morning, bound for ordination to priesthood. I was acutely aware that I was still free to leave the Paulists and my commitment to ordination. Giving up the chance to be a parent had been weighing on me, and shortly before our train trip to the rendezvous with the bishop, I had had a dream in which the imagery spoke of death to a son. Patches of Delaware and New Jersey flashed by the train windows while I turned all this over in my mind. Until the precise moment in the ordination ritual when the bishop asks each man to come forward, I was free to back away. I stepped forward on May 11, 1964 in the Church of St. Paul the Apostle in New York City.

The ordaining bishop was New York's archbishop, Cardinal Francis Spellman, a soft-spoken, diminutive man who wielded large authority in the United States Catholic Church. After he had laid ordaining hands on me, relatives and friends gathered around to receive my first priestly blessing and to be photographed. And then we new priests emerged into New York's May sunshine. Soon thereafter, my Paulist superior handed me an envelope containing a letter of assignment. I was to spend that summer at a small Catholic parish under Paulist care in Layton, Utah.

After a short post-ordination vacation and visit with my family, I flew west to Salt Lake City. There, with people far from integrated into Mormon society, I tried my hand at a variety of priestly duties. I heard confessions, preached, visited the sick, instructed young people in the faith, conducted a door-to-door census, and anointed the dying. By summer's end I had learned to love and respect the parishioners, many of whom were impoverished Mexican-Americans employed in local agricultural work.

At the end of the summer, I was sent to Toronto, Canada, where Paulists were responsible for a parish and an information center. Hundreds of people came to this center every year to get a new understanding of Catholicism; many came seeking baptism or admission to the Catholic Church. This was exactly the kind of work which had initially drawn me to the Paulists. In the next two years I was challenged to prepare clear, cogent, and non-academic instructions to the adults in the classes held at the center.

My work in the autumn of 1964 had a special character because the Catholic Church was undergoing the greatest and most thorough reform since the time of Martin Luther and John Calvin. Catholic bishops from all over the world were preparing for another session of the Second Vatican Council.

Our professors in the seminary had kept us up to date on reform within the church through their lectures. Second Vatican Council proceedings had been deeply influenced by theological, biblical, historical, and patristic research published in scholarly reviews. Our professors had encouraged us to read the newer thinkers such as the reknowned Karl Rahner, the sprightly controversialist Hans Kung, F. X. Durrwell, and others. Even before ordination we seminarians had participated in a modest ecumenical dialogue with seminary counterparts from Gettysburg Lutheran Seminary and from an Episcopalian seminary just outside of Washington, D.C.

I found these new writings, initiatives, and debates to be very positive. I felt that Catholicism was shaking off layers of dust, a hardened crust that had formed over the centuries of controversy with Protestants. A fresh reading of our own history gave us vital orientations for the future. It was exciting to try to convey all this to the men and women who sat before me in the Toronto classroom. However my superiors had other plans for me; a long stay in Toronto was not my fate.

The Second Vatican Council's very stress on our being open to contemporary science, both natural and social, led the Paulist Fathers to invite me to do advanced studies in sociology. In the fall of 1966 I reported to the Paulist University Chaplaincy at Ohio State University, where I had been accepted as a master's degree candidate. While I continued to take a turn preaching, leading worship, and hearing confessions, my main task was study. By the summer of 1968 I had earned my master's degree and was accepted for a doctoral program at the University of California at Santa Barbara.

It was a great blessing that at both of these fine universities I encountered excellent professors of sociology, men who were enthused about its worth and yet realistic about its limits. America was aflame in those years with deep social conflicts over racism, the war in Vietnam, and university reform. Like many other graduate students under pressure, I paid inadequate attention to God during this time. My seminary discipline of prayer and meditation, Scripture reading, and devotions eroded badly. Although I continued to perform my regular priestly duties, my main focus was on studying to obtain the doctorate degree.

By late autumn of 1972 I was in Washington, D.C., for the third time, not as a seminarian but as a faculty member. Sociology of Religion texts and journals filled my bookshelves. I set out to offer courses designed to show how sociological principles could throw light on religious behavior and on churches as organizations. I don't know whether it was the new mood of seminaries or my defects as a teacher, but registration for my courses was miniscule. Sociology of Religion was an elective, and the new breed of seminarians were hard at work accumulating credits in the required courses of theology and Scripture.

When our seminary administration decided that it could no longer maintain St. Paul's as an independent, degree-granting institution, we ceased to exist as a college and our seminarians went elsewhere. I was out of work, somewhat disappointed, and characteristically unclear about what to do. My efforts at job hunting in the nation's capital led to nothing very solid in my newly-acquired skills.

While I was still trying to discern a future as priest-sociologist, my superiors offered me the opportunity to become a university chaplain at the Massachusetts Institute of Technology in Cambridge. I began in the autumn of 1974, and it was not many years later that Terry Shanahan invited me to his wedding.

Being a chaplain at MIT was an exciting responsibility, and whatever regrets I had at leaving the field of sociology so abruptly seemed to fade before the challenges of helping these Catholic students become more mature in their faith. I was particularly sensitive to those who found a new faith or new commitment among dynamic Protestant groups on campus. For this reason, too, Terry's move away from Catholicism hit me with special force.

In the next few years I realized that, spreading out before me on the campus and apparently throughout the nation, evangelical Protestantism was growing and gaining momentum. Even though I understood at one level that not all evangelicals are the same, I felt in my bones that they presented the heart of Christian belief in too simplistic a fashion. I did not think it would adequately nourish in the long run. I was also offended and distressed by the latent, occasionally overt, anti-Catholicism sometimes exhibited by its proponents. On the other hand, evangelicalism in its broad sense had clearly touched something in the American soul. Its campus fellowship groups and Bible studies were filling a need among the undergraduates. We Catholics seemed to lack anything of similar appeal. It was time for me to begin a study of this important sector of American Protestantism.

Writing, studying, and observing as a busy chaplain was not enough and I felt the need for a change, so I asked my superiors for a sabbatical year in which to take a longer look at evangelical Protestantism. Many good things had been accomplished at MIT, but I felt drained and uncreative. The chaplaincy needed a new person and a new approach. The Holy Spirit brooded nicely with me and, I dare say, illumined the path.

Providence combined with human agents when I received an invitation from evangelical historian Nathan Hatch and from Joel Carpenter of the Billy Graham Center in Wheaton, Illinois, to attend a mid-April conference on evangelicalism. A gusty spring day in 1983 was the occasion for a new level of learning and experience. An impressive array of speakers addressed those of us who attended the conference—David Wells, Carl Henry, Richard Pierard, Mark Noll, and others. I appreciated the humility and humor with which these evangelicals dissected their tradition in order to better understand it. Their analysis was not for the purpose of killing off the movement; it was done in love for the purpose of enlivening it. I liked what I heard and I liked what I saw. I enrolled in Wheaton College for my sabbatical year, September 1983 to June of 1984.

My pilgrimage to Wheaton had begun years earlier when I judged evangelicals to be wolves among my flock. Later, I saw evangelicals less as threat and more as challenge. Catholic friends, hearing that the Paulists had given me permission to spend a year at Billy Graham's alma mater, reacted as if I had been chosen for a mission to outer space. They made an immediate and simplistic connection between Billy Graham, television evangelism, and some of the media personalities they had seen whose preaching they often found either obnoxious or absurd.

I wanted to learn more fully why such immediate connections were wrong. In my own pilgrimage, I have gone from "threat" to "challenge" to "admiration" over a ten year period. The Spirit, I believe, is brooding graciously and creatively over us all.

2

A Closer Look at JESUS CHRIST

Unlike some born-again Christians who can point to a given year, month, day, and hour when they accepted Jesus as Savior, I am mute. I am unable to point to such a moment because my best image for understanding religious growth is that of an upward spiral. At each level of human development, I believe I circle around an axis—my own weaknesses and strengths and Jesus who accompanies me, offering deeper insight. Since I conceive of this spiral as tilted heavenward, I hope and trust that my grasp of the divine will continue to evolve. What I know or appreciate now about Jesus may appear shallow to me twenty years from now. And I hope that what I know now surpasses what I appreciated when I was seven or eight years old.

The age of seven or eight was important for Catholics of my generation because it was at that age that we were offered the opportunity for a most personal encounter with Jesus. If our local pastor, our parents, and the nuns who prepared us agreed, we could make our First Communion.

Since we had reached what theologians of that day called "the age of reason"—the age when it was presumed we knew some right from wrong—we were instructed for our First Confession. Then, as spiritually clean as we could be, we went to Sunday Mass and received Communion for the first time. This occasion was both solemn and joyous. To mark it, the girls wore white dresses and matching bridal veils, the boys white suits and shoes.

My memory of my own First Communion focuses, perverse child that I was, not on the solemn religious moment, but on a special treat of ice cream which we as family enjoyed afterward. More important, however, is that once launched in the piety of Sunday or weekday communion, I often enjoyed the reverent and welcome moments of intimacy with Christ. The nuns taught me that under the outward appearance of bread and wine, Jesus my Savior was present—truly body and blood, soul and divinity. I could and did talk to him freely, thanking him for my family, asking favors of him, and just enjoying the presence of this divine-human friend.

My first-grader's grasp of this mystery may have been deficient from the theologian's point of view, but it was expected that I would continue to learn and experience, moving along the upward spiral. Later in seminary I learned more, but it is not always the case that more knowledge led to holier conduct. Again and again I asked my divine friend's forgiveness through whispered confessions in the Confessional Box, and again he welcomed me to his Communion. I sense his welcome and mercy still. I will rely on it in the years ahead.

Jesus Fully Human

While our gray catechisms at school contained theologically correct questions and answers about Jesus, I feel I learned more about Jesus from the parish church than from the books. Shortly before Christmas each year, St. Jerome's janitor took the Christmas crib and huge statues out of storage. He assembled and arranged the pieces in front of the church to one side of the altar. Soft lights shone on the colorful plaster statues of Joseph, Mary, shepherds, and animals. Near December 25, the baby Jesus was placed in the small straw-lined crib. Jesus' fragility and humanity stood out in a way that the catechism book could not convey.

I also remember seeing a painting in which Jesus was depicted as a young boy. The artist had encircled his young blond head with a gold halo to remind me of his holiness, but Jesus also had a carpenter's square in his hand—a sign of his occupation, his need to work. I gained a greater appreciation of my divine friend then.

While official Catholic teaching is usually modest about things only hinted at in the New Testament, I recall popular preachers who taught me about Jesus' humanity in their imaginative reconstructions of gospel scenes. They encouraged me to believe that Jesus must have enjoyed a hearty laugh when he entered a certain town and spotted Zacchaeus, the curious and greedy tax assessor, hanging over his path on a tree branch. They also urged me to think seriously about Luke's remark that Jesus "progressed steadily in wisdom and age and grace before God and men."

Jesus' humanity is important to me because I would feel awkward or distant from him if he did not know what it meant to be a poor worker in a confusing and unjust world. I have come to appreciate very much those tantalizingly brief scriptural lightbursts when I read that he sighed or spoke with vehemence, wept, or grew angry. I am fascinated with the way he engaged people in conversation and challenged them to service, enjoying their company or sharing their pain. Never intrusive or offensively aggressive, he radiated confidence when asking for sacrifice or seeing into someone's potential.

What Christmas crèches, sentimental art, and popular preachers taught were tested by the more formal doctrinal standards of my seminary professors. As my own views deepened, some of the childishly simple notions had to be developed. I feel that as I live and experience more, as I continue to read, there is a slight but real deepening of my grasp of Jesus. Ideally, head and heart keep in step with each other.

Post-seminary experience has taught me still another dimension of Jesus' humanity—his Jewishness. Scripture tells me that Jesus and his family observed the Jewish rituals. He worshiped at the synagogue, and Mary and Joseph undoubtedly taught him to memorize and recite the words to Jewish daily prayers and told him the exciting stories of Israel's past, stories of Abraham, Moses, Noah, David, Judith, and Esther. And, as Jewish women still do, Mary probably lit a candle on the eve of Shabbas.

It was precisely Christ's Jewishness and humanity which led Catholics, in older days, to observe the feast of his circumcision on January 1. It was seen in part as his first shedding of blood for us; it was also a striking testimony to his being part of the covenant of Moses and truly Jewish. As he grew, Jesus must have learned both the wisdom of the Torah and the nation's history.

One of the apocryphal gospels tells about Jesus' boyhood through an incident in Joseph's carpenter shop. Someone working with father and son noticed that one of them had made a bad measurement. The story says that Jesus, noticing the error, did not cut a new board, but miraculously extended the length of the defective board. I like that story because it places Jesus in a human setting while maintaining that even as a boy he had divine power. My preference is to think that there were days when he went home to supper with a sore thumb, black and blue from misdirected hammer blows on crooked nails. Growth in age and wisdom should mean more manual dexterity!

Popular Catholic devotion and preaching have focused lovingly on Joseph, Mary, and Jesus under the title "Holy Family." They formed a united core, enriched no doubt by cousins, aunts, and uncles living the routine of Nazareth, a village of no great importance in a province of no great importance.

Although Joseph has only a cameo appearance in the gospel, he has fascinated generations of Catholics. His quiet obedience to divine messages protected Mary from embarrassment. He is missing in later years and we presume that he died before Mary and Jesus. As workingman, protector of a family, and obedient servant to God, his qualities recommend themselves to millions of Catholics who placed his name on their children and their cities. St. Joseph, Missouri, is a rough midpoint between Montreal's Shrine to St. Joseph and California's San Jose Mission.

I will discuss Mary's role in the Holy Family in detail in chapter 13. But for now it is helpful to remember that Jesus did not simply spring full-grown from her rib. Crying, gasping, fragile, and dependent, this child came from her womb. She who bathed him, nursed him and taught him his first steps testifies to his humanity.

We catch a brief, intriguing glimpse of the boy's growth toward independence in Luke's story of the family's pilgrimage to Jerusalem to celebrate the Passover. Jesus is studying and discussing Law with religious leaders in the temple, but his parents think he is lost among the crowds. When Mary and Joseph find him three days later, they complain about his absence, but Jesus answers with a quiet lesson—the need to be about the Father's business. Returning to Nazareth, back at their village routine, Mary and Joseph must have wondered and worried about Jesus' future.

Jesus' humanity pops out all over the Gospels. Two incidents come immediately to mind. The first is his frustration when he returns to his village to preach the Good News. His neighbors and relatives are at first delighted that they know a celebrity; their mood changes to disbelief and scorn when he tries to teach them something. Their lack of conviction defeats him. A second incident is Jesus' fear that the enthusiastic crowds will force him into being an earthly king. He runs away, wanting to avoid it. They follow, and he must explain that what they want he cannot be. Even if someone couldn't believe that Jesus is Savior, nearly everyone can grasp the attractiveness of this teacher. The human touches make him accessible.

Jesus Fully Divine

A Scripture professor I know once sent squads of undergraduates taking her classes to local Catholic parishes in the Greater Boston area. Equipped with pencils and questionnaires, students interviewed Catholic parishioners after Sunday services. One purpose of this exit poll was to discover how Catholics view Jesus. The professor told me that the results showed among Catholics an overwhelming sense of Jesus' divinity, so overwhelming in fact that his humanity seemed forgotten.

Overshadowed or not, Catholic teaching and belief about Jesus' divinity arises from practically the same sources which sustain the beliefs of evangelicals. When Donald Bloesch builds his argument for Jesus' divinity on the three pillars—Jesus' deeds, Scriptural texts, and the teaching of ancient church councils[1]—he is following the same track used by Catholics. A typical example is Bloesch's use of the prologue to the fourth Gospel as a touchstone for orthodox belief about Christ. "In the beginning was the Word," declares John, "and the Word was with God, and the Word was God."

A very able Scripture scholar who has helped me understand Jesus better is Father Ray Brown. He analyzes the importance of the titles conferred on Jesus by the early believers. I had become so accustomed to praying and addressing Jesus as "Lord" or "Christ" that I forgot that these are not names but titles, each with a significance worth considering. Many titles and phrases are found in the Old Testament referring to the promised Messiah. When these same titles are used in the New Testament, they are thrilling reminders that early followers of Jesus were applying to him pre-existent titles, seeing in him the fulfillment of Old Testament prophecies and hopes. Jewish models of saving figures were at hand, ready to be used by Christians, terms like "Servant of God" and "Son of David."

Clearly, while the titles, models, and hopes pre-existed Jesus, his own actions provided the impetus for applying the titles to him. Here Catholics, as well as other Christians, have found evidence of divinity. The raising of Lazarus and of Jairus's daughter strike me as particularly compelling. Further, when Jesus claims the power to forgive sin and is criticized for arrogance, he refuses to weaken the claim. He punctuates it by healing a paralytic on the spot.

Implicit in what I am saying is the view that there was a chronology of events which arose in God's loving purpose and which led to Jesus' birth, life, death, and resurrection. Eyewitnesses to these events, or people informed by eyewitnesses, spoke of Jesus to others; they described their experiences and told others of his teaching, his debates, and his actions.

Current Catholic scholarship, as I understand it, supports this view that the earliest evangelization, preaching, and teaching was by word of mouth. Before the Jesus story crystalized in the twenty-seven documents called New Testament, Christians told and re-told collections of stories, sayings and instructions that Jesus had given. It was at least three hundred years after Jesus' death, in the days of Emperor Constantine, that the Christian churches were able to agree on a common core of literature suitable for public reading in worship services. Prior to this time, different churches acknowledged and used for public reading different collections of these stories and sayings.

Once Jesus' identity and mission were established, the New Testament served as the sourcebook for later Christians' approach to him. Yet having a Christian sourcebook was not enough. For the churches as a group, a new spiral of debate led to a new spiral of learning. This would come through the mechanism of church councils.

Since Catholics and evangelicals buttress their ideas of Christ's humanity and divinity by referring to these early meetings of bishops, monks, theologians, and laity, it might be helpful to look at the process which gave rise to them. Catholic theologian Richard McBrien mentions three pressures which triggered the conciliar process.[2]

The first pressure for a church gathering to clarify teaching is the blessed capacity to reason—to question. The rich assortment of biblical titles given to Jesus by first-century believers already revealed what people thought about Jesus, but later generations were to reshape their views in different language, or deepen the concepts for another age. Councils served the purpose of stimulating thought, clarifying debated points and restating earlier, traditional beliefs in more contemporary language.

We get a fine insight into this process from reading the Acts of the Apostles, chapter 15. At issue was the acceptability of Gentiles as followers of Jesus, and the extent to which Gentiles following Jesus should follow Jewish law. Dissension led to debate and debate led to a meeting in Jerusalem where apostles and presbyters examined the situation. Discussion led to decisions, and decisions were seen as the combined effect of human policies and the inspiration of the Holy Spirit.

Later, church leaders followed this example and assembled in regional groupings on many occasions to help settle disputes or clarify teaching for the people. Some of the local councils were called to combat the irrationality and distortions that were infecting the church through the heresy known as Montanism. Followers of this school believed that they were a spiritual elite called to restore the church to its primitive simplicity. Already in the second century of Christianity there were men and women claiming to have new revelations which added to or overrode what the apostles themselves had taught and handed on.

The example of Montanism illustrates the second pressure to which church leaders responded by calling a council. Different Christians using the same scriptural texts arrived at different interpretations, or, claiming to be directly taught by the Holy Spirit, arrived at conclusions unheard of in earlier church circles. This variety of interpretations can be helpful, but at certain points it threatens our grasp of the truth and divides the flock. A council helps arrest this fragmentation.

There are gifted and dynamic leaders in every age ready to offer their own insights. In the early centuries of Christianity, sub-Christian speculations or mergings of various religious currents muddied Christian clarity. Dissidents launched various theological trial balloons, now stressing Jesus' divinity to the point of forgetting the humanity, now denying his divinity for the sake of saving or stressing his true humanity. History tells us of famous church councils which dealt with these complex issues. The Council of Nicea in 325, A.D., sharply rejected any teaching which made Jesus less than divine, and the First Council of Constantinople in 381, A.D., reminded the church that Jesus was, all the same, truly human.

Further debates developed regarding Jesus' personality. Since Jesus is both human and divine, was it correct to think that he had a human will and a divine will? Can it then be said that *God* died on the cross? At the Council of Ephesus in 431, A.D., Jesus was described as a coherent, single person, "true God of true God," and that as a consequence it was not wrong to say that since Mary was the mother of Jesus then she is the mother of God. I am struck by the importance of these councils. They issued carefully sculpted, thoughtfully prepared statements of the truths in question for us to follow.

Many people think that Catholics must accept the authority of the Church over the authority of Scripture. I believe that when it comes to the identity of Jesus, we Catholics cannot interpret Scripture in ways which contradict the faith of the early Church, a faith hammered into historic formulations by the councils. On this issue, we do let the Church, especially the ancient Church, have the last word.

On the other hand, Catholics must go to Scripture again and again in every age in order to be refreshed at the source of our faith and to interpret the texts about Jesus or other issues in contemporary idiom. Even the hallowed conciliar formulas can be rephrased or presented again in thought patterns and language more suited to modern times. Such a process should always bring forward the same substantial teaching or a legitimate inference from it. This leads me to mention the third pressure for assembling the church's leaders in a council.

Shortly after Jesus' death and rising, spirit-filled disciples preached the Good News far and wide. When these evangelists stepped outside the Jewish communities and synagogues, they had to develop new strategies and a new language. Scholars argue that this process of adaptation for missionary purposes shows up already in John's Gospel, especially in his use of the concept of *logos.*

When a Jewish Christian heard the phrase "word of God," the words carried a depth of meaning inherited from centuries of usage in Jewish scriptural texts. When Greeks or Romans heard that phrase, it could not give them the same depth. In fact, "word of God" or *logos* among Greeks carried a different tone or color. Among the Hebrews the "word of God" was Yahweh's own utterance, powerful and creative, a dynamic force present from the beginning. Among Greeks, "word" was divine reason ordering and upholding the universe, present everywhere in the regular movement of the stars, changes of season, and mental processes.

In short, when John chose the phrase "word of God," knowingly or unknowingly, he used words which had two different meanings, depending on context. But for either set of hearers, the effect would be a deepening of the meaning given to Jesus. Added to the Jewish monotheistic focus would be the Greek interest in an intelligent, thinking divinity.

Adaptation to a new age and new people still leads churches to assemble in prayer, study, and debate. In 1974, evangelical churches held a worldwide meeting in Lausanne, Switzerland. As Billy Graham presided over the meeting, speaker after speaker came forward to clarify, interpret, and focus the meaning of God's truth. A new generation of evangelicals felt the need to cope with new philosophical and scientific trends. Seemingly dangerous voices, or at least disturbing voices, propose "liberation theology" or the "death of God." Africans, Asians, and Latin Americans at the great Lausanne assembly pleaded for cultural adaptation so that Christian core truths can flourish apart from their Western European or North American seedbed.

Such a council, whether that of Lausanne in 1974 or the Second

Vatican Council of Rome in the early 1960s, gives me hope. Men and women of faith, anxious to fulfill the Great Commission, are praying, discussing, wrestling, and struggling to find the best way to bring the light of Christ to the contemporary world.

Jesus Who Fascinates Every Age

One of the reasons for having clear doctrinal formulations is their ability to serve as guides for later generations. Even if we didn't want to clutter our lives with new formulations, we couldn't possibly avoid it. Time passes, language shifts in meaning, cultural contexts which supported the language dissolve and new contexts appear.

In ordinary American speech there is a constant influx of new words or of old words used in newer ways. An obvious example is the word "gay." New technology and rapid communication almost force us to use words like "feedback" or "computer" or "input." Some forms of speech or hallowed phrases are astonishingly flexible—"American national interests" can mean almost whatever the speaker wants. I am reminded of a Bible translator trying to translate the phrase "giving thanks" in the language of a small tribe in the Philippines. The best approximation of the idea was a phrase in the native language having to do with a positive feeling in the liver.

It is precisely this relentless march of time and cross-cultural situations which require continuous new efforts to present Jesus. To make him understandable, we need a firm base in Scripture and in the orthodox conciliar formulas. We also need a Spirit-given ability to choose the best portrayals of Jesus which are all around us today. Novels, films, television productions, music, poetry, and even rock videos have tried to update the Savior. Even among nonbelievers, wherever the story of Jesus has appeared, there is fascination.

In his fine book, *The Challenge of Jesus,* John Shea writes:

> After two thousand years, people still journey to Jesus. They bring a vaunting ego and last year's scar, one unruly hope and several debilitating fears, an unwarranted joy and a hesitant heart—and ask Jesus what to make of it.[3]

Nineteenth-century thinkers put forward various images of Jesus, highest expression of Judaeo-Christian thought, of Jesus as epitome of being human and model for us all. The later 1960s treated us to Jesus in the rock musical *Superstar* or *Godspell*, updated, toe-tapping portraits. Anybody and everybody has had a hand at trying to write the story of Jesus. Jesus is black. Jesus is a revolutionary. Jesus is Mr. Nice Guy encouraging us to feel good about ourselves. As one irreverent joker saw it, the last word came from a crucified Jesus talking to the thief at his side, "If I'm okay and you're okay, why are we hanging here?"

I lean toward the view that Jesus' story is so deeply engrained in the Western psyche that it can still appeal, fascinate, and lead people to wonder and eventually to believe. My faith tells me that Jesus is divine. This must mean that human words will always fall short of expressing all that could be said; it also means that every age and culture, every decent poet or thoughtful film maker can find more to say about him.

I like the efforts of Dr. Morris Inch of Wheaton College, for example, who uses insights from Paul Tillich and Dietrich Bonhoeffer to describe the Savior as:

> The Wise Other, one who knows when to be firm and when to encourage,
>
> The Reconciling Other, recovering me, bringing me to myself, restoring me to His way,
>
> The Redeeming Other whose will we experience as other and yet our own,
>
> "It is no longer I who live but Christ lives in me; and the life I now live in the flesh I live by faith in the Son of God . . ." (Gal. 2:20).

From the Catholic environs, Father John A. O'Grady, a biblical theologian, offers a look at contemporary images of Jesus. For him, one of the more fruitful is J. A. T. Robinson's Jesus as the human face of God. The scriptural basis for this begins in Genesis, which describes every human being as created in the image of God; we could perceive perhaps the divine in every human visage. A more direct statement with powerful impact is John 14:9, "Whoever has seen me has seen the Father." Colossians 1:15 speaks of him as the "image of the invisible God, the first born of all creation." Hebrews 1:3 puts it, "He reflects the glory of God and bears the very stamp of his nature."

Cautioning us about the use of this image, O'Grady writes:

> Our humanity or our idea of what it means to be human is not the measure of evaluating Jesus, but rather His humanity is the criterion by which we not only judge ourselves but even come to realize our potential.[4]

Seeing Jesus as the face of God alters how I approach the Gospels. I do not have to exclaim "eureka" every time I find scriptural proof for divinity. Instead I can let the gospel stories lead me to a remarkable person in whom there is depth and dimension. Something appealing and awesome undergirds the Nazarean dinner guest, the up-country preacher, the disruptive visitor to the Temple in Jerusalem.

New images of Jesus, whether the "Reconciling Other" or the "human face of God," help me deal with a personal problem. There are times when my own psychological-spiritual grasp of Jesus' reality waxes and wanes like a far-away radio signal. I know I cannot expect, humanly speaking, to feel Jesus' presence with me at every single moment of the day with great emotional intensity. I also know that emotional factors are not the safest way of judging whether one is walking with the Lord. So my mind and heart need the freshening that can come from an insightful writer, musician, film maker, or artist.

Jesus as the "face of God" can perhaps be visualized in many ways, but one of the most awesome is the picture mosaic of *Jesus as Ruler of the World* in the dome of Washington, D.C.'s Shrine of the Immaculate Conception located on the campus of the Catholic University of America. Inside its vast spaces there is a lavish display of artistry, lighting, sculpture, mosaic, and painting, much of it focusing on Mary. Over it all, Christ as ruler of the universe presides triumphantly in a massive mosaic in the dome, his half-bare muscular arms extended to embrace the world. Thousands of bits of colored stone portray this magnificent scriptural truth, and the grandeur and size help me to think of Jesus as Lord.

If I let my mind and heart move from that portrait high on the underside of the Cathedral cupola to the daily newspaper stories of humanity's sin and cruelty, I can easily breathe the ancient Christian prayer, "Maranatha—Come, Lord Jesus." I also realize that in that serious, reserved look, the mosaic's face sends me out of the Shrine to the work of binding up societal wounds.

Jesus is perenially fascinating, evoking many emotions and images. These can in turn direct us to related truths. Our idea of redemption takes its cue from the image of the person. Jesus, the rural rebel, died because he challenged the ruling class. Or was Jesus the pure teacher of ethics who died for integrity's sake? I think that many Catholics respond positively to the enriching insights of poets, novelists, painters, film makers, and sculptors. At the same time, we insist that the definitive understanding of Jesus must arise from scriptural interpretations given their authoritative bearing through centuries of Christian witness, worship, study, meditation, and conciliar doctrines.

Jesus' Mission

A full treatment of Jesus' mission, his redemptive work, will be given in chapter 5. Here it seems important to me to point briefly to the links between Jesus' identity and that mission.

First, I personally want to keep Jesus' concreteness, his historical nature, well in focus. I want to be aware at all times of his place in Jewish history. He comes from a people with whom God made a series of covenants. In the latest and best of the divine initiatives, Jesus fully embodies God's self-giving love for his people. Our Christian Old Testament is a collection of Jewish Scriptures. In them Christians today see foreshadowings, precedents, and prophecies whereby the Israelites could hope for a new era in which they as a body or nation could walk in even greater intimacy with their Creator.

My desire to hold on or to highlight Jesus' Jewishness comes from historical and theological sources: both his human reality and his embodiment of the Father are rooted in the Jewish milieu. Further, awareness of his Jewishness should make me at least initially more sensitive to anti-semitism, my own or that of others. Lastly, I believe that Christian sacramentalism—baptism and the Eucharist for example; days of fast or feast; the notion of "doing penance" through alms, fasting, and prayer; even the models by which Paul and Timothy organized the new communities of believers—arose to some degree from Jesus' Jewishness and work in a Jewish milieu.

Second, if I accept what Scripture scholars are saying, I can appreciate how the titles given to Jesus or used by him helped clarify for his contemporaries—and for subsequent generations—what kind of mission he accomplished. His kingship raised memories of David and Solomon, and he uses this expectation to bring people to a new view of kingship. He was a prophet, but greater than Isaiah. Teaching with authority, he surpassed the judges. Son of Man he is, but in a manner that gives new vitality to the vision of Daniel. Our own belief in his transfiguration, resurrection, and return in glory fill out the mysterious image of Daniel.

Third, I understand Jesus' mission in a multi-faceted way. Jesus' work is both negative and positive. God's loving initiative seeks us out to cleanse the human race from sin. Jesus must span the gap between us and God, a gap opened by sin. However, once the gap is spanned, there is a positive facet. We are brought into a new broad, wide, and deep relationship with each other and with the Father.

This relationship with the Father is personal and collective. It is personal because each one as an individual is invited to be part of it, and it is collective because together we constitute a new people. An evangelical friend once surprised me by telling me how much he liked John Paul II's view of Jesus. Cardinal Wojtyla had written a book to help prepare his priests and people in Cracow for the renewal begun by the Second Vatican Council. In *Sources of Renewal*, the pope described the doctrinal and real unity between the Trinity and Jesus' redemptive work. Since Jesus is Son of God, what Jesus does is also a divine work.

> Redemption is the work of Christ, the Son of God made man; it is the essence of the mission of the Second Person of the Trinity whereby God entered visibly into human history and made it a history of salvation. The work of redemption is, as Christ Himself said (cf. John 16:7), the explicit condition of the "mission" of the Holy Spirit, his descent on the day of Pentecost and his continual visitation of the souls of men and the Church.[5]

In traditional Christian theology, Jesus is the bridge thrown across the divide between us and God, a divide we have made. God in

Jesus crosses to our side and becomes part of human civilization. Jesus as the peak of humanity draws us across the divide, urging us to be more than we ever think we can be, entering the life of the Trinity.

This idea appears in the Catholic doctrine of Jesus as Mediator between God and man. Cardinal Wojtyla uses this term when he writes that Jesus Christ is:

> . . . redeemer of the world, that world "which in the Christian vision has been created and is sustained by the love of its maker, which has been freed from the slavery of sin by Christ, who was crucified and rose again in order to break the stranglehold of the evil one, so that it might be fashioned anew according to God's design and brought to its fulfillment."[6]

Wojtyla's language here catches the negative and positive facets, "freed from slavery" and "fashioned anew . . . brought to its fulfillment." We believe that Jesus wants our hands, hearts, minds, and initiative in establishing the kingdom in all things: culture, politics, finance, ecology, and family life.

My fourth comment arises from this idea. Jesus' will to make the Father's kingdom more alive in our time cannot be completed perfectly, but we feel we are called to do it through mission work and evangelism. The complete "coming of the kingdom," however, must wait until the end of time. With Christ as our center, we are to be a people drawn upward along the learning spiral, stumbling and slipping, yet continually roused by the Holy Spirit. We are to be drawn eternally into and toward that around which everything circles—God's own life.

I have on my desk a magazine published by Maryknoll, a Catholic overseas missionary organization composed of priests, sisters, and dedicated lay volunteers. The July 1984 issue describes the society's work in the Central American country of Guatemala and recalls the heroism of one of their priests. Father Bill Woods served poor parishioners on a government colonization project in the jungle. An expert pilot, he ran a shuttle service, flying people and goods in and out of the roadless jungle clearings. He also taught farmers to organize cooperatives, to plant new kinds of cash crops, and to require the government to keep its promise of giving them legal title to the land they worked.

For his efforts, Guillermo (Father Bill Woods) received a number of death threats. In November 1976 his plane crashed into a mountain at high speed under mysterious circumstances. No one believes that it was an accident. He is widely considered the first priest to be martyred in Guatemala in modern times.[7]

I once heard Samuel Escobar of Peru say that the gospel is like a stick of dynamite in the social structure. That is true, but the dynamite also kills those who hold the sticks. Jesus has come to set the world ablaze.

Catholics can make their own the words of Jim Elliott, a beloved figure in evangelical circles who went as a missionary pilot to Ecuador's jungles to work with a remote tribe, the Aucas. While trying to bring the gospel to them, he and three of his companions were killed by the Indian tribesmen.

Elliot wrote a prayer while he was still a student at Wheaton College, a prayer that was answered.

> He makes his ministers a flame of fire. Am I ignitable? God deliver me from the dread asbestos "other things." Saturate me with the oil of the Spirit that I may be a flame. . . . In me there dwells the Spirit of the Great Short-Lived whose zeal for God's house consumed Him. Make me Thy Fuel, Flame of God.[8]

Conclusion

Since my Savior is truly divine, I would be disappointed if he didn't continue to fascinate every age, inspiring its artists, poets, and film makers. Since he is truly divine, I should never expect human formulations to freeze him and fix his person once and for all. For me personally, this Savior is both close and distant, a mysterious friend. The nearness I sometimes feel suddenly dissolves and I realize how far I am from him in my conduct or attitudes. Since he is divine, this paradox is exactly right.

Since Jesus is truly human, I delight in the fact that every age could in some degree make him its own. He is the chubby Bambino of the Renaissance painters, the cool corpse of Michelangelo's *Pieta*, the tortured king in Rouault's paintings, and the plastic statuette stuck on a dashboard. His humanness consoles me, and indeed, is really necessary if he is to speak to me at all.

Since he is mediator between God and man, redeemer of the whole earth, each of us is called to a renewed sense of our dignity—eternal union in the Godhead. Since he is Savior of the whole, there is nothing earthly which escapes an invitation from his spirit to be renewed, in a new heaven and a new earth. I think that he has to be this universal and all-embracing if he is to measure up to my desires and hopes for my own life and for civilization. A lesser figure, a merely great human being would not do—even though, God knows, we could use a lot more great human beings!

3

A Closer Look at THE CHURCH

A few years ago I was teaching college students a survey course on the history of Catholicism in the United States. In order to illustrate some of the Catholic-Protestant tensions, I showed them a book published in 1950, a handsomely illustrated history of American Protestantism. Its author went to great lengths to show how compatible Protestantism is with American democratic ideals. Next to a picture of a white, single-spired New England Congregational church, he described how Puritan religious thought had helped lay the groundwork for the American Revolution.

Later the author stressed how well the Protestant belief in the priesthood of all believers and in a married clergy fit American notions. A benign clergyman was photographed in his home; next to him sat his gracious wife and their children. They seemed to be reading Scriptures together. In another picture, the pastor was presiding at a meeting of the Board of Elders—good, solid-looking American males. Local town meetings found religious impulse in the lay-run congregation.

Convinced that American democratic ideals and Protestant theology matched like hand in glove, the author's sprightly text and photos of happy elders and pleasant clergyman with family seemed as though they might be a quiet critique of the undemocratic, priest-ridden, papal religionists whose obedience to a foreign monarch ran counter to American ideals. For every one of these pro-Protestant books, there were of course pro-Catholic counterparts.

Rummaging through our parish library recently, I came across a book published in 1958, *What Do They Ask about the Church?* The author, Monsignor J. D. Conway, distills hundreds of questions put to Catholics and provides them with clear, self-assured answers.

> *Question:* "How can you prove that the Catholic Church is the one true Church . . .? Christ said to Peter, "Upon this rock I will build my church." He didn't say, "I will build the Catholic Church."
>
> *Answer:* You admit that Jesus did establish a church. He called it "my church," and Peter was the rock on which it was founded. All you need to understand is that the Catholic Church of today is exactly the same as that one which Jesus established 1900 years ago. . . .[1]

My point here is not to deny that Puritan theology had a role in preparing the colonies for later political developments, nor to deny that Monsignor Conway could make a case for linking Catholicism with the church established by Christ. The point is that both Conway and the Protestant author felt the need to debate in terms which echoed the tragedy of Reformation and Counter-Reform. It was as if Catholics and Protestants had massed their troops on opposite sides of a valley. From the Catholic side the leaders waved banners bearing the message "Continuity with the First Christian Church," or "Tradition" or "Unity." From the other side of the valley Protestants waved banners emblazoned with *Sola Fide, Sola Gratia, Sola Scriptura!*—"Faith alone, grace alone, Scripture alone"—while shouting in unison, "Priesthood of all believers!"

Do we need to continue like this today? Some of the liberal Protestant footsoldiers seem battle-weary; many evangelicals find a surprising Catholic welcome when they send out small patrols. Catholics looking at the opposing ranks also see friendly faces. Since the sixties, the Christian world has altered dramatically. How could we discuss our differences today?

The wrong way is easy to describe, and we hope, a thing of the past. An ardent evangelical searches the Scripture to prove that from Pentecost the early church was democratic in style and did not practice infant baptism. Catholics look for verses showing an embryonic hierarchy and references or allusions to the sacraments. Sometimes Catholics and Protestants even use the same text with which to club each other.

Here is a method doomed to failure. My hope is that this chapter can provide an alternate model for mutual discussion. The key, in my view, is a return to the Scriptures for all of us—a meditative, prayerful return. From across the valley of division, we may find in Scriptures a new call to understand the idea of "church." In what follows I present a brief account of how Catholics have heard the call and are responding. Protestants are urging a new view as well. I confine myself to what I know better.

The Holy Spirit Calls Catholics to a New View

During the years of the Second Vatican Council (1962–1965), I was a seminarian in Washington, D.C. in an organization which was slowly opening its windows to establish contact with the outside world. My classmates and I gathered every night after supper to watch national network news about the massive bishop's gathering in Rome. Snatches of color, sound, and the reporter's text over these gave only tantalizing bits and pieces. For more depth, we followed reports in church magazines and papers. We turned also to *New Yorker Magazine*, which had added a well-informed Rome correspondent to its staff. Month after month, Xavier Rynne, a pseudonym for a Catholic priest, unveiled the maneuverings and debates behind the scenes.

The Council was a happy, holy, and very human assembly of more than two thousand bishops, abbots of major monastic groupings, directors of men's religious orders, theological advisors, churchmen from the Eastern Orthodox families, and Protestant observers. From this four-year event there came a remarkable new spirit to worldwide Catholicism, a spirit which coalesced to clarity in painstakingly drafted documents. One study of the Church, *Lumen Gentium*, invited all Catholics to take a new look at our collective identity.

At the heart of the document there is a garden of biblical delights, a profusion of Scripture references which speak about the Church. Here is a partial listing, developed by the bishops:

- sheepfold (John 10:1–10)
- flock of which God is shepherd as in Old Testament foreshadowing (Isa. 40:11, Ez. 34:11)
- tract of land (1 Cor. 3:5)
- choice vineyard (Matt. 21:33–43)
- edifice of God (1 Cor. 3:9)
- "our Mother," that Jerusalem which is above (Gal. 4:26, Rev. 12:17)
- body of Christ (1 Cor. 12:13)
- people of God (1 Pet. 2:9–10)

For my purposes I will concentrate only on the last two, "body of Christ" and "people of God." Before opening these topics, it is helpful to notice what the Council document did not stress: a model of the Church which had been prominent in our teaching since the Counter-Reformation, the "institutional model."

This model, in its typical formulation, described the Church as a "single, concrete, historical society" having a "constitution, a set of rules, a governing body, and a set of actual members who accept this constitution and these rules as binding on them. . . ."[2]

In the Counter-Reformation period, when Protestants groups were launching their massive critique of hierarchical abuses and late medieval church organization, Catholics responded by reformulating their notion of the Church. Reacting to what he saw as vague, spiritual notions of the Church, Cardinal Bellarmine gave us a definition which became hallowed for centuries, the Church as a perfect society, as visible as the Republic of Venice. We believe that its perfection is due not so much to the members as to its head, Jesus Christ.

In their popular book, *That Catholic Church: A Radio Analysis*, Rumble and Carty write that Jesus, during his public ministry,

> . . . carefully selected His twelve Apostles as the nucleus of the new community He was organizing and He conferred upon them magisterial,

> legislative, and disciplinary powers, sending them in the end with authority to make disciples from amongst all nations. . . .[3]

The Vatican II bishops did not reject this approach to the Church; the document speaks of hierarchy and refers to authority, priests, deacons, and laity. The bishops, however, did not begin with a focus on the governmental or institutional side. They began with the biblical visions of the Church. Granted that the Catholic Church has an institutional aspect, let us examine the tone and feeling which the bishops felt needed stressing.

The Body of Christ

Catholics heading toward their local church on Sundays often say that they are "going to Communion." Their first meaning is often this: they are going to participate in the life of the risen Savior through the sacrament of Holy Communion. In the Vatican II document, the bishops call our attention to another meaning—the sacrament of Holy Communion is also the union with each other in Christ. As St. Paul wrote:

> Because the bread is one, we though many, are one body, all of us who partake of the one bread (1 Cor. 10:17).

In the sacrament all of us are made members of his body and conjoined . . .

> . . . so too we, though many, are one body in Christ and individually members one of another (Rom. 12:5).

Our union with each other in Christ began before we took Holy Communion. It began in the sacrament of baptism. As Israel went through the waters of the Red Sea to become a new people, so does a new believer pass through waters to become part of Christ, members of his body. Christ is of course the Head of the body, firstborn of a new people (Col. 1:15–18).

Since he is Head, his Spirit fills the whole body, distributing different gifts for the good of all. This mysterious union of the baptized with Christ leads to the teaching that all the members ought to be molded into Christ's image until he is formed in them. Made one with his sufferings as the body is one with the Head, we endure with him so that we may be glorified with him.

One aspect of this unity of Christ and his members came home to me personally one day like a thunderbolt. It happened while I was at the seminary during daily chapel celebration of the Lord's Supper.

Following the piety of the time, my classmates and I walked forward from our pews in an orderly line to the front of the chapel. There, kneeling along a low railing, we waited for the priest, assisted by an acolyte, or altar boy, holding a metal plate. He walked along the opposite side of this railing distributing the consecrated bread. The acolyte walked ahead of the priest, holding the plate under our chins. When the priest drew near we raised our heads and extended our tongues. Holding the bread carefully between his thumb and forefinger, the priest placed the wafer on our tongues, saying in Latin, "May the body of our Lord Jesus Christ bring you unto eternal life." If he missed our tongues or if we moved inappropriately, the acolyte's plate was the safety net to catch the consecrated bread. Moving quickly, trying to accommodate the numbers of seminarians at the rail, the priest muttered the formula hurriedly, "Corpus Domini . . .", the latter part trailing off into his throat.

Having received the consecrated bread, we rose from our kneeling position at the railing and returned to our pews with eyes downcast to savor a few moments of intimacy with the Lord. Our piety focused powerfully on the actual and miraculous presence of the Risen Savior in the consecrated bread, the "body of Christ" distributed, received, and honored.

This was the atmosphere in which my thunderbolt came. A newly-ordained deacon had been assigned the preaching that day, and he spoke of the sacrament of Holy Communion. At the end of his remarks, he had invited us to modify our customary behavior. "When you return to your pews today," he urged, "do not close your eyes for private prayer. Rather, look around you at the other people who are moving forward devoutly to communicate or look at those who are returning to their places. Look at them and see in *them* the body of Christ. *They* are Christ's body."

When I had received the sacred bread, I returned as usual to my place. But instead of withdrawing within myself to enjoy the customary intimacy with Christ, a suggestion made to me years before when I was prepared for First Communion at the age of seven, I kept my eyes open and head erect. The seminary chapel and its worshipers took on a new aspect. My fellow seminarians—with whom I played sloppy basketball, waited on tables, washed dishes, and studied theology—were the body of Christ. My "communion" with Jesus was never the same again. I continue to love the presence of the risen Lord in the Eucharist, that sacrament of the Lord's Supper which commemorates Christ's sacrifice on the cross. But I have never forgotten the other truth driven into me by that deacon's sermon. The sermon had reminded me that my moment with Jesus had to open outward to love his body. Sins committed against others constituted an assault on Christ.

Crucial to the Catholic perspective on this is our awareness of the organic character of Christ's body in the world. Contemporary Catholic theologian Monika Hellwig points to this in her meditation on the Pentecost account in Acts and in John 19:30: "Jesus delivered up his spirit." She writes:

> The whole meaning of the Pentecost story seems to be that they must also breathe in the Spirit and become alive with it in a new creation which draws together the fragments of the broken Adam into one body again—one body which is in a profound sense the body of the new or second Adam, the body in the world of the Risen Christ.[4]

Her view of church builds on the Greek word *ekklesia*, gathering or assembling. Our task as the Church is that of:

> . . . gathering the scattered people of God into the unity of harmony, of worship of God, or concern for the common good, of mutual service in the generosity of self-forgetfulness of Jesus Christ.[5]

Some today argue that one of the Church's continuing challenges is that of being a herald, announcing what Christ has done and making him vitally present in every age. The body of Christ imagery can help highlight this approach, as I would like to illustrate.

A priest once told his congregation a story which speaks to the vivid and realistic depth of Christ's body on earth. As a military chaplain in World War II, he had traveled into a battle-ravaged village in France. Air raids and artillery shelling had reduced the houses to rubble; the village church was particularly badly damaged. Miraculously, there was one surviving Christian symbol in the middle of what had been the church—a large statue of Christ. The peculiar feature of this statue was that a random explosive had stripped the figure of arms and hands.

The chaplain saw in this mutilated statue a symbol of who we are. Boldly he said, "Christ the Head needs our hands and arms." Action by the members of the body is in some sense action of Christ. Clearly, great trouble could arise if we were to identify what we do all the time as Christ's actions. Who would dare to throw responsibility for our sins, ignorance, and failings on Christ?

The ideal situation would be that in which the leaders, anyone in authority, would be servants of the community and its members. All the others would be working for the common good, not for their own individual advantage. The failure of leadership to be what it should be has been the backbone of criticism and protest in the Catholic Church. One of the more memorable protests came from the fourteenth century reformer and mystic, Catherine of Siena. Taking aim at the clergy of her day she wrote that priests

> . . . go about fancily dressed, not like clerics and religious, but like lords or court lackeys. They are concerned about having grand horses, many gold and silver vessels, and well-adorned homes. . . . Their heart babbles out its disordered vanity, and their whole desire is feasting, making a god of their bellies. . . .[6]

When Pope John XXIII convened the Second Vatican Council, he relied on another biblical image to speak of the Church. Ephesians 5:25–28 describes it as the bride of Christ, but the Pope acknowledged that every so often the bride had to be reformed so that without wrinkle or stain she would be attractive to unbelievers.

To summarize, the biblical image of the Church as the body of Christ gives us a higher view of our union in Christ through faith and baptism; it also keeps our attention focused on Christ as Head and on his Spirit at work among us. As members of his body, what is good for one is good for all, and what is damaging to one is damaging to all. Leadership must take seriously the distribution of gifts and respect varying charisms while remaining servants of the whole.

The People of God

Here, as was the case with the scriptural image of the body of Christ, the bishops of the Second Vatican Council meditated on the deep implications of God's Word. In typical Christian fashion, they began with foreshadowings of the idea in Jewish Scripture. A review of Exodus or Deuteronomy makes it clear that, as the bishops wrote:

> It has pleased God, however, to make men holy and save them not merely as individuals without any mutual bonds, but by making them into a single people. . . .[7]

The way God dealt with Israel serves as a model or clue to the way he would deal with others. He made a covenant with them and taught them his will. He also promised to broaden the covenant and to renew it. The bishops believed that Jewish prophecy, like Jeremiah's vision of a new covenant (31:3–34), found fulfilment when Christ began to draw people to himself. A new nation or people arises, born of imperishable seed, born of water and the Holy Spirit (1 Pet. 1:23, 2:9–10). A new Israel takes shape—visible, corporate, organically related. It is a People, not a mob; it has functions, purposes, and structures.

Giving further flesh to this People of God model, the bishops retrieve traditional descriptions of Jesus—Prophet, Priest, and King. As a People, we believers are to be sharers in Christ's triple roles.

The People of God and Priesthood

Thomas Jefferson once attended a Catholic mass and later wrote to his wife how pitiful it looked—the priest muttering in Latin while layfolk murmured prayers in their own tongue as they fingered their rosary beads. The "foreignness" of what Jefferson observed may have been sharpened by three centuries of Catholic-Protestant tension in which "priest-craft" was a war cry. Martin Luther's revulsion at the abuses of late medieval religion and clergy led him to stress the priesthood of all believers. Catholics of the Counter Reform came out of their corner ready to counterpunch, stressing just the opposite.

Lost in this debate was an appreciation of both positions: a special priesthood and the priesthood of all the baptized. The bishops at the council sought to achieve a better balance as they spoke of the layperson's role in being part of Christ's priesthood. "The baptized, by regeneration and the anointing of the Holy Spirit, are consecrated into a spiritual house and a holy priesthood."[8]

Because of this consecration every baptized believer "can offer spiritual sacrifices and proclaim the power of him who has called them out of darkness into his marvelous light." Further, all the disciples of Christ, persevering in prayer and praising God, should present themselves as a living sacrifice, holy and pleasing to God (Rom. 12:1).

In popular Catholic piety, this biblical insight surfaced with the notion of offering self as sacrifice, or of offering one's entire day to God. In our parish elementary school, the nuns opened our class day with the Pledge of Allegiance to the Flag, and a prayer which began, "Oh, my God, I offer you all my prayers, works, and sufferings of this day. . . ." In those days, neither the nuns nor we would confuse our priesthood with that of the ordained, but the prayer reveals a priestly mentality, a mentality of offering sacrifice.

At Catholic baptismal ceremonies, while proud parents or sponsors assist, the priest not only bathes or pours water, he also anoints. He dips his finger in scented oil and traces a cross on the crown of the candidate's head. As he does, he recites:

> God the Father of our Lord Jesus Christ, has freed you from all sin, and given you a new birth by water and the Holy Spirit, and welcomed you into his holy people.
>
> He now anoints you with the chrism of salvation. As Christ was anointed Priest, Prophet and King, so may you live always as a member of his body, sharing everlasting life.[9]

Anointing is an Old Testament gesture used for kings and prophets. The formula combines the body of Christ imagery with peoplehood and Christ's triple role.

The People of God and the Prophetic Role

Since we share in Christ's priestly and prophetic roles through baptism, it is helpful to see how the prophetic side is developed. The bishops of the council see this in several ways. First, we can spread abroad a living witness to God, especially by a life of faith and charity. Just as Jesus and the prophets before him wanted people to direct their attention to God, to obey his will, to respond to his invitation to a deeper covenant bond, so Catholics as a people are to give witness to these truths.

Second, the People of God exercise their prophetic mission in prayerful speech and praise. The bishops remind us of the command in Hebrews 13:15:

> Through him let us continually offer God a sacrifice of praise, that is, the fruit of lips which acknowledge his name.

Third, prophets have the vital role of teaching the truth. The whole People of God, when united in belief—from the bishops down to the last member of the laity—exercise a prophetic function. Teaching is best understood in the broadest sense. It includes not merely verbal activities—preaching, training children to understand the Bible, or the catechism—it refers to the whole complex of actions, words, and writings through which we prepare our children for mature discipleship and through which we "teach" the world around us.

It is as if the People, when united in belief, have a sixth sense, an intuitive feel for God's truth and the Spirit's leading in given situations. The People cling without fail to the faith once delivered to the saints. Here is a hint at the controversial quality of our prophetic work, infallibility, possible only because we believe that we as a People have been anointed by the Holy One.

The People of God and Christ's Kingship

When the bishops discuss Christ's kingship as embodied in the People of God, they have in mind the traditional "marks" of the Church. These marks come from the creed which states our belief in a church which is "one, holy, catholic, and apostolic." Jesus, called "heir of all things" in Hebrews 1:2, is Head of the new and universal People of the sons of God. Holiness, unity, and universality arise from the work of the Holy Spirit. As the bishops put it:

> He it is who, on behalf of the whole Church and each and everyone of those who believe, is the principle of their coming together and

> remaining together in the teaching of the apostles and in the fellowship, in the breaking of bread and in prayers.[10]

The Holy Spirit is the one who brings believers together under Christ's kingship. It is the Holy Spirit who keeps a world-wide fellowship united by faithful transmission of apostolic teaching and by prayers and sacrament. Vatican II documents show our conviction that God calls all men and women to be a new people, rescued from their divisions and dispersal by Christ.

It is useful to add here that Christ's universal kingship has mission implications. In another Vatican II document, *Decree on the Missionary Activity of the Church*, the bishops note:

> The pilgrim Church is missionary by her very nature. For it is from the mission of the Son and the mission of the Holy Spirit that she takes her origin. . . .[11]

The bishops remind the Catholic world of Jesus' mandate in Mark 16:16, and of the Church's challenge to save and renew every creature, so that all things can be restored in Christ, and in him mankind can compose one family and one people.

Citizens of every race are called to form the People of God, citizens through baptism of a kingdom which is of a heavenly nature. We must be careful to avoid saying that the visible Church on earth constitutes God's kingdom. That would be an error. The very fact that we pray, "thy kingdom come" reminds us that the visible Church, witnessing, priestly and missionary, constitutes only a beachhead for the kingdom. We await the full revelation and establishment of the reign of God when the Savior returns in glory.

Conclusion

Catholics today find themselves called to move from the one-sided stress on Church as Institution to an appreciation of the Church as body of Christ and People of God. Both of these biblical images help us to concentrate on Christ as origin and principle of ongoing life and power. These images have the advantage of being scriptural, and they speak to our Catholic belief—namely that God did not intend people to be saved as individuals, but as a collectivity, diverse yet ordered, linked to him, and vivified by his Holy Spirit.

The bishops' invitation to a refreshed and wider sense of the Church also helps us to think with joy and hope about the Communion of Saints, a fellowship which includes the acknowledged saints who have gone to the Father and the dead whose faith is known to God alone. We believe that a collective bonding with them in Christ leads us to continue to ask the saints victorious to pray for us to the Father; chief among these saints is Mary, Jesus' mother. In their time, these men and women were the People of God; now they are a part of the crowd of witnesses urging us on.

Some time ago I joined some evangelical Christians for a worship service. At one point, we joined the choir in singing lustily Samuel Wesley's hymn "The Church's One Foundation." I couldn't help thinking of the Communion of Saints and the Catholic instinct about collective bonding as we came to the words about the church in "mystic sweet communion with those whose rest is won."[12]

4

A Closer Look at SCRIPTURE AND TRADITION

One of the great stereotypes facing Catholics and Protestants is that which divides us along the Bible-tradition valley. Some Catholics will admit that they don't know much about the Bible, saying that such knowledge is a "Protestant thing." Some might even be a little proud of biblical ignorance, saying that all one needs to know about salvation is taught by the Catholic Church, which has passed the truth down for generations.

Some Protestants assume that Catholics base much of their belief on traditional, non-biblical views and possess little appreciation for the Bible. Other Protestants think Catholics are not free to interpret the Bible for themselves, bound as they are by centuries of papal teaching, council pronouncements, and blind obedience to a local priest or bishop.

Lyman Beecher, a famous nineteenth-century evangelical preacher, once said regarding Catholics:

> . . . none may read the Bible but by permission of the priesthood, and no one be permitted to understand it and worship God according to the dictates of his own conscience.[1]

Beecher's information seems to have been only partially correct. Catholics were indeed forbidden to read *unauthorized* translations of the Bible, especially the King James Version. But as early as 1829, Catholic bishops in the United States urged the laity to read Scripture for guidance and instruction—as long as the translations were those approved by the Church at that time: either the Douay-Rheims English translation of the Latin Vulgate or the English version by Bishop Challoner.

The bishops were so concerned about uninformed reading, unapproved translations, and private interpretations that they made it their business to establish a first-class biblical course at Washington, D.C.'s Catholic University. One of the bishops, Philadelphia's Francis Kenrick, had even produced on his own a new translation of the four Gospels from the original languages.

In our day, we Catholics are able to explain our views of Scripture in such a way that our Protestant brothers and sisters can better understand us. To help in this process, I propose to show how much Scripture means to Catholics, and secondly, to show the differences and similarities in our use of Scripture.

Our Esteem of Scripture

Luke 4 tells us that one Sabbath, while visiting a synagogue in his hometown of Nazareth, Jesus read from a scroll of Jewish Scripture, commenting on its meaning to those present. This scene testifies to the Jewish use of Scripture, a practice which the Christians have continued and expanded. Faithful to this tradition, Catholics continue to gather for Sunday worship in which Scripture is read and explained.

Growing up in the United States Catholic Church before the reforms introduced by the Second Vatican Council, my fellow Catholics and I attended services where the priest at mass read the assigned texts from Scripture in Latin. We could follow his reading in our own hand-held, miniature service books. He then presented the Scripture verses in English and preached his sermon from them. In my boyhood, the same text was heard annually on a given Sunday. Since the reforms of the council, however, the selection of assigned texts has been widened. A particular passage now appears only once in a three year period instead of once a year.

Scripture in public worship, whether Sundays or weekdays, is central to our Eucharists. Scripture has also been the backbone of our non-eucharistic worship. From very early times Christians developed the habit of daily prayer, continuing Jewish practices. Often they prayed as a group in local churches and cathedrals, singing God's praises through the psalms. Other Scripture might then be read and a sermon preached, followed by prayers.

These laymen's prayers became the priest's breviary, his time-honored daily prayer. Today many Catholics use a simplified collection of psalms and New Testament readings for their own daily devotion, interrupting their work day to pray at various times. This helps them consecrate the hours of the day, particularly the beginning and ending of the day.

Throughout this book I will be trying to show how Catholic beliefs arise from and are supported by the Bible. Scripture has been and remains our primary, although not exclusive, source for Catholic doctrines. Our central Christian tenets as expressed in Church pronouncements, creeds, and repeated preaching, rest on scriptural foundations. The theological giants who have shaped our teaching—the great Greek theologian John Chrysostom, the North African Latin bishop Augustine, and the medieval genius Thomas Aquinas—had to anchor their faith in the revelation handed on to us by the apostles, especially that which they recorded in Holy Scripture. Our commitment to the Christian and Jewish Scriptures goes further, however, than doctrine. It also extends to questions of morality.

The Ten Commandments served as boundary markers for acceptable moral conduct as my peers and I were growing up. When I disobeyed a teacher, a parental substitute, I was reminded of the commandment to honor my father and mother. When I shaved the truth, I was reminded that I should not "bear false witness." My church, my teachers, and my parents saw these as basic. Beyond this they tried to instill in me the kind of charity praised by Paul. They prayed that I would show the fruits of the Holy Spirit, and they encouraged me to have the characteristics found in the Beatitudes. Scriptural morality continues to be the backbone of Catholic ethical teaching. An example is the scriptural prohibition of murder, a command that leads us to protect fetal life as well as the lives of thousands targeted for nuclear holocaust.

Beyond the formal reliance on Scripture in doctrine and morality, there is at work among us a remarkable renewal of interest in Bible study and devotions. The Second Vatican Council gave this renewal great approval and new life. At the council, the bishops said that Scripture and tradition constitute a mirror which we hold up to our faces to see how we measure up. We were urged to compare our current conduct, teaching, policies, devotions, and prayer practices with the high standards and directives found in the Bible.

It was due to this reforming council that our Sunday and weekday worship Scripture readings were enlarged. We were at least to have our ears pricked with a richer selection of texts than in the past. Thanks to the council, our sacramental practice was also refreshed and strengthened by a better and fuller use of Holy Scripture. The reforms touched popular devotions as well, asking local churches to make sure that the content and practices associated with them would be solidly based on Scripture.

All this urging from the council made an impact. I now find Catholics praying an ancient devotion, the rosary, with greater attention to the Scripture story which accompanies the recitation of the prayer "Hail Mary," the Doxology, and the Lord's Prayer for every ten beads. Each of the rosary's fifteen Scripture stories commemorates some major teaching or event in the life of Christ or the Blessed Mother.

Another world-wide devotion dating from the eighteenth century is prayer and reverence for the Sacred Heart of Jesus. This was a favorite devotion of my aunt, who once gave me a wallet-size leather-covered picture of Jesus. He was crowned with thorns and his pierced heart glowed mystically from his chest. Some of the piety around this devotion needed renewal, and contemporary pamphlets show more clearly the biblical roots for meditation on Christ's love and suffering for us.

Another ancient Catholic devotion, the Way of the Cross, signifies a miniature walk with Christ from his condemnation by Pilate to his Crucifixion. On my desk I have another contemporary pamphlet containing the scriptural references for this devotion. Beyond these specific devotions, it must be said, millions of Catholics use Scripture for personal enlightenment and Bible study. It is at the heart of countless prayer groups, large or small.

I would like now to discuss some background for our approach to Scripture. History shows us that Christians have often differed in their understanding of things. They frequently offered contradictory Bible texts to illustrate their views, or they used the same texts interpreted differently. I mentioned briefly in chapter 2 how well-meaning, Bible-loving Christians debated with scriptural weapons about Jesus' identity. We know, too, that Reformation theologians trying to cleanse a shabby Christian world used biblical texts to support their calls for reform. Their Catholic counter reformers battled back with texts which supported their own views.

Once the classic Protestant-Catholic battle lines had been drawn, history tells a dreary tale of continual sniping, debating, and crossfire, with both sides vigorously maintaining their views of Scripture in general and of certain texts in particular. This scriptural stalemate was shaken only in the nineteenth century when first a trickle, then a torrent of scholars began to investigate more closely a wide range of topics which affected our understanding of the Bible. There was a dramatic information explosion about archaeology, ancient languages, history, religion, and science.

Exciting discoveries and fascinating scriptural theories mushroomed upward into a century already on fire with other new ideas and philosophies. Both Catholic and Protestant authorities worried about the spread of Darwinism and the use of modern science and historical method to deny the possibility of miracles or resurrection from the dead. Many began to feel that the truth, the historical accuracy, and the divinely-inspired character of Scripture were being threatened. Since some scholars, Protestant and Catholic, worked in these new disciplines and found much in them that was credible, tensions arose within the churches.

Among Protestants, these tensions became increasingly noticeable toward the end of the century, in the division between the so-called "liberals" and the "orthodox." Liberals in varying ways wanted to use the new findings in history, literature, comparative religion, archaeology, and textual analysis. Sometimes they explained away miracles and apparent contradictions in the texts. Sometimes they gave new and disturbing interpretations of certain passages, denying fundamental truths. "Orthodox" pastors, seminary professors, and scholars tried to blunt the trendy use of the new hypotheses and findings. With the help of many concerned laity, they also began to issue a set of pamphlets on the "fundamentals." By the late twenties and thirties of our century, a sharp cleavage had opened up. Liberals flailed away at the orthodox. Defense of orthodoxy through the pamphlets soon got the label "fundamentalist."

While these struggles were raging within Protestant circles, Catholics felt the same tensions—but in less dramatic and more hidden ways. It was nervousness over the new theories and findings about Scriptures that prompted Pope Leo XIII to establish the Pontifical Biblical Commission in 1901. Its appointed officials were to be watchdogs over biblical professors and biblical courses. Some Catholic scholars of those days found it was healthier to keep their newer speculations and findings out of print. Would-be professors of Scripture were to attend only the approved biblical institutes. Once they were professors, they were to teach only the approved curriculum.

The pope's new Biblical Commission had two main effects. The first effect was the slowing or shackling of free debate and writing. This was painful for the scholars and researchers, some of whom had risked life and limb to rescue precious scrolls or to photograph ancient inscriptions. A second effect, however, was that the "new Scripture" did not percolate down from scholarly reviews to the local pastors and their people. The mass of Catholics continued to rely on the preaching and teaching they heard from the local church. In all likelihood, that local church knew little of exotic controversies waged for or against the view that Moses was the author of the first five books of the Old Testament.

Less than fifty years after Pope Leo XIII established the Biblical Commission, a new spirit was in the air. The commission kept to its charted course, defense of Scripture's truth and accuracy, but the extreme tensions and nervousness had eased. Commission watchers must have been surprised when in 1941 it issued a statement condemning not the new biblical research, but those persons who distrusted the new disciplines too much.

In the middle of World War II, Pope Pius XII gave a quiet blessing to new biblical scholarship with his 1943 encyclical *Divino Afflante Spiritu.* After his death, in the years leading up to the Second Vatican

Council, there was a ripple of conservative reaction against new biblical theories. When the council opened, some scholars felt that their work was under a cloud caused by some Roman officials. How would the bishops in the council deal with newer biblical research and findings?

Well before the bishops gathered in Rome, an advance committee of theologians had drawn up a document on Scripture. Designed for submission to the bishops when they arrived, it was entitled "On the Sources of Revelation." The advance committee chose this title because many older scholars believed that God had revealed his truth in two separate but criss-crossing streams: Scripture and tradition. The second source of revelation was therefore tradition—Jesus' teachings and actions, as well as those of the first believers, which are not recorded in the Bible. John 21:25 reminds us that after all,

> There are still many other things that Jesus did, yet if they were written about in detail, I doubt there would be room enough in the entire world to hold the books to record them.

The older scholarly view among Catholics held that Jesus taught and organized the early church in ways not retained in written revelation. Jesus' wishes and ideas were enshrined in early church practice and in teaching by the apostles, which was handed down from generation to generation.

When the bishops began their deliberations at Vatican II, the advance committee's document on Scripture was presented almost immediately. Some felt that since its contents were so well established, it would be passed routinely. Hopes for quick approval were dashed, however, when dissatisfied bishops voted to send it back to the committee for revision. The Church's official statement on Scripture and revelation was to make several trips back and forth between the committee and the whole assembly before it won approval. Finally ratified in November 1965, this document, *Dei Verbum*—"Dogmatic Constitution on Divine Revelation"—is now twenty years old, and remains a key teaching for us.

For our purposes it is important to look at two major issues: the link between Scripture and tradition, and the ways in which Scriptures can be used in study and spiritual growth.

One view of revelation which the Vatican II bishops wanted to restate came from the Council of Trent in 1564. At that reform council, the Church had declared that the gospel "is contained in written books and in unwritten traditions." This phrase helps explain why the advance committee in 1962 had entitled its document "The Sources." At Trent, the bishops declared that the Church venerated the written books *and* unwritten traditions with an equal attitude of piety and equal reverence. The bishops' view was that "insofar as the ancient apostolic traditions convey the gospel, they were on a par with Scripture."

Notice that the phrase "insofar as the ancient apostolic traditions convey the gospel" leaves open the larger issue: exactly *which* traditions in fact convey the gospel. In the heat of the battle with Protestant critics, Catholic bishops of the sixteenth century were not likely to embrace the other idea that in a certain sense all revelation may be held to be contained in Scripture.[2] The value of tradition, ancient and apostolic, was too great and its reality too powerful to let the issue be stated that way.

The final Vatican II document on Scripture gives a formulation which simply leaves the older "two source" statement aside. Of interest for us, however, is the document's second chapter, which describes the process of handing on the teachings of Jesus. This "handing on" language is the English equivalent of the Latin *traditio*, and the bishops saw it happening in stages.

The first stage is the time covering Jesus' own lifetime to the moment when apostles and others, inspired by the Holy Spirit, recorded Jesus' life and teaching. In this first stage, particularly after Jesus' death and resurrection, issues arose which required an application of principles inherent in Jesus' teaching. The customary example is the conflict in the early churches about accepting non-Jews as converts without requiring them to observe Jewish dietary laws or being circumcised. The early believers had apparently no clear, formal directive from Jesus about this. Peter, who had a dream about the subject, interpreted this as a revelation and it led him to adopt a more open stance. Yet the resolution of the problem seems to have been a church decision, not one directly dictated by Jesus.

This first stage of tradition contains far more than formal policy decisions recorded in Acts. The apostles' preaching as well as their behavior must have amounted to a living enactment of revelation. Their sermons, now that Jesus had risen, were an essential link in the transmission of revelation.

The second stage of "handing on" arises when, as the Vatican II bishops put it, "apostles and apostolic men who under the inspiration of the same Holy Spirit committed the message of salvation to writing."[3]

The notion of stages in transmission helps to remind us that before there was any official collection of Gospels, Epistles, or apocalyptic literature into the twenty-seven books we call New Testament, the churches were nourished by divine revelation in both written and unwritten forms. Scholars say that in cultures where many members are illiterate, there is often a well-developed capacity to transmit lengthy and complex material through memorization and story-telling. Since biblical scholars incline toward the view that the Gospel of John is a relatively late composition, yet one of the oldest, we have to believe that the early churches learned revelation from unwritten sources.

After the "oral" phase came the written records of Jesus' sayings, experiences of the apostles and Mary, key events in Jesus' life, and the disciples' accounts of his resurrection and sending of the Holy Spirit. As the Vatican II document puts it:

> That the Gospel might be kept integral and alive without interruption in the Church, the apostles gave themselves successors, the bishops, to whom they handed on "their own teaching responsibility." This holy transmission and the Holy Scripture of the two covenants are therefore like a looking glass in which the pilgrim Church on earth contemplates God, from whom she receives all, until the time when she will be led to see him face to face as he is (cf. 1 John 3:2).[4]

These twentieth century bishops did not wish to repeat the sixteenth century language about equal piety and equal reverence for written books and unwritten traditions. Still, they call our attention to the Spirit-given nature of the "transmission" when they call this process "holy."

I hope the following important point will be helpful in trying to understand this issue. Sometimes Catholics have been tempted to argue, especially in debates with Protestants, that what was transmitted by the apostles was a collection of clearly tailored, precise doctrinal formulas. Catholics need to be reminded that the bishops speak of the transmission under three headings: teaching, life, and worship. Teaching, however precise, was only part of the message handed on. The ways the apostles and others organized their communities and their manner of worship need to be studied as well. One "teaches" or "reveals" as much by action as by words.

Having looked at the Church's latest declaration about Scripture and tradition, I pass now to the way the bishops approached the problem of interpretation. Here they leave no doubt of their belief that God is the author of the books of Scripture. They also say that the human writers and editors ("redactors" in technical language) are truly authors. In some circles there is a burning question about the degree to which the human author was inspired by the divine Author. There are many different views about this, and the bishops simply did not enter into any detail about it. They are content to say that God expressed himself through the literary qualities and methods of men, whom he guided through the charism of inspiration.

For the bishops of Vatican II, Scripture teaches truth—firmly, faithfully, and without error. What is the truth in question? Is it scientific truth? All the bishops say is that Holy Scripture is free of all error as regards the truth of salvation, but not necessarily in merely philosophical or scientific matters.

Scripture Interpretation

The bishops avoided detailed regulations or restrictions on legitimate freedom of research, but they do provide four general principles which should be kept in mind when interpreting texts.

First, because Jesus, his apostles, and their contemporaries were Jews steeped in Jewish Scriptures, we Christians need to keep in mind the interconnections between Christian Scriptures—the New Testament—and Jewish Scriptures—the Old Testament. One collection throws light on the other.

A second principle is the importance of interpreting texts with a certain attitude of faith. We see the Old and New Testaments as historical records of the events of salvation, profoundly spiritual writings in which the Word speaks to man through the Spirit. Therefore, the texts are adequate, reliable guides to salvation history and are open to a "spiritual" interpretation which goes beyond the literal text.

A third principle of interpretation is the value of understanding the authors' use of various literary forms. I remember that when I was a boy, someone gave me a wonderful book about the birth, boyhood, and adventures of Daniel Boone of Kentucky. A child's history of Daniel Boone cannot be expected to give the depth found in a biography intended for adults. Children's literature, although capable of great depth, has its own styles and rules.

For a biblical example, consider the apocalyptic literature. Scholars tell us that Daniel, Revelation, and parts of the Gospels contain material written following a certain conventional style. This style involves content which cannot be read or interpreted in the same way one reads Titus or Timothy. An appropriate understanding of Revelation has to be built on a grasp of this particular type of literature. In short, various literary forms have an impact on what the author intended to convey.

The fourth principle which the bishops offered regards the "spiritual sense" of a text. Catholic tradition has always paid special attention to the Spirit-inspired, deep meaning which permits a text to speak to the needs of succeeding generations of readers and hearers. Once we have discovered the historical and literal meanings of a text, we should be alert to the possibility that there is also a deeper, richer meaning. Before the Middle Ages, Christian thinkers found such rich treasures for instruction and devotion in a variety of "spiritual senses."

While we hope that many contemporary Protestants are well beyond Lyman Beecher's nineteenth century misreading of Catholic views of the Bible, some still feel that Catholics are not free in their interpretation of Scripture. I would argue that individual Catholics should and do read Scripture for their own instruction and guidance. I would also argue, however, that *reliable* interpretation takes place within a church.

Catholic theologian Avery Dulles makes a point here that I wish to adopt as my own. The proper use of Scripture, as a source of faith for the Church, is within the Spirit-governed Church. In other words, no Catholic bishop or individual, no matter how saintly, is free to interpret texts or expound their meaning without reference to the wider, living body of Christ. Nor, for that matter, can an individual go very far in these interpretations without consulting the interpretations of the Church of the past. Someone once said that the truest form of democracy allows our ancestors a voice.

Prayer formulas, ways of worship, creeds, council teachings, writings of recognized authorities—all of these need to form at least the background to contemporary interpretation. Part of the reason is that we believe divine revelation in its best and definite form occurred in Jesus Christ and in the apostles' transmission of his teaching.

Every age, in God's providence, has "inspired" leaders in politics, science, and religion. But we would find it strange to think that the original, sacred truths could be radically re-shuffled every century or so. I think that Clark Pinnock has put this very well when he speaks of the value of tradition. From his evangelical perspective he says:

> Today the church is flooded by a strange new world of Bible theories. Each publishing season one is greeted with many novel interpretations which the ordinary believer is not able to assess. Tradition serves in this case to insulate the community from the firestorms of theological speculation, and gives her teachers time to devise appropriate defensive strategies.[5]

Senses of Scripture

Earlier in this chapter I referred to the bishops' fourth principle of interpretation, focus on the "spiritual sense" of a text. I would like to describe briefly four senses which Christian interpreters have used in the past, senses which are still helpful today: literal, allegorical, tropological, and anagogical.

The *literal* sense arises immediately and directly from a text. Generations of Christians and Jews have found nourishment from the beautiful phrase in Psalm 139:

> O Lord, you search me and you know me,
> you know my resting and my rising . . . (vv. 1–2).

The immediate and literal meaning goes right to my heart. In contrast, look at this phrase from Psalm 118:

> . . . the nations all encompassed me:
> in the Lord's name I crushed them . . . (v. 10).

This doesn't seem to speak literally to me.

The *allegorical* sense can be a very exciting thing. Allegory means that a subject or an idea appears in the texts in a symbolic way. The readers of the text have a creative task, applying what is said symbolically to the underlying issue or concern. A contemporary Catholic writer, Benedict Groeschel, gives Psalm 80:9 as an example:

> A vine from Egypt you transplanted;
> you drove away the nations and planted it.

It is hard to believe that the writer is referring to a single vine of some rare grape. "Vine" and "vineyard" are allegorical references to the People of God.

Another example from Groeschel may also help. In Psalm 30 we read these verses:

> To you, O Lord, I cried out;
> with the Lord I pleaded:
> "What gain would there be from my lifeblood,
> from my going down into the grave?" (vv. 9–10).

Literally, one might argue that the particular lines express someone's anguish. Could the text also be a prediction of the suffering and death of Jesus? Whether or not it is such a prediction, can we not see the psalmist's cry as symbolic of Christ's own predicament?

Beyond the literal and allegorical, there is the *tropological* sense. This means that texts can be read as a call to conversion or a cry of encouragement in the struggle against sin. There are many psalms which describe great conflict between Israel and its enemies. Israel can be symbolic of my own God-given strength and desires, while the idolatrous and murderous pagans are symbolic of my sins, vices, and deep-rooted egotism. Israel's victory, seen in the tropological sense, is a sign that I can overcome my own internal enemies with God's help.

The *anagogical* sense adds something very precious to our prayers; it is an uplifting spiritual interpretation. For brief moments we can get a feeling and conviction that we are praying with the angels or the saints. The psalms offer many examples. They call us to feelings of deep joy, thanksgiving, and exultation. They lift us out of the humdrum of life. They help focus our prayer on the voice of hope which arises from the life of Christ within us. Here is an old favorite with an anagogical capacity:

God is our refuge and our strength,
an ever-present help in distress.
Therefore we fear not, though the earth be shaken
and mountains plunge into the depths
of the sea . . . (Psalm 46:2–3).

Using the Imagination

In addition to these four aids to interpretation, there is yet another way to derive profit from the Scriptures; it is through use of the imagination, one of God's great gifts to us. To stretch your enjoyment of Scripture, try reading a text and bringing your imagination to bear on it. Take as an example the story of the Good Samaritan. Put yourself imaginatively in the scene. What kind of day is it? Would you be a priest, Levite, or Samaritan? Would you be the victim? Perhaps you have felt often what it means to be a victim. How would you react if you were the innkeeper presented with the task of caring for the victim?

This imaginative technique, called by some "going to the place," is also used in preaching. I once heard an evangelical preacher speak about Jesus' walk from the Upper Room to the Garden of Gethsemane. Sounding like someone who had walked the path himself, the pastor portrayed Jesus at prayer in the dark of the garden. As the apostles snored at his side, he could see a snake-like procession of soldiers bearing torches coming down the valley. Judas was at their head.

It was an effective way of preaching, and while the pastor's arrangement and description of the scene didn't go against Scripture, they certainly gave us things which are not in the text. But his purpose in using this imaginative form of preaching was to help us enter into the scene with heart and soul. Here, in my view, is an example of the way Protestants and Catholics meet in their use of Scripture.

Many Catholic devotional practices and popular preaching over the ages have used imaginative touches to help hearers grasp the drama and significance of a biblical event. The Way of the Cross, the meditations accompanying the recitation of the rosary, preaching about the life of St. Joseph or about Jesus' home life in Nazareth have all relied in varying degrees on imaginative touches. Like every good gift, the imagination which God gave us all can be abused. But, provided we do not commit theological atrocities, there should be no theoretical objection to its use in scriptural exposition and prayer.

Is the Bible a Divine Armory of Sacred Truth?

Some of the most fruitless and ultimately frustrating experiences Catholics and Protestants have had are encounters in which they try to convince each other of their own point of view by use of Scripture, quoting a profusion of texts to prove their points. Barely listening to each other, the combatants let the arrows fly back and forth. Sometimes they are both relying on the same text, each giving it his or her preferred weight and interpretation. The Protestant may debate unaware that he is using an interpretation which comes not from his own heart or personal inspiration but from his own church tradition. It might be as old as John Calvin or as recent as B. B. Warfield. The Catholic, too, may be presenting the view of Augustine or Cardinal Bellarmine of the sixteenth century. Both sides read and interpret from a tradition. What is more frustrating than the failure to grasp this is the tendency for them to rattle off snippets of a verse or bits of a chapter to invoke a different meaning than the original author intended. One Catholic writer has criticized this "game" as the "prostitution of the Scriptures." The Bible surely is a divine armory of truths, but we must be more responsible in our reading of the verses and their context.

Behind this frustrating manner of debate there was a conviction that Holy Scripture provided a divinely-revealed body of clear and distinct ideas from which doctrinal conclusions could be deduced, as the Westminster Confession put it, "by good and necessary consequence." Revelation for Protestants and Catholics has often been understood in terms of tidy propositions, valid always and everywhere, containing divine teaching.

Both Catholic and Protestant theology of the last one hundred years developed a theory of revelation that was in many ways quite similar. God had revealed himself in nature, and by our own observation of nature, by our use of reason, we could arrive at some knowledge of our Creator. But because of original sin, this knowledge was defective and had to be supplemented by revealed knowledge—supernatural knowledge. Revelation was "the body of propositional truth contained in Scripture and apostolic tradition. This revelation was committed to the Church and is authoritatively taught by pastors of the Church who speak in the name of Christ himself. . . ."[7]

Unfortunately, this approach has lent itself to the practice of formulating propositional declarations of truth which are lifted directly from a text, rearranged, and used in a chain of logic. Sometimes this has led us to abuse the texts, to force something from them that the biblical authors might not have recognized. How can we avoid this to better appreciate the Scriptures and to avoid fruitless arguments?

Jesuit theologian Avery Dulles suggests a new approach to Scripture which he calls "symbolic mediation." He believes that this would help us avoid two exaggerations. One exaggeration is the "liberal Protestant" tendency to make everything in Scripture that is difficult or miraculous merely a symbol or myth—meaning invention, fiction, or fantasy. It would, however, serve as a corrective to the idea that every apparently straightforward sentence in the Bible, unless the contrary can be proven, expresses a revealed truth.

Dulles sees a symbol as a special type of sign, distinguishable from a mere indicator. Dulles's view of a symbol is a sign pregnant with lively and life-giving meaning which is present, but not explicitly spelled out in living color. A text can have, as one writer puts it, a "surplus of meaning." A traffic sign is an *indicator* that has one meaning. A curved arrow, for instance, means there is a curve in the road ahead. Our country's flag on the other hand, is a *symbol* that evokes a variety of different meanings, and often can move us to tears. In the same way, gestures—the lives of certain people and revered historical sites—can have a wordless effect. Jesus is a historic person who is also God's communicator with us. His actions alone are full of meaning, capable of shaming us or encouraging us. His whole person is meaningful in a way that words cannot communicate.

To approach the Scriptures along the path of symbolic mediation is to set aside the temptation to juggle texts or connect them like dominoes to prove some point. A symbol is never a sheer object. Symbols do not lead to speculation, but instead give participatory knowledge.

Symbols can involve us, move us, and transform us, while sheer ideas may not. Symbols can stir the imagination, release hidden energies in the soul, and give strength and stability to the personality. They introduce us into realms of awareness not always accessible in tidy, logical language. Sacred Scripture is revelatory because God has inspired it, but it is also revelatory because its symbols touch us in deep and complex ways.

Dulles does not deny that the New Testament has propositional truths about Jesus. He suggests, however, that both the New Testament literature and Jesus as a person should be "dwelt in" or appreciated for the plenitude of meaning which is present without explicit, tidy, logical formulas.

Could this perspective help us in our approach to the Bible? An illustration may answer that question. Some years ago while working as a chaplain on a university campus, I got to know a young Christian who had begun a Bible study for his fraternity brothers. One semester, he invited me to participate in the study. When I asked him why he wanted me, he explained that there were some Catholics who attended. They sometimes got into discussions with their Protestant friends about Catholic theology which my friend couldn't handle. He wanted an authoritative spokesman on hand from the Catholic tradition.

I agreed to attend the Bible study on the condition that my friend retain the leadership. (It is so easy for clergy to take over with long sermons!) He agreed and I began attending. Since he was new at leading the Bible study, he had equipped himself with a teacher's guide or "how-to-do-it" manual for such studies. Typically we opened with a brief prayer and then read a chapter or two of the particular book we were studying. Then my friend read aloud questions from the teacher's manual.

It struck me as odd that among highly-educated literate folks, the manual's questions were designed to fish out the obvious and restricted answers, almost parrotlike repetition of a scriptural text rich with theological meat. My friend's conviction and zeal made it hard for him to accept answers from his fraternity brothers which differed from those given in the manual. He seemed unwilling to trust answers which were not in the guide or in his own Scripture commentary. It was as if each line or two of text could be read and understood in only one way.

When group attendance at the study began to sag to near death, I suggested that something was perhaps amiss. I suspected that it was the rigid constraints of the leader's guidebook. I couldn't help contrast this study with another Bible study group in which I took part at the same time. In the other Bible study, there was also a leader equipped with a "how-to-do-it" manual, but the manual was of a different kind. The first questions in that manual were never "What does this passage *teach* about Jesus?" They were rather along the lines of "How did you understand this passage?" or "How did this verse strike you?" This leader felt that before extracting a teaching or lesson, we in the group had to let the proclaimed text speak to us, to disturb, puzzle, exalt, or anger us.

Each person in this study came weekly with his or her own life experience. Each read or heard the text from that situation and base. Jesus, a parable, a healing, or the Crucifixion became in the group a symbolic communication, ripe with possibilities for nourishment and action. The variety of interpretation and the various resonances the text evoked arose from the different perspectives of members in the group. Scripture used in this way mediates God's revelation with symbolic meaning in depths beyond the mere words.

I am not saying that "Scripture only means what it says to me." I am not saying that our experiences are to be the judge of Scripture. My point is that no one, be it St. Augustine, Martin Luther, or Pope John Paul II, comes to these texts without their own life experiences and cultural filters. I am arguing that really good literature has something to offer men and women of every age. Holy Scripture is truly great literature, particularly since we believe it to be God's Word recorded in human words.

My experience of these two different Bible study groups convinced me that while no one can deny that Scripture has teachings and doctrinal messages, neither should we deny that God wishes to speak through the Bible in differing ways to each and every hearer. For this reason the key figures and events—Moses and Jesus, the Exodus and the Resurrection—and key objects—manna in the desert, bread at the Last Supper—carry a surplus of meaning not explicitly stated.

My final topic for this chapter concerns our current practice in Sunday worship, a practice refreshed by the Second Vatican Council's reforms. When the people have gathered on Sunday and have been brought to a group consciousness by a hymn, a generic confession of sinfulness, and an opening prayer, they sit to listen to an Old Testament passage chosen to match thematically the New Testament text assigned for the day. At the end of the Old Testament reading, the people are to respond by singing or reciting a psalm which is chosen to deepen or prolong the mood of the Old Testament selection.

The people then listen to a portion of one of the Epistles. For most of the year's liturgical cycle, these are read sequentially, Sunday after Sunday, independently of the chosen themes. During the seasons of Lent and Advent, however, Epistle selections reinforce the themes.

When the reader concludes the Epistle, priest and people stand in honor to welcome the gospel into their midst. Sometimes the priest or deacon who is to proclaim the gospel moves ceremoniously to the pulpit or lectern, escorted by acolytes bearing candles. While he does so, the people, the cantor, and the choir may be singing a short chant. Once the Bible is in position on the pulpit, the priest or deacon may pause to honor it with swirling clouds of incense. He then sings or says, "The Lord be with you," to which the people respond, "And also with you."

The implication of this brief prayer, mutually exchanged, is that what they are about to hear is not a message about Jesus, but Jesus himself, speaking through the sacred text. This text is then either sung or recited while the people remain standing out of respect for Jesus' special presence in the event. The singer-reader then says,

"This is the gospel of the Lord," to which the people reply, "Praise to you, Lord, Jesus Christ." Their praise is to the Lord, not to a book or to an effective reading. They are indicating that they have heard more than the human words.

I am not suggesting that every Catholic worshiper is paying deep attention to all of this every Sunday. There are places and times when this act of homage is done in a routine and coldly formal way. My point is that the ritual seeks to express and sharpen our sense of the power of the gospel as more than a text—as the presence of Christ, mediated through the text proclaimed by believers to believers. The Second Vatican Council's reforms of ritual make it clear that the priests are expected not to preach on their favorite football team, the leaking roof, or political controversy, but on the Scriptures of the day. This is the nourishment needed.

Conclusion

Catholics, as I hope I have made clear, have a distinctive approach to the Scriptures. The latest official stance on this and tradition is found in the Second Vatican Council's document on revelation, which encourages us to take the Scriptures seriously. We believe that the Bible is authored by God, but is simultaneously the work of inspired human authors. The council bishops, relying no doubt on the latest scriptural research, describe the New Testament as a collection of twenty-seven documents, the final product of a three-stage process.

In the first stage, the disciples taught what they were hearing and had learned from Jesus. They also taught through example by their manner of life, prayer, and ways of organizing the Christian communities. They were already in the process of beginning traditions and passing on to the next generation of believers what God had revealed in Jesus.

The next stage occurred when the churches studied, taught, remembered, and read in public worship a circulating collection of written materials, more than we now have. The selection of twenty-seven from this wider collection is the third stage. This too was a gradual one, a time of testing the written material against the community's instincts and memories, determining whether the written pieces reflected what many had learned and were living from the unwritten traditions.

Finally, around 315, A.D., there emerged a stable collection of documents accepted by most churches as most suitable and reliable for use in public worship. This three-century process, increasingly accepted by Christian scholars, is for Catholics a striking testimony to the view that vital and faithful churches existed before the New Testament as we know it now. The New Testament is therefore in a real sense the product of the church and tradition, passed along from the apostles to subsequent generations. This view strengthens the Catholic tendency to read Scriptures against a backdrop of tradition in a context radiant with the faith, prayer, theology, and holiness of our Catholic ancestors.

Tradition, in the sense used in this chapter and by the bishops at the Vatican Council, is the creative and inspired process by which God's revelation of himself in Jesus was remembered, told, retold, and adapted by Jesus' followers, particularly by the apostles and the succeeding leaders of the Christian churches.

5

A Closer Look at REDEMPTION

At the beginning of this book I wrote about my own journey of faith. I cannot claim that it is typical of all Catholics. All I can claim is that it never seems to fit the model which has the highest public profile among many Protestants.

When the evangelical asks the average Catholic over lunch or on a university campus, "Are you saved?" the Catholic is usually puzzled. This is because Catholics and Protestants attribute different meanings to the process of redemption.

Evangelicals generally view salvation as a single event—a voluntary, conscious, deliberate choice to renounce the old man and accept Christ as Savior. Some Protestant churches place their emphasis on this personal acceptance of Jesus as the key to redemption. Others stress the importance of adding the sacrament of baptism. The evangelicals I've met believe that redemption from sin hangs on this one occasionally dramatic acceptance of Jesus' work on our behalf.

Catholics, on the other hand, view redemption, insofar as it is our response, as a continual process which begins when one is christened, brought into the body of Christ. I consciously accepted Jesus into my life in a special way at the age of eight when I made my first Holy Communion. Six years later I again pledged myself to serve Christ in the sacrament of "confirmation." We are *being* redeemed, becoming little by little more alive in Christ, through the sacraments of the Church and our personal search for deeper knowledge of Christ. Thus, we see salvation not as a one-time conscious experience, but as a continual and life-long active process.

Both Catholics and Protestants make a distinction between two moments in Christian history. The first moment is the series of events associated with the historical figure, Jesus of Nazareth—the angel's message to Mary, his childhood, his baptism by John the Baptist, his first public miracles and preaching, his arrest and imprisonment, and his death and resurrection. Some have called this entire story the "Christ Event." Catholic liturgical texts focusing on Jesus' suffering, death, and resurrection, speak of the "paschal mystery." Whatever the terminology, Christians believe that Jesus represented and made concrete God's initiative of love and reconciliation to the entire world. We further believe that this one man's life has had an eternal, universal effect—an impact which has changed and continues to change the story of mankind.

But modern men are nineteen hundred years beyond these initial and decisive events. Therefore, there is for each age and for each person a second moment. These things which Christ achieved become effective five hundred, a thousand, or even five thousand years later.

My third ground-clearing remark has to do with the problem of language. One Protestant acquaintance with experience on the mission field in Japan told me that the concept of being "saved from sin" is strange to Japanese hearts. Their culture, with its strong family or corporate bonds, does not provide an immediate open door to our typical talk about *personal* sin. Even the word "redemption," with its overtone of being bought back, is problematic. When we start speaking to such people of substitutionary atonement, it may become even more difficult.

Even among ourselves we run into the problem of definition. One Christian writer I consulted provided eight distinct definitions of redemption. Is it "ransom from the devil," "liberation from slavery," or "atonement for dishonor?" Is it all of these or none of these? In a world where people suspect that there is no devil or where people don't even agree that sin is an enslavement, the language problem complicates the effort to explain this key Christian concept.

Rev. John Stott began his Lausanne Congress discussion on the topic by explaining what redemption is *not.* It is not psycho-physical health, even if Jesus did cure some people and wishes it for us all. It is not socio-political liberation, although Jesus was very concerned about justice. It is not "human development" in the sense of secular, worldly human potential movements. What, then, is it? Stott answered this question by giving a triple frame to the definition. Redemption is a reality of the past, the present, and the future.

In the *past,* we were saved from the wrath of God, from his just judgment upon our sins. Christ bore our guilt and was condemned in our place in order that we might be justified. This compares roughly with the "first moment" which I described earlier—the events of Jesus' life, death, and resurrection which altered human history. Stott then urged his hearers at Lausanne to bring the second moment more to the forefront, to concentrate on our new condition.

Redemption in the *present* tense means that for each human being who has been converted there is a new reality. We are sons and daughters enjoying free and happy access to our heavenly Father. Catholics believe that salvation is therefore as much a present reality and process as it is a gift received, a notion that Stott also stressed:

> I am not yet saved, for sin still dwells within me and my body is not yet redeemed. . . . Nevertheless during this present time, gradually, but surely the indwelling Spirit of Christ is subduing the flesh from within me and transforming me into the image of Christ, from one degree of glory to another (2 Cor. 3:18; Gal. 5:16–26).[1]

When Stott spoke of gradual subduing of the flesh, the transformation into the image of Christ, he opened the discussion to salvation *future.* His statements imply that since we are able to move from one degree of glory to another, there is something unfinished about the redemption now possessed.

Stott went on to say that we can't claim to be saved from self if we do not go on to abandon our liberated self in selfless service. Finality and completion are not yet achieved. We look forward to a new heaven and a new earth, to our deliverance from the whole process of decay in creation and from evil. Then we shall experience, along with the whole of creation, what Paul calls "glorious freedom of the children of God" (Rom. 8:21).

The three-part framework for defining redemption reminds me of an acclamation made by Catholics during their Sunday worship. When the priest has retold the narrative of the Last Supper, he holds up the consecrated bread and the cup of wine. He invites the people to proclaim a mystery of faith. In response, the people typically either sing or say aloud, "Christ *has* died, Christ *is* risen, Christ *will come* again." We are recognizing that redemption is a process which Christ began in the past, which he continues in the present, and which he will bring to completion in the future.

The same awareness pops up at the beginning of our worship. The priest praises Christ with a triple formula, to which the congregation answers, "Lord, have mercy; Christ, have mercy; Lord have mercy." One such formula reads as follows:

> Lord Jesus, you *came* to gather the nations into the peace of God's Kingdom. (Congregation responds.)
>
> Lord Jesus, you *come* in word and sacrament to strengthen us in holiness. (Congregation responds.)
>
> Lord Jesus, you *will come* in glory with salvation for your people. (Congregation again responds.)

Each of the three phrases shifts the frame of reference: he *came*, he *comes*, and he *will come*.

Above and beyond details of our liturgical rite, it is good to recall that the entire Catholic calendar of observances includes past, present, and future. The Christmas season, from late December to early January, and Lent remind us of Jesus' coming to us and suffering. Easter reminds us that Jesus is victoriously alive. Advent helps us focus on the end of time, Jesus' second coming, by using prophetic texts calling us to repentance.

Acknowledging that salvation has a future aspect, many Catholics find it hard to get excited about some television evangelists who preach continuously about the last days or the coming judgment. An intricate exegesis of Daniel and Revelation interwoven with comments about the Arab-Israeli war or problems in the North Atlantic Treaty Organization seem to us too far afield.

We affirm in our creed that Jesus will come again to judge the living and dead. We pray in the very prayer Jesus taught us, "thy kingdom come," and we believe that God's rule cannot be simply equated with any particular ideology, government, or revolution sweeping one country or an entire continent. Salvation is the past, present, and future work of God. He does invite us to cooperate in this process, but concerning the last days, no man knows the day or the hour. For us, the issue is, "How well do we use the space allotted?"

Saved from What?

Stott's description of salvation past spoke of being saved from God's wrath, just judgment, and guilt. Why should God be wrathful? What is the guilt we have incurred? The usual answers speak of guilt for our sins and wrath at humanity's misdeeds. Theological language speaks of the original sin of Adam and our own personal sin.

A great Christian thinker once said that even if the Bible didn't have anything about original sin, observant people would have invented the concept. We are confronted daily through the newspaper or television news with a painful and never-ending scenario of cruelty, war, greed, and injustice. Millions of newborn children, through no fault of their own, arrive in a world already seriously polluted, eroded, war-torn, and often occupied by the wealthy for the benefit of the wealthy. In many countries, children grow up in societies where access to education, food, housing, and medical care is either non-existent or twisted to favor only the middle and upper classes. Even within families, children are born in unsafe or unjust situations because of decisions made years before by their parents or grandparents. This, it seems to me, is the reality we experience. The situation speaks of cosmic disorder, of mysterious division and injustice between peoples. It is, in biblical terms, life outside the Garden of Eden.

Catholic Scripture scholar Pheme Perkins says that the New Testament authors saw all of humanity trapped in sinfulness. These writers looked around and saw a world dominated by evil powers, but whose rule is broken in the victorious exaltation of the risen Christ at the right hand of God the Father (Col. 1:18–20). This is a way of speaking of "salvation past," rescue from the grip of these evil powers. Yet this rescue operation is not meaningful unless there is follow-through. The victory is also the foundation of a new community, the church (Col. 1:18). Only God's action can break through the death-grip of sin—both the effects of Adam's fall and the effects which we ourselves contribute.

For Perkins, the key term to describe this gracious and powerful victory of God is the word *reconciliation.* I like the term because it reminds me of healing between husband and wife, parents and children, and feuding nations and races. Reconciliation is God's turning in love toward a sinful humanity. It speaks of a salvation that has been given in Christ *before* humans make any move toward the Father. Perkins writes:

> This divine action is described as having universal consequences. . . . But, this cosmic dimension is also expressed in the community, since those who have been saved by Christ constitute a group in which the old divisions of hostility between Jew and Greek have been overcome. . . .[2]

The ancient churches of the Christian East described redemption in yet another way. These ancestors of ours in the faith were not afraid to speak of salvation in terms of divinization. As the old adage put it, "God became Man so that men might become God." As 2 Peter 1:4 says, we are "partakers of the divine nature. . . ."

To conclude my efforts to define redemption, I want to quote extensively from Pope John Paul II's first encyclical *Redemptor Hominis,* where he approaches the topic from the point of view of "new covenant," and "new creation." These paragraphs contain the redemption past aspect, what Jesus did, as well as the positive side, redemption present.

> . . . do not forget even for a moment that Jesus Christ the Son of the Living God, became our reconciliation with the Father. He it was, and He alone, who satisfied the Father's eternal love, that fatherhood that from the beginning found expression in creating the world, giving man all the riches of creation, and making him "little less than God," in that he was created in the "image and after the likeness of God."

In Jesus, the pope writes, a new covenant is offered.

> He and He alone satisfied that fatherhood of God and that love which man in a way rejected by breaking the first covenant and the later covenants that God "again and again offered to man."

The pope then describes redemption of the world as:

> . . . this tremendous mystery of love in which creation is renewed—(redemption) is, at its deepest root, the fullness of justice in a human heart—the heart of the first-born Son—in order that it may become justice in the hearts of many human beings, predestined from eternity in the first-born Son to be children of God and called to grace, called to love. . . .[3]

I use this long quote to show that the very language which we use to describe salvation affects the way we view our own present state and our own calling. I find it uplifting to focus, as does the pope, on our new condition—called to grace and justice. By speaking of redemption in connection with humanity's struggles and pains, the pope can introduce that dimension to the Church's mission. He has reworked the ancient "divinization" theme for a technological age plagued with injustice:

> . . . in Christ and through Christ man has acquired full awareness of his dignity, of the heights to which he is raised, of the surpassing worth of his own humanity, and the meaning of his existence.[4]

Much of the pope's later writing and speeches build on human rights and social justice, a concern flowing directly from the pope's understanding of the new condition we share through redemption.

I hope that it is now clear that when a Protestant asks a Catholic acquaintance, "Are you saved?" and doesn't receive the expected answer, the reasons are evident. The best answer a Catholic could give would be, "I was saved, I am being saved, and I hope to be saved at the end."

Getting in Touch with Jesus' Saving Work

Beyond the issue of the richness of definition there is the question of getting in touch with salvation. Whether one refers to this process as "reconciliation" or "atonement," we still has to figure out how Jesus' work enters our lives. In what follows, I will clarify the differences between Protestants and Catholics on this point.

Both Protestants and Catholics believe that salvation comes to us because God wills that all men and women should be saved. He wants us to be reconciled with him and with each other. It is his love that moves him to extend to us new life, new creation, and new covenant. We Catholics believe that to do this, God sends his Holy Spirit, breathing where it will, attracting us, startling us, convicting us, getting our attention—whether we are atheists or animists, secularists or sinners.

We also believe that Jesus, through the mystery of the Incarnation, is in some deep sense united with every person. The entire human race has been shifted by Jesus, oriented toward the source of life and love. Clearly, individuals and communities often resist this shift. God therefore asks for our cooperation in evangelizing, in bringing all humanity to awareness of his love in Jesus Christ and his gift of new life through the Spirit. The Great Commission asks us to share the gospel truths and bring others to the community of believers.

Consider the meaning of the word *conversion.* Is it primarily a single dramatic moment? Is it a long process? If it is primarily a single dramatic moment, consciously recognized, does this mean that the world is sharply divided into two camps, the saved and the unsaved? Are there no gradations between being converted and unconverted? I personally get nervous with this kind of division. It seems to judge millions of human beings as unsaved because they have not had the decisive, conscious moment of choosing Christ. I prefer to believe that in every human being, the Spirit is breathing, gradually calling individuals to clearer vision, sounder values, and eventually consciousness of God's love in Jesus.

I find it helpful to rely on John Stott's discussion of conversion. He sees conversion as a turning to the Lord, a movement of the heart triggered by God's own Spirit. It does involve repentance and renunciation, but Stott does not linger on this aspect. He accentuates the central aspect of repentance as commitment to what God himself is doing in human history.

Stott also speaks of a "new beginning," to be followed by the life of discipleship, growth into Christian maturity, membership in the church, and involvement in the world. God in the Holy Spirit is the agent of our gradual growth in Christ—the ongoing work of salvation—through these four aspects. It should also be noted that by our membership in the church, growth in maturity, discipleship, and involvement in the world, we do our part to lay the groundwork for salvation to come—the establishment of the kingdom of God.

Perhaps an unfortunate aspect of much evangelism is the focus on the actual moment of decision, so much so that these four important sides of salvation are lost in the shuffle. Effective preaching does lead to a change of heart, but these other aspects—membership in a church, discipleship, growth, and involvement in the world—are just as important as the realization of Christ as Savior. I know that Dr. Billy Graham has been deeply concerned about the question of follow-up, and that at one point he asked Navigators' founder Dawson Trotman to help the Graham campaigns with the training and development of follow-up personnel. Without that, the approach which focuses solely on the moment of conversion runs the risk of being both pragmatically ineffective and biblically unsound.

When the apostles preached at Pentecost under the Spirit's impulse, they urged repentance and change of heart, but they also urged their hearers to be baptized in the name of Jesus for the forgiveness of sins. In turn, these newly-baptized believers would receive the outpouring of the Holy Spirit. The practical or concrete outcome of their repentance, baptism, and forgiveness was the formation of a very visible community—proto-church. The heart of this community was discipleship, holding goods in common, helping the poor (involvement in the world), constant prayer, and celebration of the Eucharist. Catholics believe that this early church exemplified the true meaning of redemption with its focus on all four elements instead of just the singular moment of conversion.

For Catholics, the notion of conversion would certainly include the possibility of an instant change of heart, but we would include the rich array of elements that John Stott describes. In a world sensitive to native customs and cultures, conversion should not mean rejection of anything that is noble from one's past or from one's heritage. All of God's good gifts should enter into the new life. And we believe that new life—effective linkage with Jesus' past saving activity, present saving work, and future coming—requires personal faith, baptism, confirmation and the Eucharist, the historical sacraments of initiation into the body of Christ.

Within Catholicism, voices have been raised to criticize a type of thinking and behavior which makes too sharp a divide between "religious" life or "spiritual" things and the world. It is at this point that John Stott's idea of involvement in the world as an important dimension of conversion should be remembered. Catholics who have been critical of Catholic passivity in the face of social evil urge us to go back and look at the prophets of the Old Testament. Again and again fidelity to the covenant with God meant work on behalf of justice for the poorest, the most abandoned and helpless.

Works Righteousness

Because I have mentioned the importance of involvement in the world as one of the dimensions of being converted, I think it is useful here to speak about "works righteousness," a phrase which has become in some quarters a "battle slogan." Many say that Catholics believe they are saved by works. Protestants believe that works availeth not, only Jesus' loving embrace. Righteousness, or justification, is not our achievement.

In classical sixteenth century reformation controversies, Lutherans and Catholics waged verbal and physical war over a number of topics, one of the most prominent being that of justification. One way of describing justification is "getting into effective touch with Jesus' saving work." Lutheran traditions speak of justification or righteousness *imputed*, accredited to us through Jesus. Another way of describing it is "forensic righteousness," declared right with God by Jesus.

Catholics preferred to speak of God's own righteousness being shared with each of us, implanted in the believer, making us righteous. The Lutheran approach stressed God's loving initiative and power; no human effort could snatch righteousness from God's hand. The Catholic approach fought for recognition of God's gift of himself to each of us, our sharing in the new life and the divine nature—*divinization.*

This may seem at first glance too technical a problem to concern us here, but the truth is that it is very much related to the notion of redemption. Disgusted with the late medieval Catholic accumulation of relics, pilgrim mileage, and frenzied commission of masses,

Lutherans wanted nothing to do with the "works" mentality. "We cannot," they cried aloud, "earn heaven."

Some of their Catholic contemporaries were as scandalized by relic collectors and indulgence buyers as the Lutherans, but rejected what they felt was too slashing an attack. It seemed to many Catholics that the Lutheran tradition, and perhaps later that of Calvinists, resulted in overkill. They so stressed our unworthiness, our corrupt character, and our weakness that it seemed as if nothing we did was pleasing in God's eyes. Are we merely rotten worms, even though we are a new creation? Couldn't the Holy Spirit have moved us to decent thoughts or actions to some degree even before we were baptized?

For Protestants who still worry that Catholics lean too heavily on "works" as the means of salvation, it might be helpful to know that Catholic and Lutheran theologians have been meeting over the years to iron out their differences on this crucial topic. The method was to assemble good biblical scholars from both traditions. Together these experts went through the Scripture with a fine-tooth comb, studying closely the phrases or words which speak of righteousness. As a result of their study and discussion, both the Lutheran and Catholic participants in the dialogue have developed a mutually acceptable statement about justification.

That statement, fine tuned and biblically based, provides a balanced formula which respects the Lutheran sensitivity about salvation as God's initiative and gift as well as the Catholic concern that new life in Christ blossoms into good works. Sinful humanity, alienated from God, has been given righteousness, becoming thereby a new creation. Salvation past is God's gift of himself in Christ with the cooperation of Mary. Salvation present is Christ's continual giving with our cooperation. Woe to those who at the last judgment will not hear the King's words, "When I was hungry, you gave me to eat; I was thirsty and you gave me to drink; I was a stranger and you took me in; naked and you covered me; sick and you visited me; I was in prison and you came to me" (Matthew 25:35–39).

The attentive reader may have noticed that I have stressed the importance of baptism as part of the redemption process. I have also mentioned the importance of faith. Infant baptism causes particular problems for evangelicals because the infant is not in a position to understand what is happening, nor can he or she make any personal commitment to Christ. While this topic will be explained more fully in chapter 6, I need to comment briefly on infant baptism here. Perhaps a short story will help; it is a story revealing a mentality about life.

A woman I met not long ago was telling me of her experiences as an elementary school teacher among Canadian Indians, quite some distance from Canada's flashier cities. The young woman, coming as she did from white schools and typical education courses, was often totally baffled and frustrated by her Indian pupils. In her efforts to stimulate their classroom performance, she would offer prizes to the child with the best record in spelling or math. The Indian reaction to this was not the usual one.

When the teacher offered an award to a pupil, the child turned right around to distribute the prize to classmates. These children did not understand that by their own efforts they had won something they could claim as their own personal treasure. It was inconceivable to the winner and to the others that any person should be rewarded to the exclusion of the others. What one had, all had.

Since so much of North American life is based on the notion of the individual's worth and rights, this young woman had to make a large mental adjustment in a culture where the tribe or group gets more attention than the individual. This is a mentality which focuses more on the collectivity than on individuals. The ancient Church practice of infant baptism reflects a society in which identity, worth, and security came through membership in a family, clan, or tribe. Biblical passages which describe the baptized as part of Christ's body, as a new people, royal priesthood, kingly nation, or branches on a vine convinced Catholics that infants, before they as individuals could understand, should benefit from the life of Christ by baptism into his body. It would be inconceivable that the grace of God offered in Christ's family be held back from the newest arrivals.

Pastoral practice is increasingly troubled by the practice of baptizing infants whose parents seem to lack the elements of conversion which we have mentioned here. It is harder and harder to assume that any child is born into a stable family, much less a stable family of deep faith in a Christian culture. As a result, some church leaders will defer baptism of an infant until the child's parents or godparents can be helped to understand more fully what Catholicism involves and the depth of their commitment when they promise to raise a child in the faith.

To require training for parents and godparents, deferring baptism for a year or more runs the risk of offending Catholics accustomed to a different practice in countries traditionally and culturally Catholic. Some pastoral teams in parishes, unwilling to drive people further away from the Church, will require less by way of preparation, and will baptize the infant, trying to make the entire experience as biblically rich and as welcoming as possible.

Conclusion

In this chapter I have tried to clarify why Protestant-Catholic conversations often collapse shortly after they start: a one-sided concept of salvation, usually salvation past, dominates.

When Catholics speak of conversion and salvation, they are speaking of more complex concepts. John Stott's helpful three-part framework for defining redemption is a useful way of thinking—our human understanding of history requires it. From God's point of view, if I may presume to speak of it, past, present, and future would have a different meaning. For God, there is an immediacy and contemporaneity about it all.

We believe that redemption means unity in fellowship that is visible. As Paul wrote to the Corinthians, we are united in Christ's body. The New Testament Christ heals, forgives, empowers, teaches, and shares his Spirit. We see this as everlasting redemption. If today he is our High Priest interceding for us, then salvation encompasses past action in history, present process, and foretaste of salvation future.

In the previous chapter I told how Catholics saw themselves as a People of God, united to Christ through baptism, sharing through that sacrament Jesus' roles as Prophet, Priest, and King. We are to be a worshiping people, a prophetic people concerned with truth in all its forms, and a kingly people, extending Christ's rule throughout all the earth—extensively and intensively, into all areas of society.

6

A Closer Look at BAPTISM AND CONFIRMATION

In this chapter I will present a brief discussion of four topics: sacraments in general, conversion, baptism, and confirmation.

Sacraments in General

I find no better place to begin than with the definition of sacrament found in the *St. Paul Family Catechism,* written by a team of nuns from the order the Daughters of St. Paul. Given an episcopal permit and published in 1983, this book defines sacraments as "an external sign instituted by Christ through which He gives us His grace."

Some Catholics believe that this formulation of grace being given through the sacraments supports the view that "mere performance" transmits grace, or that the sacrament operates like a water tap, open and close to get outburst of grace. Any misunderstanding of sacrament along this line must be set aside in light of a related question and answer from the catechism:

> Do all the sacraments give grace?
>
> Because of the merits of Jesus' passion and death, all the sacraments give grace if they are received with the right dispositions.

We believe that mere *performance* of a rite is inadequate. When we participate in a sacrament, we are to have "right dispositions." The catechism describes these as faith and love, trust in God's mercy, and sorrow for sin.

The importance of faith, trust, and hope in receiving the sacraments has been standard Catholic teaching. The problem has been that in debates, some Catholics would tend to heavily stress the divine side—the offer of grace, *ex opere operato*—while paying too little attention to the faith side—the human capacity to be present to God's offer of grace.

Our Catholic belief says first that a sacrament is connected with Christ, his Passion, and his death, and second, that proper participation in the ritual bestows grace. The catechism's formula is an umbrella over a very rich, complex, and lengthy history. We have to take a brief look at this history of Catholic reflection about sacraments in order to understand how and why Catholics believe as they do.

The word "sacrament" is the English translation of the Latin word *sacramentum,* and this in turn was a translation of the Greek word *mysterion.* A concept found both in ancient Greek philosophy and religion, *mysterion* appears in the writings of St. Paul. It is also found in Mark 4:11, referring to the reign of God breaking into the world through Christ. This "inbreaking" of the kingdom is grace bringing salvation to believers.

Paul uses this word *mysterion* in a new way. Taking it beyond Greek usage, the ritual of a secret cult, he uses it to describe God's gift of life in the person of Jesus Christ through his death and resurrection. This whole is a mystery unveiled by the Spirit of God, to be proclaimed by the apostles (see 1 Cor. 2:10–15).

For some later Christian writers, the ritual enactment of the saving work of the crucified, risen, and glorified Lord could also be called *mysterion.* The next crucial moment in the history of the concept came when the theologian Tertullian used the Latin word *sacramentum* to speak of this idea. *Sacramentum* in Latin culture seemed like a particularly inspired translation because it connoted the idea of a sacred commitment by the gods and a reciprocal commitment by the believer. In short, God's covenantal relationship with Jews and Gentiles and our covenant with him in Jesus could be described as sacraments.

By the fourth century of the Christian era a new emphasis emerged, described by one scholar as follows:

> . . . the main interest now became the realization, the making present, of the saving deeds of Christ through ritual celebration, to make possible a participation in the essentials of salvation.[1]

There seems to have been at this time no hesitation in referring to the historically unique events of Jesus' crucifixion and resurrection as being repeated in the ritual enactment.

Crucial for later discussion of sacraments by medieval and Reformation theologians was the contribution of St. Augustine. He used the word *sacramentum* to apply to more rituals and prayers than the seven later adopted as official sacraments. Augustine described baptism and the Eucharist as sacred signs of the divine reality of grace. Yet they were not, as some later followers of Augustine thought, merely signs or symbols. For Augustine, as Alexandre Ganoczy asserts,

> the sacrament of Christian ritual effects what it symbolizes. It communicates that to the recipient which the analogy points up: baptism communicates cleansing, justifying faith; the Eucharist communicates the unifying power of the true body and blood of Christ.[2]

In short, Augustine preached a sacramental realism.

It seems that from Mark, Paul, Tertullian, and Augustine, the theological challenge has been that of describing the reality and power of the Christ Event, the mystery, and its enactment in ways that are helpful to the particular people and culture being addressed. Further, the challenge is to do this without falling into "magical" manipulations of the divine or into "mere symbolism" or "visible lessons" about Jesus. While some medieval theologians laid heavy stress on the reality of these things, some Reformation theologians backed very far away, stressing the notion of sacraments as "commemorative only," or subjectively "spiritual" events.

Despite contrary efforts prior to the Second Vatican Council, popular preaching and teaching about the sacraments retained the flavor of the Catholic-Protestant debates. We Catholics therefore stressed proper performance of ritual, the centrality of the priest or bishop as ministers of the sacrament, and God's unfailing promise to give grace in the act. We did not forget the importance of dispositions, but these occupied lower ground in our defense mentality.

Newer Formulations of the Sacramental Concept

Catholics are currently blessed with fuller, richer formulations about the meaning of sacraments, and in this section I can give only a sample. Rev. Richard McBrien's fine work gives a good summary of the meaning of sacraments.

1. By the external gestures, words and objects we Catholics proclaim our faith, express our belief in the unseen reality beneath the signs.

2. Sacraments are signs through which we worship, but at a deep level. We believe that Christ, the risen Savior, pays homage to the Father, and that because of our unity in the Son, we can share in that worship.

3. Sacraments are signs of unity of the Church. The unity in question is a unity of faith being expressed in common by a congregation, or the recipients of a sacrament, and by the minister. We believe the same way about the meaning of the rite and we believe we encounter Jesus in it.

4. Sacraments are signs of *Christ's presence,* and ultimately that of God the Father. When we participate in the sacraments we believe that we are part of Jesus' own healing, forgiving, or cleansing. Christ's human actions, especially in the Eucharist, are not confined to the historic moment in which he first acted. Christ is both God and Man and there is an eternal, time-transcending activity which we touch in the sacraments.[3]

To sum up, McBrien repeats a point made earlier. Sacraments do not cause grace magically. They are "free acts of God and they are free acts of ours." They work only to the extent that we bring faith and devotion to them.

Another contemporary restatement of the sacramental concept is that of Georgetown University's Monika Hellwig, who defines sacrament as "embodiment." She writes:

> Human persons cannot meet or experience God except as embodied. The chosen people Israel, with its holy land and its holy law, its sabbath observance and its great festival celebrations, was such an embodiment from early times, offering its mediation in Scripture and tradition even to Jesus himself. . . . For Christians, the fundamental sacrament or embodiment of God's presence and merciful power in the world is the person of Jesus. . . .[4]

Hellwig's perspective is that the Spirit of the risen Jesus draws us together to be interdependent in pursuit of a common purpose in life "the followers of Jesus become in their turn part of the mystery, the sacrament or embodiment of God in the world." We are members of Christ's body or the gathering of God's people.

Catholics therefore see God as embodied in Christ, who is in turn embodied in a limited and yet real way in the Church. What the Church does when focused in a ritual embodies Christ. Thus, Jesus is a fundamental or primordial mysterion, a sacrament.

A third contemporary restatement of the notion of sacrament comes from Alexander Ganoczy.

> Just as an individual "reveals" his own "mystery" in moments of communication with other individuals, and thereby gives existence to his innermost being, so in like manner does God use physical forms of encounter in order to communicate his saving being to the individual.[5]

As is perhaps evident from this approach, "sacrament" again involves a very humble use of earthly things to convey the divine. Underneath or behind, interwoven with what believers do together in the ritual, God is present with a particular offer of himself in Christ and the Spirit.

All the foregoing formulations, ranging from the simpler, traditional one from the catechism through those of McBrien, Hellwig, and Ganoczy express our Catholic belief. They also seek to present the idea of *mysterion-sacrament* in its full Christian depth while avoiding excessive stress on the performance—seen as magic, a "visual aid," or a spiritual symbol. Perhaps these terms will make the Catholic view of sacraments more clear.

Conversion

Several years ago, I had the privilege of attending a national meeting sponsored by Campus Crusade for Christ. Thousands of young men and women came to Kansas City, Missouri, for teaching, seminars, and motivational sessions. Many of the young collegians in attendance had never personally "witnessed" to their faith in Jesus Christ, and one conference goal was to train them to do this. In collaboration with the Salvation Army and some local churches, the young men and women were given the opportunity to witness in Kansas City neighborhoods.

The key training instrument and doctrinal tool for Campus Crusade witnessing is a pamphlet called *Four Spiritual Laws.* As an observer at the Kansas City meeting, I was much impressed by the zeal of the young men and women who set out one frigid winter afternoon to share their faith with strangers. Later the same day, before thousands of students in the municipal auditorium, some of these men and women were encouraged to tell of their experiences. Many came forward to the television camera to tell us how they had shared the good news about Jesus and how their hearers had often accepted Christ.

These young collegians had helped trigger a movement in the hearts of people, but only local churches connected to the follow-up program would be in a position to know how the movement developed.

As defined by John Stott, conversion requires more than this first stage. Following the acceptance of Christ comes repentance, renunciation, and a new beginning, followed by discipleship, Christian growth, membership in a local church, and involvement in the world. Stott's view parallels a contemporary Catholic perspective on the same subject. I am referring to Rev. Brian McDermott's treatment of grace in which he speaks of five stages: acceptance, conversion, discipleship in community, witness, and service.[6] Let's look at these stages.

God's loving offer of himself to us humans is always in action, but it has a particular point and effect in our birth into a family which provides for us an initial welcome and acceptance. Modern psychology stresses how important this psychological-emotional acceptance is for children. Without it they lack the capacity to trust in the reliability of parental love. The first stage of grace is being able to trust our own worth and the capacity to know a world which has some basic order and stability.

God's grace and gift to us of this kind of beginning can deepen to a realization that every human being, in goodness or guilt, can find in the Creator a loving person. The love extended by God has the power to draw "the falsely self-assertive and harmfully dependent ego" into a relationship that is life-giving.

Following this initial gift and movement, there is the possibility for what Stott calls "repentance" and "renunciation." McDermott writes:

> Sorrow, shame and confusion . . . emerge almost organically (yet as fruit of God's love and thus freely as well) when the acceptance experience puts down roots deep into the soil of the human spirit.[7]

McDermott reminds us that both Protestant and Catholic Christianity proclaim that "we in our entirety need conversion and transformation, not only because the natural in us needs to be graced, but because *all* of us is threatened by the dark power of sin."

> Not only our sin in the sense of our obviously destructive side, but also the gifts, talents and experiences of yesterday, need to be drawn out of isolation or tendency toward isolation into life-giving relationship. There is a centripetal tendency both in our goodness and sins, an egoism that is an egoism of goodness and of sin.[8]

While McDermott's stages speak directly of growth in grace, they are also phases of conversion and therefore the work of God's self-gift in Jesus. As with Stott's model, McDermott's begins with initial turning to the Lord and continues through repentance, discipleship in community, witness, and service.

My own reading of evangelical sources leads me to believe that sudden or instantaneous conversion is more rare than the gradual kind. Many evangelicals active in radio and television media regard some of their work as sowing and watering, not as harvesting of converts. Catholics use this sense of conversion in their efforts to evangelize adults through the Rite for the Christian Initiation of Adults (RCIA).

Many Catholics are currently working in their parishes to apply to modern life what had been an ancient Christian initiation program for would-be converts. This revised version being tried in the United States and other countries presupposes that God's grace is drawing people to him. Thus, the Church's task is to help people recognize this, to enhance its effectiveness, and to help them in the growth process. To understand this, it is useful to catch the flavor of the process whereby adults became Catholics in our recent past.

Prior to the Second Vatican Council, particularly in North America, adults asking for admission to the Catholic Church usually had two options. The first and most common was a set of meetings in private with a priest who gave instructions according to his talent and in the manner best fitted to the inquirer's needs. At some point mutually agreed upon by the priest and the person, baptism or a formal profession of faith in the Catholic Church would follow.

A second option, promoted especially during the post-World War II resurgence of religion in the United States, was classroom instruction. A priest gathered a group of would-be Catholics for a weekly teaching session on Church doctrine, practice, and customs. While private supplemental instructions were also given, the basic experience was a classroom setting with group discussion. Depending on needs and resources, courses ran from a few weeks to six months. At the end of the course, the priest and potential convert discussed whether or not baptism or profession of faith as a Catholic was in order.

One of the drawbacks to this system was that the course of instruction, whether private or in a group, was too often isolated from the parish into which the convert might be integrated. Another drawback was that, even with lengthy courses, personal interviews, and counseling, priests rarely had time to follow up on the new Christian. Some of the newly baptized lost their initial enthusiasm in a parish that seemed less lively or less interested in their needs than the priest who had instructed.

The current RCIA concept tries to provide systematic instruction, personal counseling, and better integration into the sponsor parish. Candidates are to be sponsored throughout the program by a Catholic in good standing. Insofar as possible, sponsors really do "sponsor," accompanying the potential initiate through various phases of conversion, repentance, growing maturity, discipleship, and so forth. When properly done, the process introduces the candidates to the parish leaders, the lay council, and heads of parish societies or committees. These have a chance to speak from their hearts about their faith, and they witness to the would-be convert.

A typical program begins with an outreach program in late summer or early autumn. People who have a desire to become Catholics then enroll for the first stages of the program. *Catechumenate* is the ancient Christian title for this process. The teaching and the exposure to living examples of Catholicism continue through autumn, winter, Lent, and Holy Week. Those who have decided to join the Church and whose application for membership has met with approval may be baptized at the Easter services. If already properly baptized in another denomination, they may make a solemn profession of faith at this time. Well-run programs also include a post-baptismal follow-up which assists the new convert in preparation for Pentecost.

The advantage of this program is that during the process, a person becomes integrated into a support group or finds a niche in the local congregation. And, unlike the earlier program, there is less chance for post-baptismal floundering when early enthusiasm wears off. A further advantage is that a well-designed program challenges the congregation to examine itself. *These people want to join us? Are we that attractive? Dare we invite them to join when we are so lukewarm?* Parishes which have had these programs for a number of years are more alive, and they are much more aware of the Great Commission.

To be sure, every person drawn to Christ has his or her own individual needs and experiences. This is the natural seed-ground for their faith, but as important as it is to honor this, conversion must go deeper. As John Stott reminds us, it includes discipleship, church membership, and a personal witness. The very process of initiation should provide the neophyte with a chance to demonstrate his or her own attitudes and values. As a parish's sponsors and staff themselves become more skilled in this work, they are better able to help discern if a candidate is ready for initiation or needs a fuller grasp of what being a Christian means.

Current Catholic practice of baptism for adults is a faith-filled acknowledgment of what God has been doing with them in Christ.

Initiation is a process which leads through baptism to confirmation and the Eucharist, a participation in the Christ-Mystery and his death and resurrection. In addition, the process of initiation recognizes and respects the gradual stages which constitute conversion and growth in grace.

Baptism

In the dry language of the catechism, baptism is the sacrament which achieves the following:

- removes original sin and all personal sins, particularly for adults
- makes us children of God, brothers and sisters of Jesus
- makes us heirs of heaven
- makes us members of the Church with the right to participate in other sacraments

In the wake of the Second Vatican Council's revision of our sacramental practices, the church's official ritual describes baptism, confirmation, and the Eucharist as a packet—Sacraments of Initiation.

The catechism's short formulations of the Sacraments of Initiation are beautifully expanded in the following paragraphs from the Rites of the Catholic Church.

> *a.* . . . through them men and women are freed from the power of darkness. With Christ they die, are buried, and rise again. They receive the Spirit of adoption which makes them God's sons and daughters and, with the entire people of God, they celebrate the memorial of the Lord's death and resurrection.
>
> *b.* These sacraments incorporate men and women into Christ. They are formed into God's people. They are raised from their natural human condition to the dignity of adopted children. They become a new creation through water and the Holy Spirit. Hence, they are called, and are indeed, the children of God.
>
> *c.* Signed with the gift of the Spirit in Confirmation, Christians more perfectly become the image of their Lord and are filled with the Holy Spirit. They bear witness to him before all the world and eagerly work for the building up of the body of Christ.

d. Finally they come to the table of the Eucharist, to eat the flesh and drink the blood of the Son of Man so that they may have eternal life and show forth the unity of God's people. By offering themselves with Christ, they share in his universal sacrifice; the entire community of the redeemed is offered to God by their high priest. They pray for a greater outpouring of the Holy Spirit so that the whole human race may be brought into the unity of God's family.[9]

These extended formulas pick up the key images—body of Christ and People of God—with which the bishops spoke of the Church. The language also points to baptism and confirmation as a sharing in the priesthood of Christ, as in paragraph *d,* "By offering themselves with Christ, they share in his universal sacrifice." Paragraphs *c* and *d* have the language of Christ's prophetic role, in which we share witnessing of him to all the world. The bishops' teaching that the laity also shares in Jesus' kingship through baptism finds expression in paragraph *d,* "They pray for a greater outpouring of the Holy Spirit so that the whole human race may be brought into the unity of God's family."

Unlike the catechism, the ritual's formulation does not speak of removal of original sin, but it does speak of being freed from the power of darkness. "With Christ, they die, are buried, and rise again." Catholics believe that our whole Christian life is a process of repeated dying and rising with Christ—ongoing redemption—a process which includes repentance, renunciation, and a new beginning. Yet, baptism has a special place in this process. As Charles Davis has written:

> The reason is that in it we achieve the essential transition from the old order to the new. The baptized essentially belong to the new order of the Resurrection. They have entered a new existence and possess eternal life. They have passed from darkness to light, from slavery to freedom, from the kingdom of Satan to the kingdom of Christ.[10]

Although Davis's book was written over twenty years ago, I appreciate his description of the new relationship which begins in baptism. The catechism's simple formulation—that the sacrament makes us children of God—receives richer treatment from Davis, who describes the relationship children of God have in the Holy Trinity.

> To the Father the relationship is that of sonship; he is the ultimate source of our life, and we participate in the knowledge and love that united Father and Son in the life of the Trinity.
>
> To the Son, our relationship is that of brother. He is the model of our life of grace, the pattern after whom we are formed when we are given a share in the divine life. We are joined to him, so that it is his life we possess, his relation to the Father we share.
>
> To the Spirit our relationship is that of host. The Spirit is our indwelling Guest, and it is because we have received the Spirit as Gift that the Father and Son are present with us. Our personal relation to the Spirit leads us to welcome him as the Guest that comes as the pledge of love from Father and Son, and who by making his dwelling within us joins us to Christ our brother and leads us as sons to the Father.[11]

Davis reminds us too of the central role of faith in this sacrament. Baptism perfects and confirms initial faith. As conferred on adults, it is a sacrament of faith in which he or she irrevocably commits himself or herself to Christ and accepts Christ's message. This is why in the revised process for the Christian Initiation of Adults the sponsor and other Catholics help the potential member to determine if there has indeed been some repentant turning from sin. The Church for her part solemnly and joyously welcomes and accepts the new believer, adding her faith to that of the new convert.

It is good to keep in mind that the Church's oldest tradition saw the rite of initiation as a three-part process: baptism, confirmation, and the Eucharist. They closely combine to bring the believer to the full stature of Christ and to help him or her carry out the mission of the entire People of God, both in the Church and in the world.

Infant Baptism

My discussion of baptism and the other sacraments has focused primarily on adults because, on one hand, contemporary Catholic consciousness has again begun to appreciate the missionary dimension of baptism and the need for evangelization. On the other hand, history shows that the Catholic view of baptism, sharpened or even skewed by the debate with Protestants, had overlooked the degree to which the rite for the baptism of infants drew from the more ancient initiation rites for adults. We had allowed the practice of infant baptism to shape in an exaggerated way our whole mind-set on the subject. We had, in short, forgotten some of our own history.

If, as I have argued, it is true that the effective participation in a sacrament requires proper dispositions, among them the need for faith, how can I in good conscience continue to baptize infants? Readers may recall that in the chapter on redemption I opened consideration of this issue by pointing out how abnormal it would have appeared to our Christian ancestors, prior perhaps to the Renaissance, to delay baptism of infants until their early adolescence.

People were born, raised, instructed, and integrated into the Christian life and culture primarily as members of a family, clan, or village. Rights of individuals or the strong emphasis on individuals, as separate from everyone else, is a concept very unfamiliar to those centuries and very odd today in many parts of the world.

An individual as such had no status. Food, housing, job security, dignity, culture, medical care, and moral support came not from government programs or entitlements, but from membership in a group—be it peasants, serfs, burghers, tradesmen, clergy, nobility, household slaves, or monks. In such a society of feudal unities, baptism of the infant was as normal as promising a five-year-old son to someone else's four-year-old daughter for future marriage.

The family or village as the primary unity and identity is still a very powerful concept and reality. At the 1974 Lausanne Conference on Evangelism, Marge Alcala Isidro spoke of the vital work being done by family groupings in the Philippines. She mentioned one husband-wife team who led another couple to the Lord.

> Later the children came to know the Lord. Mr. Isidro had the privilege of baptizing the entire family.[12]

Another speaker at the same conference mentioned how difficult it is to make headway among rural Japanese. This is because they live in tightly-knit groups under the leadership of a patriarch whose advice and decision-making power are decisive. For individual villagers or farmers to step outside of that system is abnormal.

These considerations are not advanced to defend infant baptism as such; they are advanced to show how foreign our Western European and North American "individualistic" concepts are. A Wheaton College professor who had spent some time in West Africa told me of similar situations there in the villages where tribal life means that individuals must submit, to a greater degree than we could understand, to the needs and standards of the entire group.

However, even in medieval Europe, baptism was not conferred without any consideration of faith. The child being presented for the sacraments was to be raised by Christian parents and godparents in what was then seen as a Christian society or village. Parents are still the first religious educators of their children, even though churches try hard to help with this task. In the Philippines today, as in some other countries, evangelical families have home altars around which they gather for prayer. The "domestic shrine" is found in many Catholic homes as well; it is a focus of prayer for family members.

One of the purposes of having godparents is to give parents support in raising the child in the faith. The Church wants to be sure that someone will lead the child to a personal act of faith in Christ. Baptism is ordered by its own nature toward the act of faith. In the action of baptism, the infant is literally carried into the church; at a deeper level the infant is carried by the faith of the Church. By baptism the infant begins to be a member of the body of Christ. Parents, godparents, relatives, and parishioners are supposed to create the conditions in which the child, as he grows in knowledge and spiritual maturity, can make the first steps of faith.

A Christian couple at whose wedding I officiated last year have just sent me a birth announcement. They have had their first child, a son weighing six pounds. The announcement card has on its cover a pen and ink sketch showing a large adult hand in which a tiny infant's hand lies. The cover has the inscription, "The Handiwork of God," and when the card is opened one reads, "in ours." Any child born to accepting, loving parents experiences a basic grace—the love of God poured out through a mother and father. Acceptance, security, assistance, care—all those beautiful things which already exist before any religious ritual is performed constitute grace.

Careful parents choose a name, a style of birth, a neighborhood, a housing style, a pattern of sleep and work, entertainment, and culture. Unaware of the thousand key choices already made on its behalf, the newborn's life is deeply dependent on them and on the people who will care for him or her for many years. Baptism of the infant is another of those choices, bringing this precious creature into the "domestic church," itself a cell of the local congregation. Sleeping or fretting, nursing, gurgling, and splashing water, the little one is in Christ through baptism. The littlest of the children have come unto him in their own manner.

Psychologists agree, says William Bausch, that "the most critical task of the child's first year on the planet is whether he will learn to trust or distrust the world." If this is true, then the quality of the faith, hope, and love of parents is crucial. Bausch makes the point as follows:

> For believing parents, the Christian life is profoundly the basic hope and trust in life. In Jesus all will ultimately be well and victorious. Since baptism plunges us into Jesus' death *and* resurrection, moves us into the "last times," and outpours the Holy Spirit—how could believing parents not share that as a life's basic thrust? Believing parents could no more not insert their children into a hope-giving redemptive community of believers than they could deny them their basic immunization shots without their consent. And here we catch the essence of why Christians started baptizing their infants to begin with. It was *out of their common life in faith* that they came to accept the appropriateness of celebrating baptism with infants and children even though the *process* of faith and conversion is essentially an adult experience.[13]

The Necessity of Baptism

In John 3:5, Christ made the statement, "Unless a man is born again of water and the spirit, he cannot enter the kingdom." This has been taken with utmost seriousness by the Catholic tradition. In locations and eras when infant mortality rates were extremely high, theologians and pastors saw no other safe procedure than baptism of infants. Catholic missionaries went to the uttermost reaches of the world, at great personal risk, to baptize and instruct.

Despite the courageous missionary outreach by both Catholics and other Christians, we know that most of the world in our day is not Christian, and that most of the world's people since its beginning have not been Christian. Are these saved?

Scripture tells us that God wants all people, past, present, and future to be saved. We believe that despite our missionary failures,

God offers all people some chance to be saved. That is, all men and women in some way unknown to us, have at least some moment in their lives a glimmer of the divine and the benefits to be gained by adherence to it. In varying forms, Catholics have suggested that such people, following this invitation of grace, can be saved. We have often called this "baptism of desire."

One famous description of this type of baptism appeared in a 1949 instruction from the Holy Office in Rome (now called *Congregation for the Doctrine of Faith*) to Boston's Cardinal Richard Cushing. He was at that time concerned about the teaching and preaching of a popular, dynamic, and gifted Boston priest who was insisting that "outside the Church," very literally, there was no salvation. The Vatican, to whom Cardinal Cushing turned for advice, answered with these words:

> . . . it is not always required that a person be incorporated in reality as a member of the Church, but it is required that he belongs to it at least in desire and longing. . . . It is not always necessary that this desire be explicit. . . . God also accepts an implicit desire, so called because it is contained in the good disposition of soul by which a man wants his will to be conformed to God's will.[14]

This 1949 Vatican instruction received fresh expression in that part of the Second Vatican Council's document entitled *Lumen Gentium* dealing with how different peoples are related to the People of God. After references to other Christians, Jews, and Muslims, the bishops describe the relationship of other peoples:

> Those also can attain to everlasting salvation who through no fault of their own do not know the Gospel of Christ or His Church, yet sincerely seek God and moved by grace, strive by their deeds to do His will as it is known to them through the dictates of their conscience.[15]

Notice that God's grace is mentioned; we believe that every person is at least offered an opportunity to participate in Christ's work of salvation.

> Nor does divine Providence deny the help necessary to those who, without blame on their part, have not yet arrived at an explicit knowledge of God, but who strive to live a good life, thanks to His grace. Whatever goodness or truth is found among them is looked upon by

> the Church as a preparation for the Gospel. She regards such qualities as given by Him who enlightens all men so that they may finally have life.[16]

Some mission-minded Protestants may be less concerned about the possibility of salvation without water baptism than they are about the possibility of salvation without a personal, conscious commitment to Jesus. Their fear is that these concessions make void the great mandate to teach and baptize all nations.

This objection or fear would be valid only if one forgets that for the Catholic Church, neither "baptism of desire" nor "universal grace" removes the obligation to preach the gospel.

> But rather often men, deceived by the Evil One, have become caught up in futile reasoning and have exchanged the truth of God for a lie, serving the creature rather than the Creator (Rom. 1:21, 25). Or some there are who, living and dying in a world without God, are subject to utter hopelessness. Consequently, to promote the glory of God and procure the salvation of all such men, and mindful of the command of the Lord, "Preach the Gospel to every creature" (Mark 16:16), the Church painstakingly fosters her missionary work.

In short, God has his marvelous ways of revealing himself to all. But he has also pointed out to us the clearer, surer path to himself—namely through Jesus and the community of Jesus' disciples.

Confirmation

Scholars are not in total agreement about all aspects of the history behind the sacrament of confirmation. What I offer here is what I consider a useful approach to the topic. We believe that the Catholic Church has tried to understand and follow the directions sketched in two texts of Scripture. Both texts associate the gift of the Holy Spirit and a rite of imposition of hands after baptism. The first text is Acts 8:14–17, and the second is Acts 19:5–6. As Charles Davis put it,

> In these texts of the Acts (including the Sermon of Peter) a distinction is made between the effect of baptism and the effect of the imposition

> of hands. Baptism remits sin and is the entry into the Church; the imposition of hands gives the Spirit. This presentation would seem to mark an early, undeveloped stage in the theology of baptism.[17]

Davis's phrase "undeveloped stage in the theology of baptism" signals what is a rather complicated scholarly debate about the origin of confirmation. Was it very early a distinct rite or merely another phase of baptism? One writer suggests that if one saw the issue in terms of a series of steps which together constituted the beginning of church life—namely washing, anointing, imposition of hands, and the Eucharist—it is possible that early theologians gave little attention to the distinct parts. Or perhaps they gave unequal attention to the parts.

The word "baptism" was used at one time for the whole series of actions, prayers, and exorcisms, excluding the Eucharist. According to Davis, the word "confirmation" appears first in Gaul in the fifth century. Along with its independent status and theological significance, confirmation's placement has been variable. In some places and eras, confirmation followed immediately on baptism and was administered by a priest. In other places it was conferred in later childhood or adolescence by a bishop.

Contemporary scholar Alexandre Ganoczy says that after the fourth century,

> . . . Nearly all of the Greek Fathers . . . ascribe the privilege of "completing" the baptismal ritual and "perfecting" baptismal grace to apostolic authority. From this, the Western Scholasticism of the Middle Ages deduced the exclusive right of the bishop. He alone is entitled to apply the holy oil of confirmation and to validly bestow confirmation, being its "proper minister."[18]

In an era when infant baptism predominated, confirmation may have been delayed precisely until later childhood or early adolescence so that a more personal commitment to Christ could be developed. A young person therefore "confirmed" the commitment made by his parents and godparents at infancy.

The Second Vatican Council described the sacrament of confirmation as a means by which believers are "more perfectly bound to the Church and are endowed with a special strength of the Holy

Spirit. Hence they are, as true witnesses of Christ, more strictly obliged to spread the faith by word and deed."

McBrien's *Catholicism* asserts that confirmation, which "comprises the post-baptismal rites of anointing, imposition of hands, and the words, 'Be Sealed with the Gift of the Holy Spirit,' is a *ratification* of Baptism."[19] He adds:

> It is not only a sacred, grace-bearing sign for the good of the recipient, therefore, but it is also a principle moment when the Church reveals to itself and to the rest of the world as a particular kind of community, filled with the Holy Spirit and committed to the Spirit's release for the transformation of the whole of creation.[20]

My own confirmation was a long time ago and the bishop who conferred it is probably already with God, but I remember the excitement connected with it. Nuns in the parish school were in charge of preparing us for the sacrament. Well in advance we were taught that this was an important step, that we were approaching adulthood, and that we were to behave as Christian adults. They stressed as well that the Spirit's coming was designed to make us "soldiers" of Christ. Heroism and steadfastness were expected of us after this sacrament.

We were also nervous as the day approached, not only because we had to make sure our sponsors were there; the bishop, to fulfil his task, would also be asking questions of us, "testing" us on our knowledge of the faith. The nuns prepped us for this of course, and also for an archaic part of the rite. As the Bishop passed along the front of the church, pausing to confer the sacrament on each, he gave each person a light touch or blow with his hand. The nuns told us, as I recall, that this was a reminder that we had to suffer for Christ's sake, like good soldiers. In addition, we were allowed to take another Christian name, beyond our baptismal name.

Having the bishop visit the parish, having the church especially decorated for this occasion, being in front of parents and sponsors—all of this was memorable. It gave flesh to the view that the bishop "confirmed" the faith which pastor, nuns, parish, and parents and godparents had already been trying to encourage.

Conclusion

When we look at the long and rich history of Catholicism's approach to the sacraments, we detect the outlines of what Robert Imbelli has called "Catholic consciousness" containing five elements:

1. *Sensitivity to the bodily, the corporeal.* There is in our past and present a firm commitment to the earthly—bread, wine, oil, embraces, and the bishop's hand. These humble things provide access to the divine.

2. *Catholic language is "we-language."* Ours is not the lonely, "existential" stance of the individual before God. Each is responsible for his or her actions, but it is precisely *we* who stand before God. We are the People of God, the body of Christ, one flock, the collective bride of the divine Groom.

3. *The very word "catholic" means that our view of religion embraces all aspects of human existence:* private and public life, nature and culture, personal and institutional, from liberation theology to "right to life." Catholic consciousness at its depth recognizes and gives voice to the possibilities and pitfalls in every contingent human expression. As Robert Imbelli says,

> Catholic consciousness and language integrate both life and death in a reciprocal exegesis which counteracts the fatal human tendency to deny death and snatch at life.

4. *Catholics, and other Christians too, should believe and exhibit the cosmic dimension of their faith.* We have a tremendous responsibility to become those children of God for whose appearing, according to Romans, the whole of the created universe groans in expectation. As Imbelli says,

> The fate of the earth is entrusted to humankind; and this incarnational responsibility finds an ultimate ground in Catholic sacramental consciousness.[21]

5. *There is in the Catholic tradition the conviction that life in Christ is a process, a transformation from glory to glory and final transfiguration.* Reverence for saints is part of this conviction, for these men

and women form part of our cheering section. Their lives provide models of the interaction between human achievement and divine grace. Their own struggles and journeys have been crowned with the Lord's reward. It is in their efforts and in our own that the self has been transformed.

For these reasons, our views of sacraments, our notion of conversion, and our practices of baptism and confirmation seem to us biblically based and as divinely incarnate as is God's Son.

7

A Closer Look at

Worship and the Eucharist

Over the years among Catholics there has been a half-joke that we "*have* to go to church on Sunday under pain of mortal sin." The saying reflects the Catholic stress on regular worship and Sunday church attendance. In this chapter I will complete my treatment of the sacraments of Christian initiation by discussing worship and the Eucharist. Let me begin by showing the reasons why Christians of the early centuries were not considered fully alive in Christ until they had begun to take communion.

We know that baptism frees us from the power of darkness and makes us a new creation, adopted sons and daughters of God. Jesus calls us to brotherhood with him and calls us his friends. Baptism is the first major step in that friendship; united to him we begin to share his life. We can offer spiritual sacrifices because we are one with Jesus the High Priest—we have become a holy priesthood. This friendship and a share in Christ's priesthood point together to the Eucharist.

Friendship can be understood from a look at John 15:14–17. We are to imitate him by laying down our lives for one another, to be united with each other, and to do as he commands. One of these commands is to celebrate the Eucharist. Luke 22:19 is another text to consult for this.

The Sunday eucharistic worship should be seen as a continued sign of our friendship with Christ and his concern for us. Friendships have and need their rituals, gestures, favorite words and phrases, and shared time. We know what pleases our friends and what does not. There is the comfort of the familiar, the joy of an affectionate presence.

My own earliest memories of Sunday and weekday worship in the parishes of my boyhood contain lively images of the familiar, time-honored ritual, fast-moving and solemn. The priest, clad in special clothing, faced away from us in the pews, usually toward the east. He seemed to be our delegate, articulating our corporate prayer to the Father before the face of Christ, the rising sun. It was solemn and awesome.

When I was in my teens, people in the pews took a more active part by following the ritual in a little book, or joining in the Latin responses and chant. This increased involvement was due to the encouragement of Pope Pius XII. While many simply prayed their private devotions during the Mass, others followed the movements of the priest and the acolytes and listened for the bells which signaled more important moments. Our bodily gestures, too, were synchronized as we rose, knelt, sat, rose, and knelt again in unison, each position carrying its own interior value.

The joy of Christmas and Easter alternated with the solemnity of Advent and Lent. Vestments, colors, incense, bells, and glittering candlelight both enchanted us and accentuated our sense of the transcendent. The biblical imagery of Jesus reclining at the table with friends was overshadowed by the picture of angels and saints worshiping at the throne. When the Second Vatican Council made its changes, a new mood and thrust was inaugurated. Some found these changes hard; others delighted in them.

The priest no longer seemed to pray on our behalf, facing east. He prayed with us, faced us, and acted in the Lord's place to invite us to the table. We even tried to learn a new name for this worship. What had been "Mass"—solemn, high, low, or whatever—now became "liturgy," meaning a collective enterprise, a joint work of the whole people celebrating God's work and participating in it.

At its best, this new liturgy was an exhilarating experience. I remember and treasure its power, especially at a university parish in California during the sixties and seventies. A husband and wife team led the people with wonderful spirit. Rousing song, beautiful guitar music, and an animated congregation lifted and sustained the faith of us all. It was, however, more than an effort to be trendy. Their leadership and our response arose from the culture and from the nation's problems and hopes of the day. In the past few years, newer somber moods have taken over. And Catholic churches today are experimenting with a music that differs from *Godspell* or *Jesus Christ Superstar.*

At one time, we Catholics went to church very conscious that we were following the third commandment about keeping the Sabbath holy. That is still an excellent motive, but we should be able to see more to it than that. Our gathering at the Lord's table is our own gesture of love; it is he who calls us to "take and eat," something he insists on in John 6:51–58.

Our approach to this is nourished, too, by the Bible's accounts of meals in which Jesus participated besides the Last Supper. At one meal he allows a woman of dubious morality to anoint his feet with perfume and wipe them with her hair, an acceptance of her love without rejecting or condemning. It is at the house of Zacchaeus that Jesus accepts the conversion of that flagrantly corrupt government official. Jesus feeds the hungry thousands even though, or perhaps because, they are weak in understanding. He prepares a meal for his stunned apostles when he appears to them by the shores of Galilee.

These meals speak of friendship, forgiveness, union, and mutual help. It is a common thing in many world religions to mix fellowship, faith, and food. Our own Jewish roots include the dramatic example of the Passover, and Jesus built on that history and tradition when he stressed the meal of the new covenant, sealed in his blood.

The Catholic emphasis on eucharistic worship is linked to these biblical moments. Our concern also comes from the early church's practice described in Acts 2:41–42. The first believers gathered regularly to "break the bread." Another biblical insight is found in I Corinthians 11. Paul criticized the manner in which this church celebrated the Lord's Supper. Because they lacked the proper dispositions and were eating and drinking unworthily, he said that they were infirm or asleep, weak in Christ, or even dead to Christ.

Looking beyond the official New Testament canon to other Christian writings in the first and second centuries, we find more evidence of their stress on the Eucharist. Since our ancestors in the faith saw something valuable and precious in this sacrament, we dare not let it fall out of our own lives.

Joined to Christ's body by baptism and anointed by his Spirit, we hear his call to be nourished by him, to proclaim with others the power of God who has called us out of darkness into his marvelous light. Our friendship with each other in him and with him in the Father needs nourishment and contact. Eucharistic worship, we contend, has a particular strength and value. It is one of the great gestures of love we can make together for and in the Lord. It is also a prime moment when he can communicate with us. Let me examine that communication now under three headings: community, Scripture, and sacramentality.

Community

Community is something everyone seems to want and which seems too often to escape our grasp. At its best, Sunday worship in our local church is *liturgy*, the expression of union in Christ and our collective collaboration in a work of worship and praise. Together in prayer, song, taking an offering for the poor, and presenting bread and wine, we form a community and express a communion in this event.

From beginning to end there is supposed to be community participation. Ushers, musicians, prayer leaders, the presiding priest, ministers of the Eucharist, the choir, acolytes—each has a role to play. And the service should bring out from the neighborhood all the varied social classes and ethnic diversity we have—old and young, babes in arms, and upwardly mobile young preppies.

The new rite encourages us to greet each other in the Lord. Newer churches have arranged their pews in semi-circles so that worshipers can in fact look at each other, seeing a brother or sister in Jesus. Prayers of intercession try to open our minds and hearts to the needs of many beyond our own community. World-wide community is part of the goal.

Scripture

The second heading by which Christ communicates with us is Holy Scripture. Catholics who attend church regularly on Sundays will be exposed to a rich selection of Old and New Testament texts. Between the Scripture readings, we are encouraged to sing one of the psalms in a meditative response to what we are hearing. Catholics today also hear a wider selection of gospel passages than we did in the past.

Priests for their part have been advised to preach, as Augustine once put it, "to break open the bread of Scripture" for the people. We confess that not every priest stepping up to the pulpit is as well-trained or prepared as he might be, but we have at least provided our people and our priests with an abundance of Scripture commentaries and printed guides to better sermons.

A friend of mine once described her pastor as an absolutely hopeless preacher, tolerated by a patient congregation. Well-meaning critics urged him to subscribe to what is called a "homily service." The service provides its subscribers with sample talks based on the Scriptures appointed for that day. This pastor began receiving these model talks in the mail and, contrary to the recommendations of the creators of this service, he began reading them from the pulpit, word for word. Parishioners noted a dramatic improvement in the Sunday sermon!

Sacramentality

Christ communicates with us through others, through the Scriptures preached and explained, and at a non-verbal level through sacraments. Someone has written that Catholicism has a unique insight: God can be found in the created world and he doesn't mind using the simple stuff of this world to communicate. Wine, oil, water, touching with hands, an exchange of vows—all can be vehicles of the divine or windows on the holy.

In chapter 6, I spoke of sacraments as external signs instituted by Christ through which he gives us his grace. I said that underlying this belief and definition is the conviction that the entire *mysterion*, God's loving intervention in our lives through Jesus' life and death, is a sacrament. We further believe that this great mystery can affect us, provided we have faith, in non-verbal ways—ashes, bread, oil, wine, and the rest.

We give a special place of honor to the rituals used or hinted at by Christ and developed by the first generations of believers. This is important because, as one writer put it, "No human really sees God face-to-face on this side of death." Only a handful of mystics have achieved total absorption into their relationship with God; the rest of us listen for echoes of the divine presence which draw us beyond ourselves into the mystery. Sacramental worship is a life full of signs which point to invisible riches.

Jesus, we have said, embodies the Godhead, and he links us to himself as members of his body. Joined with Christ, we become aware of his presence when he forgives sin in baptism, heals the sick by anointing, or supports the husband and wife in matrimony. Frail human beings and simple elements of bread and wine collaborate so that the Eucharist becomes for us the fullest sign of incorporation into Christ. It is in this that I want to develop controverted views of the Eucharist.

Eucharistic Aspects

Views about the Eucharist have in recent centuries been perhaps more divisive than unitive. There are two major cleavages on the subject. The first deals with the way Jesus is present in, around, or with the consecrated bread and wine. The second deals with the link between the Christian celebration of the Lord's Supper and Christ's death and resurrection. Each of these positions has its own subdivisions.

Consider first the manner of Jesus' presence in relationship to the bread and wine. There are two broad approaches, one being that of *sacramental realism.* This traditional formula insists that Jesus Christ is actually present, body and blood, soul and divinity, under the appearances of bread and wine which have been duly consecrated by the priest. Russian Orthodox, Greek Orthodox, High Anglicans, and Roman Catholics, among others, hold to this view.

There are Catholics alive today who, when preparing for their

First Communion, were told not to chew the slim, papery wafer which the priest placed on their extended tongue. The reason given by some teachers was that chewing Jesus with the teeth would hurt him. Medieval Catholicism reported incidences in which people at worship saw the host bleed. There have been moments in the history of this realism when reverence for the consecrated elements overshadowed the truth that these elements were food to be eaten.

When I was growing up, the Catholic sense of the mystery of Jesus' presence under the appearances of bread and wine was very strong. On entering the church we were taught to *genuflect,* going down on the right knee while facing the front of the church. The main object of this reverential salute was Christ's presence in the sacrament, reserved from the previous celebration of the Eucharist in a *tabernacle.* The very term for this strong box was designed to evoke the Exodus. The tribes carried the tabernacle on their journey and God dwelt in it. We were encouraged to "visit Jesus" at this time. Kneeling in a semi-dark church, we felt close to him and prayed fervently while a red light flickered near the tabernacle.

When I was growing up, we could only receive Communion at the hands of the priest. He was allowed to handle the host and chalice with his thumb and forefinger, which had been especially anointed at the time of his ordination. To receive the sacrament we followed the medieval gesture of reverence and knelt at a low rail in front of the church. From the other side of that rail the priest distributed the host. For centuries the custom of taking from the chalice had been non-existent. That was reserved for the priest.

When we couldn't take Communion, for lack of spiritual readiness, there was a "spiritual Communion" in the service of Benediction of the Blessed Sacrament. The main drama of this was in the actions of the priest. He placed a large, specially prepared, consecrated host in an ornate, portable, cross-shaped or sun-shaped showcase. Suitably vested, under strong lighting and accompanied by heartfelt song, organ, incense and prostrations before the Sacramental Savior, the priest lifted the showcase high and made a huge sign of the cross over the congregation. When he finished, he knelt reverently and led the people in a series of praises to God, Jesus, and Mary.

Catholic devotion to the Eucharist was not fed solely by medieval stories of bleeding hosts. A priest told us a World War II story about a Catholic chaplain saying the Mass in the front lines of battle. After he had consecrated the elements, but before communion by the soldiers, they came under enemy fire. One soldier leaped up and covered the sacred elements with his body, which took a fusillade of bullets. He was described as a martyr for Jesus.

For millions of Catholics, sacramental realism means that we are following as strongly as we can what the New Testament said about the bread and wine. It also means that, presuming attention and faith, we can enjoy precious moments of personal encounter with the Lord. It does not exclude other moments of great intensity, but it does sustain us spiritually and deepen our sense of God's love for us.

The other major view held about the Lord's presence in the consecrated bread and wine makes that presence less substantial, more spiritual or commemorative—a sort of *sacramental symbolism.* Some versions seem to imply that the priest or pastor's actions have no effect unless people in the pews are believing. Catholics find this view less than convincing. Perhaps a Bible illustration will help show why.

St. Luke's Gospel, chapter 24:28–32 tells how the disciples, after Jesus' death on the cross, walked disconsolately the road from Jerusalem to Emmaus. On their way they were joined by a stranger who asked them for the latest news. When they began telling him about the death of Jesus and how much it disappointed them, he began explaining how Jesus' death matched the Jewish prophecies. They were enjoying the lesson so much that when they arrived at an inn around sunset, they begged the stranger to stay with them for a meal. They then "recognized him in the breaking of the bread." For many Catholics, this recognition of the Lord in the Eucharist is a biblical way of saying "sacramental realism."

This sense of Jesus' presence does not usually include these days a vision of the bleeding host. When I learned about the Eucharist from the nuns at the parochial school, they made it very clear that I was not engaging in cannibalism. We were never led to believe that we were literally tearing at the Lord's dying body on the cross, nor at his resurrected body. We were, however, eating, drinking, and being nourished of him. Emotionally speaking, there is in this a closeness and a comfort for us that exceeds words. If our attendance at worship is our little gesture of love for him, his presence in that sacrament is his very grand reaction.

The second major issue to be considered also includes the manner of Jesus' presence, but it is much larger. All of our ceremony, lights, incense, precious vessels, songs, and prostrations are in this wider context. Our reverence would be excessive indeed unless the sacrament was related in a specific way to Jesus' death and rising. But the nature of that link has been another sore point between Catholics and Protestants. Some Protestants, including many evangelicals, have recoiled from the popular, late medieval view that said the Mass was "another" sacrifice of Jesus for our sins. Since Jesus had died once and for all, no human ritual could repeat this. It was particularly unthinkable that some priest could do mumbo-jumbo and call down Jesus into those humble bits of bread and drops of wine.

When I first began to think of writing this chapter, it seemed to me that the gap between Catholic views and those of many Protestants was too broad to be bridged. Catholic talk of the Eucharist as a sacrifice and Protestant insistence on the Lord's Supper as a memorial did not harmonize. I found myself trying desperately to describe the Catholic approach in ways that would be both biblically responsible and helpful to those who disagree with us. In my search I stumbled on what I think is a glimmer of light, but I leave it to you to judge.

While at Wheaton College in the autumn of 1983, I attended many weekday chapel services in Edman Chapel. Once in a while, for variety I attended a worship arranged by graduate students in the Billy Graham Center. It was there one day that I heard Dr. Julius Scott of the Wheaton Bible Department leading a Bible study. If memory serves me correctly, his title that morning was, "What is the Lord Doing Now?"

To answer that question, Dr. Scott led us through a close study of the Epistle to the Hebrews, which describes Jesus as the eternal High Priest, offering sacrifices and interceding for us. Dr. Scott also spoke of the vision found in Revelation 5 of the Lamb triumphant before the throne of God. Dr. Scott seemed to be teaching that

Jesus continues to plead our cause before the Father. It is as if the triumphant Lamb still can exhibit the wounds, "reminding" the Father of his suffering and death on our behalf.

Since I had been raised with the teaching that Jesus, in the Eucharist, does indeed continue to plead our case before the Father, I was delighted to hear Dr. Scott speak of this. I wrote a note to Dr. Scott and we had some discussion of this. I thought, naïvely perhaps, that his biblical study opened the door to understanding our Catholic view. If Jesus was constantly interceding for us, and if he was doing this as Lamb slain, Lamb triumphant, why couldn't we be one with him in this continual pleading and reminding through our ritual?

Dr. Scott asked me for information about the Catholic view and I supplied some, but the breakthrough I had hoped for did not appear. We had the pleasure of a good conversation but no agreement. In what follows, I will do my best to make the Catholic view of the Eucharist as understandable as possible. Some of the material I shared with Dr. Scott reappears below.

The Sacramental Concept

In the preceding chapter I mentioned how important it is for Catholics to live by what Monika Hellwig has called "embodiment." Since God took on a human body through his Son, Jesus Christ becomes a sacrament of God's loving offer of life. And since God's Word entered into all of human life, all of creation has the potential for sharing the divine.

Washing with water, laying on of hands, anointing, and feeding are physical gestures which Jews used in religious ways. Christians have continued to use these gestures and elements in baptism, Confirmation, and the Eucharist. But even more important than the use of these elements is the view that the followers of Jesus become in their turn part of the mystery, the sacrament or embodiment of God in the world.

In short, God is embodied in Jesus, and Jesus is embodied in his people, called by Paul the "body of Christ." Therefore, relying on the sacramental principle alone, whenever the Church sets its mind and heart to something, especially in worship, the divine is in the picture. But to understand the Catholic way of linking the celebration of the Eucharist with Jesus' death and rising, another consideration is in order.

Again the Salvation Issue

Earlier I used John Stott's helpful definition of salvation in three moments: past, present, and future. How does one "get in touch" with salvation, past, present, or future? Catholics argue that the Scriptures command us to bring adults or infants into contact with Jesus through baptism. This is because Jesus is embodied in the Church. Access to Jesus, while not impossible apart from the Church, is easiest, best, and biblically justified through sacraments of initiation, baptism, confirmation, and the Eucharist.

By faith we believe that we are part of Christ's body. His promise to build a Church, to send the Spirit, to be with us all days until the end of the earth, to be within our midst where two or three are gathered together in his name—all this leads us to the view that there is a particularly powerful meaning and depth to our participation in ongoing salvation through the work of Jesus' Spirit. This depth and meaning acquire special intensity in the Church's gestures and rites.

A sacramental view and a view of salvation as an ongoing process need to come together if evangelicals are to understand our view of the Eucharist. From the evangelical side, some have lamented the lack of sacramental understanding in their own churches. One writer puts the blame on the loss of continuity with the teaching of many of the early church fathers and Reformers. The result is the deterioration of sacramental life.

One important father is St. Augustine, a fourth century bishop from Hippo, North Africa. Martin Luther, John Calvin, and generations of serious Christian thinkers were influenced by this man's genius. Best known for his famous semi-autobiographical *Confessions*, he should be as well known for his Bible commentaries and views of sacrament. Protestants and Catholics might find in him a common reference point about which the Eucharist could be discussed.

A contemporary student of Augustine, Alexandre de Ganoczy, says that this bishop's view of a sacrament was a subtle and balanced blend of remembrance, symbolism, and realism. His major thrust was the view that the sacrament of Christian ritual effects what it symbolizes. Baptismal washing symbolizes cleansing of the heart, but Augustine would also say that it also *effects* or causes cleansing. The Eucharist brings the unifying power of the true body and blood of Christ.

Mark 7:31–37 tells the story of Jesus curing a deaf-mute. Jesus fingers the man's ear, touches the man's lips with spittle, and breathes a command, "Ephphatha"—"Be opened." What the gestures tell is effected. Touching and breathing are not merely symbols or signs; they actually convey healing. Following Augustine's logic, the Eucharist nourishes us with Jesus.

Haunted still by Dr. Scott's Bible study, I think it is safe to say that the risen Savior's present activity keeps before the Father the once and for all death and rising which brought redemption. Presumably, Jesus' current activity also brings redemption, salvation present. Dr. Scott's biblical spotlight bounced around in my mental attic and reminded me of a traditional Catholic formula. Somewhere in my Catholic training one or more teachers described the Mass as an "unbloody" sacrifice. This phrase was designed both to link it with Calvary and, at the same time, to show its difference from Calvary. Calvary was the once-and-for-all "bloody" sacrifice. The Eucharist or Mass stems from this as an "unbloody" sacrifice.

On Calvary Jesus was offering, as a High Priest does, and at the same time he *was* the offering. In the Catholic parochial school they taught me that in the Mass, Jesus offers himself *sacramentally* to the Father. He continues as High Priest and he continues to be the offering. It is not the same as Calvary, yet is related at a very deep level.

Traditional teachings like these as well as devotional books since the sixteenth century Council of Trent struggled to maintain both the unity and the difference of the Mass and Calvary. We agreed with the Reformers that Calvary couldn't be repeated literally or historically. Yet, remembering Augustine's notion of sacrament, that a ritual *effects* what it symbolizes, we believe that the Eucharist is our way of being with Jesus as he makes ongoing intercession for us. He is broken for us and his blood is poured out, ritually making that intercession accessible. We cannot rest content with a ritual enactment that is "mere memorial."

Catholic theologians have benefitted immensely from the revival and renewal of biblical studies. One of the results is their interest in a new understanding of a word that is crucial in describing what the Eucharist is. Not surprisingly, it is a word from the Lord. At the Last Supper he commanded his disciples to celebrate the Eucharist "in remembrance" of him. Contemporary Bible scholars have been asking about the meaning of that phrase. Some of their conclusions are helpful.

"Remembrance"—in Greek *anamnesis* (lezzikaron)—had a stronger meaning in Jewish piety than the contemporary ceremonies or dramas enacted for tourists. When modern New Englanders re-enact the first Thanksgiving with the Indians or when Civil War buffs re-create the battle of Bull Run they are remembering, but in a shallower sense. In Jesus' culture and time, remembrance was a stronger notion.

Kevin Irwin's book, *Liturgy, Prayer, and Spirituality* (Paulist Press, Ramsey, New Jersey, 1984), teaches that while the covenants between God and the chosen people were forged and sealed at a given historical moment, the reality of covenant was experienced again and again by succeeding generations gathering for Jewish liturgical rites.

Irwin states this dramatically when he says, "Through the liturgy God was remembered by the people and God remembered them as his own. God's remembering has effect: it gives life." A rabbi friend once told me that when his family celebrates Passover, they are not just recalling why the night is special; they are being liberated in the very celebration.

Understood in this sense, liturgical memorial is not merely or even mainly re-enactment, re-doing, or repetition; it is perpetuation and direct contact with God's continual work. As some liturgical experts have put it, "through liturgical memorial we break the boundaries of historical time to experience what is timeless and eternal—life with God."

The Jewish celebration of Passover, according to Ramsey, has three dimensions. The past is remembered in the telling of the Exodus from Egypt. In the very celebration devout Jews can experience God's ongoing liberation of them. They also set an extra place at the table, reserved for the prophet Elias. His return will signal the time of God's judgment and the fulfilment of his covenant promises.

The Catholic understanding of the Eucharist has these same three dimensions. We re-tell the past, God's covenants of friendship with Jews, and then with the Gentiles through Jesus. In the ritual we confront the High Priest interceding for us, the Lamb slain but risen, triumphant before the throne. We pray the words that Jesus taught, "thy kingdom come," summoning the future. And we ask for continuing grace and ongoing transformation—salvation future.

The Real Presence

Centuries of debate about the depth and manner of Jesus' presence have continually embittered the theological and ecumenical scene. Richard McBrien reports that, along with growing convergence among denominations about the Eucharist as sacrifice, there is wider and stronger consensus about *real presence.* Anglican-Catholic discussions, Orthodox-Catholic, Lutheran-Catholic, Presbyterian Reformed-Catholic, Disciples of Christ-Catholic—all have come to affirm the presence of Christ's body and blood under the signs of bread and wine. There is agreement on the "what," but not on the "how."

From the Catholic perspective two comments are in order. The traditional way of speaking of the real presence, a tradition from the sixteenth century to our own, used the philosophical and theological language of Aristotle and St. Thomas Aquinas—"transubstantiation." Catholic theologians have tried to describe more fully how Jesus is present in philosophical and theological language that is more contemporary. But Pope Paul VI rebuked these efforts because it seemed to him that the newer language fell short of the reality intended. Needless to say, his criticism spurred writers to new creative depths. The older language, Jesus present under the appearances of bread and wine, asserted that the substance of the bread and wine had been changed into the substance of Jesus' person. The external appearances—weight, feel, and dimensions of the bread and wine—remained. Catholics are open to better formulations, but so far none has emerged to win general approval.

A second consideration needs to be highlighted here. The teaching of the Second Vatican Council repeated the traditional teaching about Jesus' presence in the Eucharist. It also reminded Catholics that Jesus' presence is broader than this. When the Scriptures are prayerfully proclaimed in faith to the faithful, and when their challenge and comfort are explained to the people, Christ is present. Our own rites help to promote this belief.

At a typical Catholic Sunday Eucharist, the deacon or priest prepares himself to proclaim the gospel selection by saying a quiet prayer.

> Lord, cleanse my heart and my lips
> that I may worthily proclaim your
> holy gospel.

As he moves from the center of the sanctuary toward the pulpit, the people stand as a sign of respect, and they sing or say a short greeting to the gospel. Once in the pulpit, before actually reading the text, the priest tries to make it as clear as possible that what follows is in some sense the presence of Christ. He says, "The Lord be with you!" and the people respond, "And also with you!" At the conclusion of the selection the priest says, "This is the word of the Lord," and the people reply, "Praise to you, Lord Jesus Christ!" In short, there is a presence of Christ in the gospel proclaimed.

The typical Catholic-Protestant debates about sacrifice and real presence have tended to obscure the scriptural presence of Christ. Catholic defense of pious customs concerning the Eucharist grew more ardent, and many beautiful customs and devotions developed around Jesus' presence in the sacrament.

From the Catholic point of view, however, the other ways in which Jesus is present were somewhat overshadowed. One result was the tendency to view the sacrament somewhat like a lucky charm. Ritual reforms from the Second Vatican Council have tried to balance the picture by reminding us of other ways in which Jesus is present.

Conclusion

In our thinking about the Eucharist, we Catholics have been trying to describe our faith in terms which are biblically sound and more understandable for modern times. Our Sunday eucharistic meal achieves greater depth for us as we see how Jesus used meals to forgive, reconcile, instruct, and nourish. Newer biblical research about the Jewish meaning of "remembrance" supports our belief that eucharistic worship is a faith expression of believers gathered to remember, to summon the future promised by God, and to participate in our High Priest's continual intercession and worship of the Father. The ritual of the Eucharist allows us to break through barriers of time and space.

We follow the ancient Christian tradition which sees the Eucharist as a sacrifice which perpetuates or continues that of the cross, but we do not mean that Jesus' death and rising literally occur again and again at a priest's command. Our Eucharist is a remembrance which allows us to be present with Christ as God continues to act.

While we continue the belief in the "real presence" of Christ in the consecrated bread and wine, we have tried to deepen our appreciation for the presence of Christ in every prayer of the Church, in the assembly of believers, in the actions we do together, and in the Word of God proclaimed. Freshened concepts of the Eucharist have invigorated our understanding of the Church's ancient initiation rites, baptism, confirmation, and the Eucharist itself, the classic sacraments of new life in Christ.

In these days, Catholics feel a special call to let their solidarity with Jesus take flesh in their solidarity with the poor. Luke 19's story of the tax collector provides an example of conversion linked to social justice. The years of bribes, grafts, and overcharges are reversed by Zacchaeus as part of his happy reunion over a meal with Jesus. To take communion with the Lord, to be in that union, is to have his sense of responsibility and love for all men and women.

8

A Closer Look at SPIRITUALITY

While chatting one day with a faculty member at Wheaton College about the topic of spirituality, he recommended that I read A.W. Tozer's *The Pursuit of God.* I found a copy of the book in a nearby bookstore and was delighted to see in Tozer a man of wide learning and a love for the mystics. He clearly saw a need for a deeper walk with God and was not afraid to quote Catholic writers whose remarks he liked on the subject of the pursuit of God. I believe that the issue of spirituality is one on which many Catholics and evangelicals can agree. I offer this chapter as an exploration in the subject.

What is Spirituality?

Tozer wrote in 1948 that his era had no lack of Bible teachers to set forth correctly the principles of the doctrines of Christ, but "too many of these seem satisfied to teach the fundamentals of the faith year after year, strangely unaware that there is in their ministry no manifest Presence, nor anything unusual in their personal lives."

He praises the dissemination of Bibles and the proper exposition of Bible truths from the pulpits, but says, "it is not mere words that nourish the soul, but God Himself."

This phrase reminded me of a heartfelt cry made by the great Jesuit theologian Karl Rahner in one of his books. He prayed not for more words about God, but for the presence of God himself. Spirituality in its broadest sense is the pursuit of God, a paradox, says Tozer, because of God's pursuit of us as well.

Richard McBrien speaks of Christian spirituality as

> the cultivation of a style of life consistent with the presence of the Spirit of the Risen Christ within us and with our status as members of the Body of Christ.[1]

Another fine definition comes from Donald Bloesch:

> In the biblical or evangelical sense, spirituality refers to the life of the whole person in relationship to the Spirit of God. It concerns the vertical relation between man and God but as it impinges on the horizontal relationship between man and his neighbor. Spirituality is the life of man in the light of his faith in God. It has to do not just with Christian doctrine, but with the practice of the Christian life. Its meaning is not simply service and stewardship but a devotion and commitment to the living God that is lived out in daily life.[2]

Richard Lovelace of Gordon-Conwell Seminary bases his view of spirituality on Romans 6, which speaks of a new nature created with power to grow in newness of life. The Holy Spirit's work is that continuing regeneration and renewal which will be completed only in the final resurrection. John Stott's notion of continuing salvation mentions the indwelling Spirit of Christ subduing the flesh from within us and transforming us into the image of Christ, from one degree of glory to another (2 Cor. 3:18; Gal. 5:16–6).

From these definitions I think it is fair to isolate three characteristics. First, the "work" or achievement of spirituality is divine. As Tozer says, our pursuit of God is already God's pursuit of us. Second, all the writers mention that the particular task falls to the Spirit of the risen Christ, the Holy Spirit. This is a transformational work, "from one degree of glory to another," making us more in the image of Christ, a continuing process of renewal. Third, neither for McBrien nor for the other writers is this growth in the Spirit a one-sided inner mysticism in flight from the world. Donald Bloesch specifically mentions, the intersection of the vertical dimension, our God relation—service, commitment, and devotion—with the horizontal, our relationship with our neighbors. McBrien calls it a "style of life." His use of the phrase in relation to the body of Christ introduces the horizontal dimension.

Although it is not glaringly obvious, there is implied in these definitions a fourth characteristic. For want of a better word, I will call it *synergy*. In Roman Catholic theology and in some theologies of the Protestant world there is the belief that God freely offers the Spirit and that the Spirit in turn offers light, wisdom, and the ability to act virtuously. But not all people cooperate by accepting these gifts.

One of the underlying mysteries in the Christian experience is the way in which the Spirit dwells in us, urging us to new attitudes and behavior, without forcing us or robbing us of our God-given individuality. We are to grow in the likeness of Christ without becoming clones. *Synergy*, our cooperation with God, is the key to this mysterious process.

During my sabbatical year at Wheaton College, I had an experience which highlighted the issue of divine-human cooperation. One Sunday I had the pleasure of attending worship at Chicago's famed Moody Memorial Church. For his sermon that day Pastor Ernest Lutzer spoke of the cross and the cost of our salvation. He encouraged his congregation to accept crosses in life with a spirit like that of Christ. It struck me that what he was saying sounded very "Catholic." By this I mean that we, too, are encouraged to sacrifice for the sake of following Christ, even to fill up, as Paul says, the sufferings of our Savior. Pastor Lutzer encouraged his people to the view that through their sufferings they might be instruments in God's hands. Their pains could help God accomplish great things.

At the conclusion of the service, Pastor Lutzer, the deacons, and the entire church interrupted the usual events to call an older gentleman forward for recognition. He had been for many years a prime mover in one of the Moody Church ministries, a radio ministry, I believe. The pastor thanked him, a deacon praised him, and the church presented him with a gift. I was struck by the praise for the way this man had cooperated with God's impulses to service. This, too, sounded very "Catholic."

Some weeks later I had an opportunity to have lunch with the associate pastor at Moody, Dr. Bruce Jones. I told him about the award given to the man behind the radio ministry, and while Dr. Jones acknowledged that they were praising his works, he wanted me to be very clear about their view that works did not "earn" salvation. All the efforts and effects were of course due to God, said Dr. Jones. I couldn't agree more, but it struck me that evangelical sensitivity on the point did not permit them to praise works or to speak of the redemptive value of suffering unless they had first separated themselves from the so-called "Catholic" view of works. I don't think I convinced Dr. Jones at that luncheon that Catholics do not believe they can "earn" heaven. We do believe, however, that God offers grace and the Holy Spirit freely, and that we may cooperate with him, bearing good fruit in *synergy*.

Cooperation with God's gifts and ongoing opportunities seems to me to be another point where Protestants and Catholics can agree. A way of illustrating this would be to look at some popular biographies of what can only be called "spiritual heroes or heroines" of the evangelical world. One of these models is Dawson Trotman, a rough-hewn man who accepted Christ at the age of twenty and went on to found the Navigators. As a young man he was more at home in pool halls than in prayer meetings. Yet as the genius behind Navigators and as a generous organizer of Billy Graham's crusade follow-up programs, Trotman left a sterling example of great deeds and generosity. I would call this *synergy*, cooperation with the impulses and power of the Holy Spirit.

Another example is that of Henrietta Mears, the indomitable teacher and crusader in Sunday School work. As the dynamo behind Hollywood, California's First Presbyterian Education Program, she made a deep and lasting impression on thousands of young men and women. Billy Graham, Bill Bright, and Richard Halversen, chaplain to the U.S. Senate, were at one time or other under her beneficent and prayerful influence. In the inspirational biography of Henrietta Mears by Ethel May Baldwin and David V. Benson, her prayerful search for the Spirit's guidance and her untiring response to it stand out. Further, her own personality traits and gifts seem to have been preserved and enhanced in this process.

Evangelicals point with pride to certain men and women who have cooperated with God's graces and have accomplished much for the kingdom. Part of the "pointing," part of the reason to sing "To God Be the Glory," arises from the visible works. We learn that Mel Trotter, an ex-alcoholic, founded seventy rescue missions, that Billy Graham's crusades, described by John Pollock in a 1969 book, drew thousands of men and women at various locations. Bill Bright in one of his own books describes how he and his wife began their Campus Crusade ministry at home in 1951 with a few college students; by 1960 he wrote that he had a staff numbering 109 on forty college campuses.

When Catholics canonize a saint, they look very hard at the person's entire life to probe about in darker corners and to uncover forgotten errors. They look however for signs, statistics or works as evidence that the person cooperated with divine graces, brought forth fruit. Thousands of Frenchmen walked, rode and struggled in the early nineteenth century to an obscure village called Ars to consult with an obscure priest by the name of John Vianney. Barely able to pass his seminary courses, assigned to a rather wretched and religiously dormant village, he soon brought it life through his manner of holiness, generosity, and straight-forward preaching. His fame spread far and wide, and people beat a path to his church for forgiveness, encouragement, healing, and advice.

Protestants as well as Catholics like to memorialize their heroes and heroines. Visitors to Montreal's Oratory of St. Joseph can see the room, even the shoes, of Brother André whose holiness made such a deep mark on Quebec. Admirers of Billy Graham and of other great American evangelical preachers can go to Wheaton College's campus to see the Billy Graham Museum. There they can hear and see the works of recent preaching giants, including displays showing artifacts of the Graham crusades. The museum is both instructive and inspirational. Billy Graham's generosity has funded it and the wonderful archives for research in evangelical history. The instinct to memorialize, to retain "relics" of a hero or heroine runs deep in the human psyche. It is not wrong; it is a way of retaining the past while transmitting its spirit to the next generation.

Biographies, memorials, and relics can of course lead to exaggeration, but abuses should not frighten us away from the practice itself. Seeing the great works, appreciating the achievements, we Catholics can make our own the Latin motto of Jesuit founder St. Ignatius of Loyola, "*Ad Majorem Dei Gloriam*"—"For the Greater Glory of God."

What About Us Ordinary Believers?

One of the hazards of observing or reading about the heroes of God is the feeling that we are somewhat left behind. When we enjoy C.S. Lewis' razor-like wit or intelligent defense of the faith, when we marvel at Dorothy Day's consistent, persistent work on behalf of the poor in New York City's Bowery, we feel second-rate. Is there hope for us ordinary mortals?

I confess that on my good days I believe that spirituality can be visualized as an upward spiral toward greater conformity to the will of God, greater likeness in the image of Christ. The upward spiral seems fitting to describe what I hope is greater maturity and experience. "Spiral" seems like a good image to me because spirals have a central core. And the core idea has two aspects.

The first aspect is that Christ, I hope, will remain my core throughout my upward life journey. The second aspect, however, is that throughout the journey, I am myself, with my strengths and weaknesses inherited, learned, and deepened by my own choices. I continue to be even the person I was at age twelve. I have said before that I cannot point to any dramatic points or places on the journey where I had a great break with sin or a sharp, mind-shaking, world-shattering insight. Christ and I are companions, a core at the center of my life, but he leads me, if I collaborate, upward in the spiral. On this spiral ascent, I confront again and again at the turning my own weaknesses and sinful tendencies. But with him at my side, we continue to move forward and upward.

There are other days, however, when I am not sure there has been any upward movement, either for myself or for others. I know some people who seem to have changed very little over the years. Is the upward spiral appropriate? Is there a transformational process, from glory to glory? Not only do I wonder about the truth of this for others, I wonder about the truth of it for me, especially on my bad days. At some periods in our lives, perhaps the best we can do is to hold fast to the Lord, like shipwrecked sailors clinging to a storm-tossed raft, refraining as best we can from evil. At other periods, with the help of God's grace and the indwelling Spirit, we can sense movement beyond mere clinging to more positive actions, fruits being produced from our Christian commitment.

Some Key Principles for Spirituality

If we believe that we are all called to be holy as our heavenly Father is holy, if we believe, as many Catholics do, that union with God in this life is at least a possibility for all and not just for the theological "superstars," then the following principles seem important.

We see spirituality as part of daily life. In Catholic piety there are saints designated for practically every known occupation—farmer, soldier, teacher, lawyer, and nurse. What we lack now are new saintly models for x-ray technicians, computer programmers, and other newer occupations. I am ready to nominate a patron saint for bus drivers.

Recently, on a muggy spring morning in Chicago's downtown traffic, I rode a city bus driven by a short, swarthy man with longish hair. Perspiring like the rest of us, he handled before my eyes an amazing assortment of trying transactions with great patience. One passenger tried to board but didn't have the correct change; since Chicago busses require it, the driver had to wait while the man made change from others already on board. Someone else appeared, calling from the sidewalk for directions. Again our driver was patient, indicated the other bus line and the other corner where it stopped. A woman got on, preceded by children of assorted ages and sizes. The children occupied seats while the mother fumbled for the fares. Again the driver was patient as he wondered if all the fares would be paid. Various passengers were transferring and they pulled crumpled transfers from hip pockets. The driver of course had to smooth them to see if the slips were valid. One woman stepped on board and before paying anything asked if the bus stopped at Chestnut

Street. The driver said it stopped at Chestnut *Place.* Was she sure of the street? She extracted written directions from her purse and re-checked the address. The driver pulled a city map from under his seat and let her check the names. She had not paid and we had traveled several blocks. Finally they both decided that this was indeed the correct bus, and she paid her fare. All the time my heroic model was handling these transactions and exchanges, he was also looking ahead and to the sides at the traffic, checking street lights, signaling lane changes, and more. It was a virtuoso performance and, if he is as patient and as generous at home with his family at the end of a hard day, he is my nominee for Saint of Bus Drivers.

Should this man not reach official canonization, Catholic piety has another example of holiness amidst the ordinary.

This is St. Therese of Lisieux, a late nineteenth century Frenchwoman who became a contemplative nun. She never got very far from her home town or her convent. She never preached to large crowds or drew visitors of importance to her cell. She did write, under orders, her own spiritual journey and spoke of holiness to be found in the humdrum of washing, cleaning, scouring pots and pans, or the slop and steam of the laundry room. Her "little way," as it was called, gave hope to many men and women around the world who desperately sought meaning in their own boring or routine tasks. She is yet another illustration of the first principle of spirituality, a process interwoven with everyday life.

The second principle is that of being "relational." McBrien uses the term to refer to several dimensions of life. The first and most powerful dimension is the same as that meant by Bloesch when he speaks of the intersection of the vertical and the horizontal—love of God and love of neighbor, love of God in love of neighbor. We remember from the writings of St. Paul that the gifts of the Holy Spirit, the charisms, are not given as personal treasures to be hugged; they are meant to be given to the community.

A second dimension to the term relational is that of membership in the body of Christ, the People of God. Catholics stress the view that Christ intended for us to be redeemed and sanctified, not as Lone Rangers, but as brothers and sisters in the Lord. Circumcised Jews formed a people covenanted with God; baptized Christians form a new people, in a new covenant. Our attitudes, behavior, and value systems affect one another for good or for ill.

John Stott has argued that true conversion leads to church membership, discipleship, and commitment. The world is all too ready to provide contemporary men and women with false guides, cult-like leaders, and visionaries who ask only one thing: "Turn a deaf ear to traditional Christian teaching and listen to me alone." Christians on pilgrimage need, like John Bunyan's hero, checkpoints at which they can make sure they are on the right path. A reliable local church can be both a checkpoint and company on the journey.

I believe that there is a third dimension to this one principle of relation. Our spirituality, while unique to each individual and the Holy Spirit who guides us, will have a strong family relationship or resemblance to the spiritual insights and the lives of the Christians who have gone before us. The Billy Graham Museum in Wheaton has films, photos, and memorabilia of the great evangelists of the past, partly to inspire the present, partly to help us see whether there is continuity between current evangelical practices and those of the past. Evangelists studying the past may need to make adaptations of style while retaining the content of the past.

Every Christian tradition provides models. And in the very uplifting of the models, younger Christians can find direction for their own spiritual growth. Donald Bloesch, calling evangelicals to a renewal in their sense of spirituality, urges them to study the distinguished writers, pastors, and activists in the Protestant tradition. Richard Lovelace reminds his readers of the importance of relating contemporary spiritual needs to the insights of the saints and geniuses of the Puritan tradition.

Roman Catholicism has carried this practice of referring present-day believers to the inheritance of the past to great lengths—some would say to excess. When I think of Catholicism's reverence for the heroines, heroes, practices, and writings of the Christian past, I am reminded of the quip once made about the Smithsonian Institute in Washington, D.C. Someone has called it the nation's attic, stuffed full of things that no one else wants, only a portion of which can be on display at any one time.

World-wide Catholicism displays only a portion of its spiritual heritage. Perhaps much of what is not on display has passed from being popular to being out of date or grotesque. Sometimes the past still moves and inspires, as the stained glass windows of Chartres, or the stark asceticism of St. Francis. At other times, these models or practices baffle those of us who live in such a different way. Beating oneself with a small whip as penance strikes many of us today as repellent, while moderate fasting, prayer vigils, and giving assistance to the needy always seem timely.

Catholic spirituality is therefore relational in the sense that it can draw from an immense range of lived models of Christian greatness, a wide range of writers, and a historic succession of personalities. I discovered a few years back a historical figure whose insight spanned the centuries to speak to my own concerns.

Several years ago, looking at my pastoral duties, I spied some free hours which matched the hours for a course on spirituality being taught at a nearby seminary. I enrolled and purchased the books. Under the tutelage of an excellent leader, I read for the first time some spiritual writers from the past who seemed to come alive for me and the class. One of the most fascinating was a fourth century monk named Evagrius, who lived in the Egyptian desert. He had been what we would call today a successful church bureaucrat in Asia Minor. Learned, trusted, and reliable, he was heavily involved in valuable church work until he felt a need to back away from it. He went to the Egyptian desert and produced some insightful chapters about the spiritual life. It is he who gave me a wonderful image to apply to the most common spiritual problem found among men and women trying to deepen their capacity for meditation: distractions. Evagrius, sitting through the cold desert nights or meditating in the dry heat of daylight, spoke of distractions. They were like great crowds of gnats and flies which buzzed around our heads, or darted into our eyes and ears. He advised tremendous self-control and patience while they buzzed harmlessly. Our twentieth century problems in spiritual growth have a family resemblance to Evagrius's fourth century problem. His imagery and his solution help me to deal with distractions in my own life.

When Donald Bloesch and Richard Lovelace, among others, urge evangelicals to make their spirituality more relational, more in touch with the greats of the past, they may not have had in mind the young evangelical I met one night on the Wheaton Campus. I entered the small chapel in the student center for a moment of prayer and noticed a young man there reading some book. When I finished my prayer and turned to leave, he did likewise. We began to chat and we discovered that we were both heading toward a special evening talk on Central America. We walked to the meeting together and chatted.

He had been raised in an evangelical home and had just returned to Wheaton after several years of work in evangelical administrative circles in Latin America. He had sensed a need for more learning and had enrolled at Wheaton. When I asked him what he had been reading, he showed me. The book, *Introduction to the Devout Life*, was written by a seventeenth century Catholic bishop and church reformer, St. Francis de Sales. He had been bishop of Geneva, was the patron saint of writers, and was a hero of the Catholic Counter-Reformation because he "rescued" some parts of his diocese from Calvinistic error.

I was astonished to find that a handbook on devotion written centuries ago by a learned and holy Catholic bishop could be helpful to a contemporary American Protestant. Some weeks later, I saw the young man again and in passing asked him, "How did you like St. Francis de Sales? He answered, "He called his book an introduction, but I feel that I am very far from being able to achieve even that beginning level of spirituality."

I believe that Protestants and Catholics can share with joy the treasures of their traditions in matters of spirituality. Christian spirituality is therefore relational in this sense, guided by and enriched by, if not controlled by, great heroes and heroines of God from the various Christian traditions.

A third principle of spirituality is the belief that our spiritual development finds focus and enrichment through fellowship, particularly through common worship. Limiting myself for the moment to public worship, thereby including the sacraments and the Liturgy of the Hours, a few remarks are in order.

Catholic liturgy has in an obvious way a strong teaching function. Sunday after Sunday, weekday after weekday, worshipers hear a sequential reading of the epistles and a wide selection of Jewish and Christian Scriptures chosen to be thematic. In addition, the very nature of our liturgical calendar—the seasons of Advent, Christmas, Epiphany, Lent, Easter, and Pentecost, along with the calendar of saints' days—is such that the major Christian truths are presented again and again and often discussed in the preaching. Observance of saints' days allows the preachers to speak of the hero or heroine being honored for the way in which they cooperated with the Holy Spirit in the work God had given them to do. This rich variety and successive display of Scripture and Christian saints provides instruction, inspiration, challenge, and encouragement for our own daily struggles and efforts.

When we celebrate the sacraments, whether in large gatherings or small, we have the opportunity to relate scriptural teaching to the occasion for the sacrament. At weddings, for example, the officiating priest will try to instruct and encourage not only the young couple before him, but also the friends, in-laws, and relations in the pews. In the sacrament of penance, there is another God-given moment when a sinner can confront his sin in addition to God's mercy. And so it is with each of the sacraments. Teaching, challenges, and nourishment are there for life's key moments as well as for the everyday.

A special case of public worship is the Liturgy of the Hours. As the term "liturgy" suggests, it is a common worship, a collective moment of prayer, song, reading, and quiet. In some parishes, religious orders, and groupings of college students, there is a daily gathering, morning and evening, to sing or recite a selection of psalms, prayers, and short Scripture readings focused on a particular "hour" of the day or night. Again, we find instruction, encouragement, and the consolation of prayer with other believers.

However, beyond the learning value in such regular gatherings, beyond the value of systematic encouragement from others, these events have a deeper dimension, namely that of worship. Just as there is a certain hierarchy of Christian truths with Jesus' redemption by the cross and his resurrection at the center, so there is a belief that certain worship moments are more important and privileged than others. Public worship, because it is public and by the brotherhood and sisterhood, seems to us more powerful than private worship. Eucharistic worship seems more privileged than Liturgy of the Hours. And even within the official liturgical cycle and calendar, there are privileged high points.

Catholics, in tune with the year's turning and the earth's rotation, observe an annual calendar. Within the annual calendar they place as centerpiece the celebration of Easter, happily coinciding in the Northern Hemisphere with the return of spring. Pentecost's gift of the Holy Spirit flows from Jesus' victory over sin and death and his return to the Father. Christ's birth at Christmas reminds us of Jesus' coming for our redemption; it speaks too of Jesus' coming again to establish the kingdom. Even within this large cycle there is a mini-cycle. Each Sunday is a kind of Easter in miniature, and different days of the week have a characteristic flavor. Monday prayer speaks to the beginning of the work week, Wednesday is the mid-week pause, Thursdays typically remind us of the Eucharist, Fridays of the Cross, and Saturdays of the Blessed Virgin.

A housewife I once heard speak about worship said that it was like eating. Sometimes worship was like grabbing a quick hamburger at the fast-food restaurant; at other times it was like a leisurely dinner by candlelight. Prayerful use of the Liturgy of the Hours is a short snack, while Easter and Sunday liturgies are more leisurely and elaborate.

Our Sunday worship is the high point in the hierarchy of Catholic worship experiences, following much of what I have said about the Eucharist and the particular meaning we give to the word "remembrance." St. Paul's notion of the *mysterion,* God's saving interaction with humanity in Jesus, translates for us into a mystery of faith. Each sacrament embodies and conveys to us something of that mystery. Prayerful and faith-filled contact with these mysteries can bring an increasingly deeper grasp of the whole mystery of redemption. These moments of sacramental worship facilitate an ever fuller appreciation, on the upward spiral, of the central Christian reality—Jesus who died for us, rose to new life, who shared his Spirit, and who intercedes for us still.

While traditional Catholic piety has laid great stress on a spirituality centered on the Eucharist, it is important to say once more that the Second Vatican Council enriched and strengthened the scriptural components in Sunday and weekday services. Further, every one of the sacraments—anointing of the sick, reconciliation, baptism, confirmation, orders, marriage, and the Eucharist—is to be presented with Scripture. These high points of public worship, including the

Liturgy of the Hours, testify to our need for Scripture's guidance. God's Word, proclaimed in these events, illumines the actions being performed. And those actions in turn reveal to us new riches in the Word.

Resources for Spirituality

Reading

As a member of a religious order, I try to follow one of its basic rules: the requirement that I devote at least thirty minutes a day to reading on some spiritual topic. When I think back over the books I have read, I feel like I am walking through a huge museum packed with a wide assortment of objects.

Monastic writers, like the fourth century Egyptian monk Evagrius, have helped me in the discipline of meditation. Thomas Merton, a contemporary monk and poet who converted to Catholicism, helped me appreciate the call to priesthood. An ancient writer, bishop, and administrator who shaped the monastic movement was Augustine. His books *Confessions* and *City of God* have nourished me.

Women of different centuries and styles have helped me on the journey. Teresa of Avila, that bustling and determined contemplative, has written wonderful things about her spiritual journey, as well as delightful letters to her friends and relatives. Catherine of Siena's searing criticism of the clergy of her day resound in my ears a healthy warning. Dorothy Day and Rosemary Haughton, modern women, have also instructed me. And here and there the works of a Quaker or a poet has influenced my thought.

A few years back I was stationed in a place that had a moldering collection of the works of John Henry Newman, and I decided that I would read all of his "parochial and plain" sermons. His intelligence, love of Scripture, and balance shone through on every page. This was a wonderful treat for me. Other theologians too have helped shape my thinking: Jesuit Karl Rahner, Redemptorist priest Francis X. Durwell, biblical scholars Father Ray Brown, Pheme Perkins, and George T. Montague's fine work on the Holy Spirit.

Time and time again these books and more were beloved companions on my spiral journey. In recent years I have included Flannery O'Connor's prose or T.S. Eliot's poetry in my "devotional" or "spiritual" reading. I am helped, too, by good hymnody and have continued to enjoy the psalms when chanted on Sunday or in the Liturgy of the Hours. Some of the melodies of the Protestant monastery at Taize, France, are memorable, as are the musical settings of the psalms by Lucien Deiss and Gelineau.

Since not everyone belongs to a religious order which requires this reading, they may lack the structured support system which I need. Still, laymen and women can find in or through their Catholic churches considerable help beyond the Sunday worship or their own private devotions and reading. To give a fuller view of these aids to spiritual growth, I want to mention at least briefly some of these activities and programs.

Charismatic Renewal

The beginnings of this renewal are usually dated from the year 1967 when Catholics at Pittsburgh's Duquesne University experienced a movement from the Holy Spirit. From there it spread to the University of Michigan at Ann Arbor, and to the University of Notre Dame in Indiana. In its early stages, the movement was best known for its stress on what the New Testament calls "speaking in tongues" or *glossolalia.*

This was far from its only emphasis, however. It provided people with an intense and personal setting in which the Holy Spirit could be invoked to revitalize their baptismal commitments and equip them for life's challenges. While plagued, like any movement, at times by spiritual thrillseekers or lay leaders who could be as arbitrary as prototypical Irish monsignors, the charismatic movement provided a popular, regular, small-group support system for Bible study, sharing, and faith.

The small groups, however, were often overwhelmed by the crowds. One of the national meetings during the mid seventies drew twenty thousand people to Notre Dame University. Toward the end of the decade the crowds declined somewhat. One reason, say the analysts, is that thousands of Catholics, renewed by the Spirit, had integrated themselves more fully in service and worship in their own parishes.

Catholics in the Charismatic Renewal opened up dialogue with Protestants, especially from the Pentecostal tradition, and some ecumenical barriers have fallen as a result. Since the meetings themselves need not involve the Eucharist, Catholics and Protestants can be together in mutual support and prayer with greater ease than would otherwise be the case.

While the Catholic priests and bishops worldwide were caught off guard by the rapid spread of the Charismatic Renewal, they sought to provide supervision and open lines of communication with its members. Very respectable church support came to the movement in the person of Belgium's Cardinal Leo Suenens, a pioneer reformer of the Church in Belgium and at the Second Vatican Council. Not all charismatic groups are exactly of the same style or mind-set, but a well-run group should include regular sound teaching by qualified persons and good communication and relations with the local Catholic churches.

Cursillo

The word *cursillo* literally means "short course" and has been used extensively to apply to a particular method of Christian renewal. This form of renewal pre-dates the Catholic Charismatic Movement. My own introduction to Cursillo was memorable and unexpected.

Shortly after my ordination to priesthood in 1964, I went to my first pastoral assignment, a small Catholic parish operated by the Paulist Fathers in Layton, Utah, only a short drive from the Mormon Temple in Salt Lake City. We priests were in charge of a congregation composed in part of Mexican-Americans, many of whom worked either at a nearby air base or as migrant or farm workers. I had hardly unpacked my bags when my pastor said that some of the laymen were sponsoring a Cursillo and that he had registered me as a participant.

Since I had never heard of this program, I joined it with some nervousness. Freed from most of my parochial duties for the weekend of the Cursillo, I moved from my rectory bedroom to a cot in a nearby church hall. There I shared meals, bathroom, and other amenities with a group of Mexican-American men, some of them middle-aged, some younger. From Friday afternoon through Sunday afternoon we were taken through an intensive process of challenge, reflection, prayer, and witnessing. The program was led by several very able laymen who had come from Arizona to direct the group.

The leader and his teammates gave a series of short but impressive talks on topics of faith, and we discussed these in more detail at small group sessions around tables set up in classrooms. When we grew weary of discussion and sharing, we were led outdoors for simple exercises or group games in the fresh Utah air. On Sunday afternoon we learned that the closing would be marked by a spirited and festive meal with songs and hearty abrazos from men and women who had completed the Cursillo elsewhere. Some of them had been praying for us during the weekend and some came from a distance to encourage and celebrate at the end. Instructed, renewed, and dedicated once more to deeper faith, hope, and love, we sang the rousing Cursillo song, *De Colores,* and promised that we would meet locally at regular intervals to support each other in the promises we had made to the Lord.

Since I was transferred at the end of that summer to Canada, I never knew how long-lasting the impact of that Cursillo was. What I do know is that the lay leader from Arizona and his team deserved immense praise and credit for managing the whole weekend with such great sensitivity to the feelings and energies of the group. From them I learned that this method had been imported to the United States by Spanish Air Force Personnel sent to Texas for training at American Air Force installations. These men saw a need for such a renewal among the Hispanics in Texas, and they launched a method they had known from Spain. From that beginning in the 1950's, the movement spread and was soon translated for Anglo use. Non-Catholics, too, are now involved.

The Cursillo's impact on me personally was primarily a lesson in humility and gratitude. I was fresh from seminary and full of knowledge about God. The men around me who had not had the luxury of my education nonetheless showed evidence of a deeper knowledge of God than I possessed. Further, even though we came from different socio-economic worlds, they accepted me with great warmth. And we were all touched by the knowledge that people all over the Southwest had been praying in particular for us on that very weekend.

Retreats

Spotted all over the United States and in other countries, Catholicism has a helpful and not-so-secret weapon in the spiritual life. It is called by different names: renewal center, house of prayer, retreat house, and so forth. It is usually in a quiet and attractive natural environment and run by people committed to providing participants with prayerful and comfortable quarters at reasonable cost. These centers have provided thousands and thousands of Catholics an opportunity to step back from their daily problems, work, and family obligations for the purpose of assessing their spiritual condition.

One of my most memorable experiences of such a retreat came in 1954 when I was at an Air Force technical training school at Chanute Field in Rantoul, Illinois. Feeling the need to escape barracks life, I signed up for a retreat to be given in Danville, Illinois. When I arrived on the chosen Friday, I learned that I was to be part of a group composed of middle-aged Catholic men from a local fraternal organization called the Knights of Columbus.

Instead of living in an open-bay barracks with fifty young and occasionally noisy men, I had a small, sparsely furnished room decorated by a crucifix on the wall and a Bible. With the other gentlemen I began a weekend of silence and solitude, interrupted by prayers in the chapel and "retreat conferences" given by a priest. Unlike the Cursillo where talks given were then discussed by a group around a table, each individual listened and then went back to his room to meditate privately on what he had heard. All of us were invited to chat with the priest and, if necessary, to turn over a new leaf by confession of sin. At the closing exercises of the retreat on Sunday, we were encouraged to make some resolutions about our future conduct.

I have forgotten what particular promises I made that day to the Lord, but I have not forgotten the faith of the other men and the beauty of our solitude and silence. All the usual props we had in life—telephone conversations, radio, television programs, chats with friends—were gone. Outside the barren trees and dark brown fields spoke of late winter's austerity; inside we faced our spiritual deprivation.

Since that wintry weekend at Danville, Illinois, I have visited other retreat centers. There is currently a great variety of methods in use, and a Catholic who wants to assess his or her spiritual condition can in many instances choose among options. When I was growing up, the wisdom of the day argued that silent retreats were best. In the late sixties newer formats appeared in which there was more group exchange, along with time for jogging, walks in the woods, and discussions led by a priest, nun, or layperson.

While the retreat is not a Jesuit invention, much of the genius and method behind retreats came from the work of St. Ignatius of Loyola. His famed writing, *The Spiritual Exercises,* described a process by which a serious searcher might deepen his or her commitment to God. A typical aim for the short form of these exercises, the weekend retreat, was to confront the participants with the question, "Under whose banner do you serve? Christ's or another's?"

The retreats I have described are usually conducted for groups. Many Catholics have enjoyed another option, spending time at a guest house attached to a monastery of men or women. In Canada and the United States there are a number of these monasteries, sometimes of the Benedictine order, sometimes of the Cistercian observance, where the spiritual pilgrim finds a welcome. One can seek personal guidance from a guest-master designated for this purpose. The visitor can also observe much or nearly all of the monastic celebration of the Liturgy of the Hours and the Eucharist. This experience need not be and often is not as programmed as is the weekend retreat done with a group.

Bible Study

Catholic parishes of pre-Vatican II days offered parishioners a full range of fraternal and spiritual organizations. For women there was the Altar and Rosary Society. For men, the Knights of Columbus offered fraternal help and spiritual encouragement. Many parishes had a Holy Name Society aimed at reducing profanity and swearing, the St. Vincent de Paul Society to help the parish needy, and youth groups centered on sports. Typically each of these was supervised by a priest of the parish while leadership, election of officers, and management of the day to day was in the hands of the laity.

Since white American Catholicism moved out of the stifling urban ghettos to suburbia, many of these societies lost their appeal. The

Second Vatican Council's reforms directed our attention to other areas. Some of these older organizations are dying but new groups have arisen, the charismatic renewal being one example. Since the 1960's Catholic Scripture scholars and Catholic publishing houses have worked to equip believers with new translations of the Scripture and an armory of pamphlets, commentaries, and books for the promotion of Scripture study.

In recent years as a university chaplain, I found one such publishing venture of particular help. *Share the Word* is a bi-monthly magazine of Bible study and thought questions leading to prayer. It is published by the Paulist National Catholic Evangelization Association as a tool for reaching out to the unchurched in neighborhood discussion groups.

Although it was designed as a means of spreading the gospel to the unchurched, this magazine has proven invaluable to me and to many parish Bible study groups. It contains a brief but helpful commentary on the Scriptures which are assigned for our Sunday worship services in a given month. With the assigned Scripture texts in one hand and a commentary on them in another, almost anyone can assemble a group for both study and prayer.

In the course of weekly meetings, I can listen as members of the group react personally to the Scriptures which we read and which will be heard again on the approaching Sunday. Since I usually preach every Sunday I am helped by their reactions. These, combined with my own ideas and the commentary, give me a creative stimulus for the sermon forming in my mind. At the close of a given study the magazine provides prayer suggestions for the group so that the occasion is not merely an educational-instructional event.

Yet another widely used and very successful format for Bible study is that of Monsignor David Rosage. He selects scriptural passages for daily reading and collects them in a paperback book. Using his book, members of a group read assigned passages for fifteen minutes each day. When they come together as a group once a week, each person has a turn at saying what he or she learned from the reading. When each has had a turn, others can comment, ask for clarification, or provide a word of support. As used by Father Vincent McKiernan of the Paulist Fathers' Center in Boston, this process has helped many people deepen their faith while becoming more able to speak of this in front of others. As someone who preaches regularly from the Bible, such groups help me not only for practical sermon preparation; they also give me new light about the bearing of a text. My religious order has another rule requiring daily Scripture reading in addition to the devotional literature. I confess sadly that I have not followed this rule as much as I did the other.

Spiritual Direction

Like Bible study, spiritual direction is one of the oldest forms of spiritual development. The apostle Paul first learned at the feet of the rabbi Gamaliel; later he would be converted to Christ and have another apprenticeship among the Christians. Solitary monks of the desert or those grouped in monasteries often sought each other out to get advice, insight, or encouragement.

In modern times there are many Catholics who enlist under the banner of some writer, preacher, or cassette tape speaker. Others seek a director or guide—be it layman or laywoman, nun or priest—to get regular, thoughtful, and systematic guidance in all that concerns their growth as disciples. Visits to retreat houses and monastery guest houses provide opportunities to consult a director. Parish priests, too, are increasingly sought out as spiritual directors. Due to infrequent travel or long distances, some people find help by an exchange of letters with a favorite guide. Not everyone, it should be added, can be a good director, and people who seek a director need to understand that a director's task is to guide, not to control, to offer light, not to produce clones in his or her likeness.

Conclusion

It has been my purpose and my hope that this selective summary of the rich resources available to Catholics for spiritual growth would be useful to a Protestant reader. I believe that much of what the Christian heritage contains of these matters can be appreciated by both Catholics and Protestants. There is also, I believe, plenty of evidence that serious-minded people are found in both sets of churches, men and women who long like the deer for living water.

Speaking not long ago in Wheaton College's Edman Chapel, John

Stott praised those who were working so hard to extend the gospel throughout the world through extensive evangelization. He also urged more intensive evangelization, a deepening of our life in Christ. Donald Bloesch has criticized any spirituality which has as its major component dead orthodoxy. Sound teaching, while absolutely essential, is more than proper doctrine. A deepening spirituality is also a teacher. A.W. Tozer noted with concern the number of pulpits which preached the basics while giving no more.

At the heart of Christian spirituality lies a fuller response to the Holy Spirit's promptings. Programs, methods, cassette speakers, retreats, preaching, private prayer, quiet time, social activism, and fasting should ideally flow out of our groundedness in the Spirit's leading. Discernment of that leading must not be our own individual judgment; we must test the spirits in relation to the Church's heritage, her current lived experience, and creative transmission of the gospel for our own age.

9

A Closer Look at RECONCILIATION AND ANOINTING

In this chapter I wish to discuss the biblical roots, history, and form of two sacraments: that of reconciliation and that of anointing the sick.

Many Catholics, both priests and laity, still refer to the sacrament of reconciliation as "confession," a label which focuses on the listing of sins in a recital to the priest. While this frank listing is indeed part of the sacrament, it is not the whole. Some contemporary Catholic writers prefer to speak of "penance" as a way of focusing on the repentance and conversion involved. I have decided here to follow the lead of Rev. Richard Gula, who prefers the title "Sacrament of Reconciliation." This has a dual advantage: it is the Church's official title, and it highlights what the sacrament promotes and celebrates—a renewed, loving relationship with God and neighbor.

All Christians face the sad truth that, despite our most sincere and ardent commitment to Christ and his teachings, we still have moments of failure. We give these moments various names—"fall from grace," "backsliding," or the generic term "sin." Catholics are of course no exception. Throughout history we have dealt with this problem, curiously enough, through revivals.

Instruction, repentance, and recommitment to Christ have marked the aims of St. Francis's vagabond friars, as well as St. Dominic's "Order of Preachers." In the eighteenth and nineteenth centuries, revivals were associated with the priests and brothers of St. Alphonsus Liguori's organization, called the Redemptorists. Their efforts to renew or revitalize Catholic groups were more often called "missions." Neapolitan lawyer-turned-priest, Liguori said that their mission work brought back huge numbers of people who had been distant from God. His Redemptorist priests and brothers trained in Europe in mission revival and brought their methods to the United States. American Catholicism was profoundly affected by the preaching of these revivals. Even today individuals and parishes show traces of the work of these itinerant Catholic preachers.

A typical nineteenth century Catholic revival began when a team of four or five priests, especially trained for this work, would be invited by the pastor of a parish to come to his place for a period of days or weeks. The pastor hoped to revitalize the cradle Catholics and to attract the unchurched. Preceded by newspaper ads, trumpeted by leaflets plastered around the neighborhood, announced from the pulpit, the mission team arrived to begin a rigorous round of services.

Each morning began with the liturgy of the Eucharist and doctrinal instructions from five to six o'clock. At six, people were dismissed to return home for breakfast, and they usually had to report to their jobs at seven. Midday services were scheduled for those who were free, but the major thrust was a series of nightly services aimed at rescuing the "carnal" Christian.

Local carpenters had erected, either outdoors in a prominent place or indoors in the center of the church, a huge "mission cross." Specially prepared parish choirs led the people in vigorous song, and then the preachers spoke. The evening preachers were chosen from the team with care—they had to be dynamic and powerful. Their lengthy talks were delivered in plain language, pulling no punches, and aimed at impressing the sinner with the dangers he or she courted. In an age without radios, televisions, or films, the people responded deeply to a good preacher's dramatic flair and vivid imagery.

If the audiences were large and the preaching effective, the revival might be extended days or even weeks beyond the originally agreed upon time. Mission teams sometimes spent nearly a month in one place in this work. As the mission became systematized and as the practitioners learned what was effective and what wasn't, handbooks appeared to instruct both the congregations and the would-be mission preacher on techniques. A special feature of the mission was the availability of Christian literature. Catholic missionaries carried this material with them, and at the end of the services they sold books, pamphlets, and devotional aids such as rosaries or medals.

A key purpose of every mission was a call to conversion, and every mission was sure to feature a vivid talk on death. The preacher challenged every person in the audience—the opportunity to turn from sin, to repent, to embrace Christ and the power of the Cross might not come again. The large mission cross, draped in a white cloth, served as a visual aid to the preaching. Some missionaries went further, erecting a *catafalque* surrounded with candles in the middle aisle. This mock casket, a solemn and graphic reminder of death, served to highlight the urgent appeal for conversion made by the preacher. One missionary, while pointing out in graphic detail how Christ's blood had run for us, grasped one arm of the mission cross and, putting his weight on it, swayed lightly from side to side as the audience visualized Jesus' death and wept with remorse.

Catholic revivals or missions were therefore in many aspects like the revivals of Finney, Moody, or Billy Sunday. The key difference perhaps lay in the way in which the repentant sinner was to give expression to his or her change of heart. Instead of the "altar call" or "sinner's bench" or the call to "come forward," Catholic preachers urged a return to God through the sacraments of reconciliation and the Eucharist. Every evening sermon contained a call to acknowledge sin, to do penance, and to be reconciled to God and neighbor through the sacraments. In Italy, some of Liguori's teams spent weeks in poor rural villages and reported remarkable scenes of conversion and reconciliation; brothers involved in feuds or vendettas embraced each other with tears.

In the United States, historian Jay Dolan recounts that a successful mission was one in which hundreds or even thousands were reconciled to God through the sacrament of reconciliation. One example was the mission preached in 1851 at St. Joseph's Church in Rochester, New York. A team of six priests, assisted by four local priests, came to minister to this parish of ten thousand people. By the end of the mission, six thousand had answered the call to enter the confessional to acknowledge their sin, repent, and promise God that they would sin no more. Reconciled with God and their community, these people would then come forward to receive the Eucharist.

As a newly-ordained priest, I remember how much in awe I was that people would come to the confessional box to unburden themselves and speak frankly of their sins to me. Separated in the shadows by a light screen we interacted in an ancient Christian practice. It dawned on me that for some of these people, my personality or my defects were less important in this sacrament than the fact that the Church, through the bishop, had delegated me to act in the community's name. Although my nameplate was on the outside of the confessional box, I acted only as a kind of instrument, a spokesman for Christ, however clumsily I conducted myself.

It has been more than twenty years since I first entered the priest's side of the confessional box. But that sense of awe still remains with me when people courageously follow what Scripture urges, "confess your sins to one another." In so doing, penitents make themselves vulnerable, and my prayer is that I will be helped by the Holy Spirit to be either silent or prudent and helpful in whatever words of advice or instruction seem necessary. As any pastor, rabbi, or priest will testify, when people bare their souls they reveal our common failings; they also, sometimes unwittingly, testify to the great work of God, the call of his Spirit to deal with the shadows and pains that menace our integrity.

To understand the particular way in which Catholicism has dealt with this grace-filled drama of sin, forgiveness, growth, and reconciliation, some history of the sacrament needs to be given. The baseline must be the biblical notion of repentance or conversion. My favorite theologian, Karl Rahner, has written that it is through the grace of Christ that human beings experience sorrow for sin, and this sorrow is a moral and religious attitude and reaction. This reaction can be called repentance or penance, and it is necessary for salvation. It is this basic attitude which precedes baptism, at least for the adult. Baptism, as Catholics have always taught, forgives sin, makes one a child of God, and launches one in the life of grace. Yet, despite being united with Christ and cleansed of sin through baptism,

Christians have still committed post-baptismal sin. What can be done with these sinners?

Since baptism is entry into a people, being made a member of Christ's body, it follows that repentance or conversion leads to and is made evident in union with the visible local body of Christ. The Scripture offers clues as to how this happens.

Karl Rahner directs our attention to two passages in Matthew's Gospel which guide us in our views on reconciliation. The first passage is Matthew 16:13–20, the famous Peter-as-rock teaching. The text is useful for the sacrament of reconciliation because it links the power to bind and loose with Peter and the Church. Again, in Matthew 18:15–18, power to bind and loose is associated with the Church. A fall from grace means a shift in one's relationship with the body of Christ, the Church.

In short, if baptism as the first birth from above involves the body of Christ, then being reborn, a quasi-second baptism, also involves the body of Christ. Reconciliation after baptism needed visible expression and this visible expression was found in the early Church.

Early Christians confronting the pain involved in seeing their brothers and sisters falling from grace debated among themselves about the means of retrieving them or reconciling them to Christ. One group argued that lapsed Christians could not be reconciled with the body of Christ until their deathbed. Another group, criticized for being lax, allowed some limited reconciliation, and permitted serious sinners to return to the Lord's Table only after arduous penance. The "laxists" won out and as early as the third century provided for the Church a model of the sacrament of reconciliation.

Types of Reconciliation

When it became evident that men and women converted to Christ as adults and baptized into the body of Christ continued to sin, often seriously, there gradually arose in the early churches two basic systems of reconciling these people. The first type is what historian Ladislas Orsy has called the *Mediterranean model,* a borrowing from synagogue practice of exclusion of sinners.[1] Intended to reconcile Christians guilty of serious sins like homicide, adultery, or denial of their Christian faith, this system included the following features:

1. A person acknowledged sin to the local bishop, who then admitted him or her to the category of "penitent." Being in this category carried with it civic and ecclesiastical liabilities. In some instances one might have to leave a certain business profession which was the cause of sin. If married, one might have to cease having intercourse.

2. "Penitents" attended church but sat in designated sections. People prayed for them and the penitents themselves fasted, gave to charities, and wore sackcloth. Over time, they could move from the rear of the penitential section to places nearer the altar. At the end of the penitential period assigned, they were re-admitted to the Lord's Table.

3. Orsy believes that relatively few people underwent this formal process. He thinks it is more likely that most were called to repentance by preaching, liturgical prayers, and use of Scripture. Fasting and giving to charities were, however, also typical ways of showing repentance for lesser sins.

4. At the beginning of the penitential period, in the case of those who had sinned seriously and had asked admission to the order of penitents, a person did in fact make a confession of sinfulness in public. This was, however, a general accusation and not a detailed listing of the sins.

5. Cases in which the bishops or Church law compelled people against their will to do public penance seem to be rare. Voluntary entry into the system seems to have been normative.

By contrast with this Mediterranean model, widespread in the fourth, fifth, and sixth centuries around the Mediterranean Basin, there arose a newer type, called the *Irish model.* Some of the most effective evangelizers of Europe were monks from monasteries of Ireland and Scotland who traveled eastward to preach the gospel. They brought with them a different system of reconciling sinners.

Unlike the Mediterranean system, which required public embarrassment and, in some cases, a very lengthy penance, the Irish monastic system permitted the sinner to do some penance in private. And the Irish model allowed for more frequent failures. Forgiveness and reconciliation to the Lord's Table could be offered repeatedly. Penances imposed by the monks were seen as healing medicine for the soul and, while often harsh, could be commuted. One writer has called this system a "tariff system," derived from Celtic and Anglo-Saxon legal practice. Their laws imposed a penalty to satisfy a crime. Assigning penances for sins had something of the same logic.

In its early phases, the "tariff penance" involved a penitent who confessed privately and received a penance which he or she then performed. After having completed the penance, the sinner would then return to inform the monk or priest who welcomed the penitent back into full communion with the body of Christ. History reveals cases where it was considered acceptable for a friend or relative of the sinner to assist in performing the penances. In later history, penances assigned were shortened so that after forgiveness, one could go to the Lord's Table almost immediately, without returning to assure the priest that the penances had been accomplished.

Monks and priests in this work came to rely on handbooks called penitentials, which were copied and circulated to assist in the process. Richard Gula illustrates the medicinal aspect or healing hope involved in certain penances. He quotes from the Penitential of Columban (600, A.D.):

> The talkative person is to be sentenced to silence, the disturber to gentleness, the gluttonous to fasting, the sleepy fellow to watchfulness, the proud to imprisonment, the deserter to expulsion; everyone shall suffer suitable penalties according to what he deserves, that the righteous may live righteously.[2]

Just as the early Church had suffered internal strife over the wisdom of permitting any lapsed person to be reconciled to the body of Christ, so did the seventh century churches argue over the wisdom of the Irish system. The older Mediterranean churches, perhaps seeing God as majestic, distant, and holy, took the view that getting back into his graces was a serious process. For the Celtic or Anglo-Saxon churches, the dominant image of God was perhaps that of the Good Shepherd who seeks the lost and urges that we forgive seventy times seven.

Some meetings of regional bishops roundly condemned and forbade the "cheap grace" or "repeated confessions" which the monastic evangelists had brought into Europe, but the practices spread rapidly and gradually won approval. In the midst of the struggle about this, one medieval authority proposed a solution: have public penance for public sins, private penance for private sins. It was a neat distinction on paper; in real life it was not so easy. One might be a public sinner in one situation and quite the private sinner in another.

As late as the thirteenth century there is evidence that the manner in which the sacrament of reconciliation could be administered included the "private" as well as the public types of penance. But in the end, the private version prevailed through and beyond the Council of Trent. It was the private version, with its stress on naming the sins, their type, and frequency—so that medicinal penance might be appropriately assigned—which dominated the field until the Second Vatican Council.

Renewal of the Sacrament

Since the confessional box for anonymity did not appear until the sixteenth century, it appears that the churches tried over the centuries to adapt their practices to the needs of the era. A tide of new insights in psychology, biblical studies, and personalist philosophy accumulated prior to the Second Vatican Council and broke through to reshape the sacraments, including reconciliation. Historians and liturgists helped the bishops retrieve the variations in the past; they, in light of modern needs, also reshaped the rite of the sacrament.

The new look provides three forms of the sacrament. The first form is the modern descendant of the monastic practice of spiritual direction and private confession. An individual seeks reconciliation to the body of Christ through the priest, who acts as the representative of the People of God. The priest and penitent can talk either anonymously through a screen or face to face. After a greeting, the ritual encourages the priest and penitent to begin with prayer and a reading of Scripture appropriate to reconciliation, repentance, or conversion. After some quiet reflection on the text, the penitent can discuss his or her situation and acknowledge sins. The priest can offer advice, and the penitent can ask for clarification. The priest then assigns a modest penance, the purpose of which is to assist the person in the reconciliation and healing process which God's grace has already begun in them. The priest then pronounces the absolution of sin while using, if possible, the biblical gesture of imposition of hands to convey the Holy Spirit's healing and empowerment. The sacrament concludes with a brief prayer of praise to God.

A second form of the sacrament involves several people, but retains the individual confession and absolution. It is becoming one of the most popular and common formats in North America. Several people gather at a convenient hour, usually in a local church where the priest greets them and brings the group to focus with prayer and a hymn. Scripture is read and made the subject of a sermon or instruction, aimed at stirring hearts and reminding the people of God's mercy. Sometimes the priest or a layperson leads the people in an examination of conscience.

The people then make a general, vocal acknowledgment of sin and recite the Lord's Prayer. Those who feel the need for a private confession of a particular sin then present themselves to the priest or priests present. From that priest they receive absolution, and they rejoin the others who have been praying or reflecting quietly in the pews. All then join in a final proclamation of praise for God's mercy and a concluding prayer of thanksgiving. After a closing blessing, perhaps supplemented by a hymn, the people are dismissed.

Had this form been permitted in the nineteenth century, the "mission team" of priests might have had an easier time. Historian Jay Dolan describes a two week mission in 1862 in a Pennsylvania town. Huge crowds of people thronged the church and many were moved to repentance, including the owner of the town's largest saloon. As a result of what he heard, he tore down his sign, demolished his counter, and ended his liquor trade. The priests giving this revival spent as many as ten hours per day hearing individual confessions of men and women being reconciled to God.

A third form is also possible, a renewed version of a form used on occasion even before the Second Vatican Council. There have been moments when, in natural catastrophes, wars, or emergencies, large numbers of people wanted to acknowledge their sins and seek forgiveness formally through the sacrament. This was especially the case among soldiers during wartime. Former atheists sometimes recovered their belief in God while in a foxhole. The Church permits a general acknowledgment of sin by a large group and grants a general absolution or forgiveness, pronounced by the priest. Like the others, this form is to include Scripture, preaching, and recitation of the Lord's Prayer.

To sum up both some of the history of the sacrament and the renewal, note the following points:

a. There is a shift of emphasis, away from "telling the list of sins" (confession) to a new awareness of the biblical notion of repentance, a deep-seated change of heart. One consequence of this is that Catholics seeking reconciliation through the sacrament are likely to do so less frequently than in the past. How often, after all, does one achieve some new insight about oneself and a new plateau of understanding of sin and grace?

b. By a variety of forms for the sacrament of reconciliation, the Church provides a helpful flexibility; group forms of reconciliation help shift the emphasis from an individualist sense of sin to an awareness of the collective impact of even one's most hidden sins. In evangelical revivals, penitents found a "sinner's bench" or "walk along the sawdust trail" to be a public gesture through which they could acknowledge their sin before God and a desire to reform. Sins affect our capacity to interact with our brothers and sisters.

c. Pre-Vatican II confessional practice allowed, partly because of the numbers of penitents, very little time or comfortable space for much dialogue between the priest and penitent. The ritual, while based on Scripture, did not include it. The revised ritual provides for use of Scripture in all three forms, and in some forms allows a better opportunity for good exchange between the priest and penitent.

d. In the new forms, both the priest and penitent(s) can emerge from anonymity and darkness. Parishes have been asked to set aside suitable rooms in which priest and penitent can speak to each other face to face. The confessional box allowed the penitent only one stance, on the knees. Reconciliation rooms provide chairs.

Only time will tell whether the renewal of the rite will achieve what it was intended to do. Current evidence is that Catholics taking advantage of the sacrament do so now much less frequently. In addition, generations of young people born since the reform of the ritual have no memory of the older practice. Unless properly instructed, like every new generation, they will be ignorant of the newer way. It is also true that some priests have refused to accept the reform of the rite. Or, having accepted the externals of the change, have not invested it with a new spirit.

The constant, however, throughout all the history I have so briefly sketched, is the Church's self-awareness based on Scripture, particularly from Matthew's Gospel, that reconciliation with God is intimately linked with God's People. Conversion or penance is an event which draws in a concrete historical group of believers. Sinfulness pulls the whole group down, holiness helps lift the whole group upward.

I have seen many positive results from the new rite of reconciliation, including some improvements over the older confessional box. First, when the penitent and I begin with a short prayer followed by a reading from Scripture, we set together a good tone at once. A well-chosen Scripture text lifts us out of our own preoccupations, embarrassment, or nervousness. The text speaks of a loving God who has reached out to the world through Christ precisely for the purpose of reconciling us to one another and to our heavenly Father.

Secondly, the new rite encourages a more personal and conversational style of interaction between me and the penitent. People feel free not only to list their particular sins, but to speak about the pressures and passions which flow powerfully beneath the surface of their lives. Spiritual growth depends in part on our capacity to recognize these deeper forces, precisely so that we can invite Christ to help us in taming them or altering them.

A third fruitful aspect has to do with the assignment of penance. Gone are the harsh penances of the third or fourth century; gone, too, are the lengthy, physical penances assigned as tariff in Celtic or Anglo-Saxon monasticism. Prior to the Second Vatican Council, the priest's training led him to impose penances which might be medicinal, faint echoes of Columban's seventh century advice:

> the talkative person is to be sentenced to silence . . . the gluttonous to fasting. . . .

But more often than not, the penances consisted of repeated recitations of prayers: "Say the Hail Mary five times," or "Recite the Lord's Prayer three times." While prayer is an ancient form of penance, many Catholics seemed to misunderstand the worth of this penance. In the revised rite, penances to be assigned should not be burdensome to the point of discouraging the penitent. It is, after all, Christ who forgives and Christ who has borne our guilt and sin. I try to tailor the token penance I assign to the kinds of sins and issues which the penitent has discussed. I see the penance as a way of helping a person in continued growth in Christ.

Because the sacrament of reconciliation seeks to promote a new harmony between God and sinner and between the sinner and the community, priests have been trained to require of the penitent, in addition to the penance mentioned above, restitution of stolen property and repair of damages, including damage to another's good name or reputation. Reconciliation which did not include these elements would not deserve the name. Catholics feel that every sin, even so-called private or undiscovered ones, has an impact on the whole body of Christ. Even one person's secret yielding to jealousy, uncharitable judgments, or pride affects the whole People. When one member is weak, it drags down the health of the whole.

The typical Catholic-Protestant confrontation over the issue of this sacrament pits the Protestant question, "Why tell your sins to a priest? Why not tell them directly to God?" against the Catholic rejoinder that, "Jesus gave to the apostles and their successors the power to bind and loose; that is, to forgive sin."

The question of "telling sins to a priest" arises in part because this is the way Catholics described the sacrament, focusing on the listing of sins. Protestant critics looked for a biblical basis for this, as well as for evidence that Catholics were not hypocritical in their frequent use of this rite. If we Catholics simply confessed, did a light penance, sinned again, and ran back to the confessional box time and time again without improvement, our Protestant neighbors could hardly be impressed. It seemed to them like a delusion at worst, or at best, cheap grace.

I believe that the priest's role in forgiving sin flows from the biblical passages mentioned earlier, texts which link forgiveness, proclamation of reconciliation, and God's love to the work of Christ's body, the People of God, and in particular to leaders in that body. I believe that, just as Jesus gave the power to teach, preach, cure, and baptize in his name to mere mortals designated for these purposes, so today Jesus teaches, preaches, cures, baptizes, and forgives through the actions of mere mortals.

I further believe that anyone who has begun to repent, before darkening the door of any Catholic church, has already felt the touch of God's grace and forgiveness. The history of the sacrament of reconciliation reveals that people aware of and repentant for lesser sins need not and did not "tell their sins to the priest." Their own prayer, their own efforts to heal breaches made in their families, occupations, or communities, their reception of Jesus in the Eucharist, can achieve the desired reconciliation.

On the other hand, the history of the sacrament as well as our own experience, shows that all sin, particularly serious kinds, affects the whole People of God. The writings of Matthew, John, and Paul advise how to deal with those who are seriously at odds with Christ. I am led to believe that a public ritual which proclaims both the return of the repentant sinner and God's forgiveness is thoroughly biblical, and a gift to the Church from Christ. Some sense of this comes through in the very prayers assigned to the priest in the ritual.

In the renewed ritual of the sacrament of reconciliation, the prayer formula to be used by the priest has these words:

> God, the Father of mercies, through the death and resurrection of his Son, has reconciled the world to himself and sent the Holy Spirit among us for the forgiveness of sins. . . .

As in John 20:19–23, the text of the prayer recognizes the presence of the Holy Spirit and the Spirit's function in forgiveness. The prayer continues:

> . . . .through the ministry of the Church may God give you pardon and peace. . . .

The Church as the People of God has a collective ministry of pardon and peacemaking. How this is done or experienced varies in different situations. If Christians as groups are seen as the "salt of the earth" or "light set on a lampstand," an individual convicted of his or her sin may more easily be drawn to Christ's forgiveness and reconciliation. The prayer concludes:

> . . . and I absolve you from your sins in the name of the Father and of the Son and of the Holy Spirit.

A Summary of Reconciliation

A Dominican nun, Sister Kate Dooley summarizes the theological principles which have undergirded the history of this sacrament:

> 1. The primary Sacrament of Reconciliation is Baptism. Baptismal life is renewed in the Sacrament of Penance and brought to completion in the Eucharist.
>
> 2. Reconciliation is by its very nature a corporate and ecclesial activity. Reconciliation with the church is reconciliation with God. Reconciliation is the work of the whole church and is not to be restricted to the office of the ordained minister, important though that office is.
>
> 3. Conversion and repentance is a process which includes both the liturgical sign and the whole of one's life. One's daily effort at reconciliation is a crucially important part of the sacramental process. Moreover, the church must undergo conversion within its own structures . . . genuine renewal must involve both personal and societal reform.[3]

Anointing of the Sick

Leafing casually through the pages of the February 1984 issue of *Christian Life* magazine, I came across a remarkable story of the return to life of a young man who had been declared dead by doctors. In the story, "Paul Cresan: Contraband Smuggler," I learned of a seventeen-year-old Romanian boy who had accidentally set himself on fire with lighter fluid. After a long hospital stay, he died. His mother refused to believe that her son was lost and demanded that his casket, which had been sealed by authorities, be opened. Although his flesh had deteriorated, and some of his bones were exposed, he came to life. Scars which had marred his face were later healed through anointing and prayer of his friends and relatives.

This remarkable story of one woman's faith in Jesus and the faith of her friends reminds us of the greatness of God's mercy and the power of the risen Christ to give life and to heal. Although the Paul Cresan story took place behind the Iron Curtain, we need not go far afield to find stories of God-given healing through the power of Christ. A reknowned Catholic revivalist of the nineteenth century, Jesuit priest Francis Weninger, always included the blessing of the sick on the last day of the mission. Jay Dolan describes it:

> He did not wait on popular demand, but solicited the presence of the sick and lame at his revivals. Weninger told the people that for some, sickness, such as blindness, may be a saving grace, just as for others good health can be a blessing from God. He cautioned them not to expect any immediate result. . . .[4]

Then, says Dolan, Weninger led the sick in prayer, asking for healing through the intercession of a deceased holy priest and by the application of a relic of that holy man. The Jesuit preacher then read a Scripture passage and applied the relic to the sick. Weninger wrote that "cures followed cures without interruption." Weninger's healing sessions took place, it should be noted, on the last day of the mission, after a time of faith-renewal and repentance for sin.

The people who had attended the mission, prayed, and been stirred by Spirit-filled preaching had already seen results. Hardened sinners or notorious backsliders in the community had returned to God. In some instances, they had even seen what seemed unlikely—the reception of a Protestant as a convert. They had seen an outpouring of special graces and they expected it to continue in the healing of the sick and the lame.

Father Weninger himself did not believe that all the cures were miraculous, yet some of them he found impressive enough to report to Rome. Two of the cures Weninger had seen were used to further the process leading to the Church's official declaration that a sixteenth century Jesuit priest could be called a saint.

Healing done in Jesus' name continues today both in Protestant revival preaching and at Catholic pilgrimage sites and charismatic gatherings. The conviction that Jesus came to heal both body and spirit is solidly rooted in the Holy Scriptures. Rev. William Bausch notes that Jesus' healings were not for the body's sake alone, but for the entire person. Jesus' miraculous signs were a way of bringing home the truth of his message about the Kingdom of God. Sickness of body and soul, along with lingering suspicion that sickness was punishment for sinful conduct, come to the Christian faith through our traditional view of Adam's fall.

Sickness and sin are related, not in the direct sense that "God is punishing me for my sins by giving me AIDS," but in a broader sense. Jesus himself took pains to correct the view that God vindictively punishes a person for his sin by a painful affliction. See, for example, the ninth chapter of John's Gospel.

We believe that sickness is an inescapable symptom of man's need for deliverance. God's original creation, as described in Genesis, breathes an air of harmony and integration; Eden turns into a nightmare of dissension and pain. From earth-shattering quakes to runaway cancer cells, there is a sense of disharmony, disruption, and distance from the loving source of life. To evade the invitation to return to God is the ultimate evil, everlasting death. This is what Jesus overcomes. This is why countless times in the gospels Jesus' cures demand faith, and he himself refers to sin in the context of healing.

Jesus still wants to heal, uplift, and redirect so that we will move courageously and more confidently on the road to the kingdom. Given our previous stress on the view that Jesus is the sacrament, the embodiment of God, and that the Church is, in turn, God's People and Christ's body, it follows that Jesus heals today through the intercession of the Church.

We recall that in Mark 6:11 Jesus appoints disciples to preach and share in his own powers. "They expelled many demons, anointing the sick with oil and working many cures." We recall, too, how Peter encountered a cripple at the temple gates who begged for money. Using Jesus' name, Peter raised the cripple to his feet and sent him on his way, cured.

I recall, some years back, watching Kathryn Kuhlman on television. During the program she brought relief to sick and crippled believers, careful always to say that what she did was in Jesus' name and power. Catholics have always cherished the text, the charter text in fact, for the sacrament of the anointing of the sick (James

5:13–15). Notice that in the case of sickness, leaders or officials of the local church are called in to pray and anoint for the forgiveness of sin, for possible restoration of health, and for revival of faith in the afflicted brother or sister.

In one of his meditations on this sacrament, Karl Rahner discusses the anointing of the sick and points out that, in one basic sense, every person faces death very much alone. Each of us is responsible for our own freedom and confrontation with life, and in times of serious sickness, the aloneness can be particularly intense.

What he calls a "merciless solitude" is, however, only part of the truth. No one escapes the presence of God. The sick person also has links, through baptism, confirmation, and the Eucharist, with the whole body of Christ. The Church practice of assisting the sick and dying has come to expression in the ritual derived from the advice of James.

A Brief History of the Sacrament of Anointing

Specialists agree that this ritual never had the prominence given to baptism and the Eucharist. But along with scriptural references to prayer, healing, and anointing, there is a recently discovered first century tablet which shows that St. James' directive was being carried out. A precious clue comes from the early fifth century in a letter of Pope Innocent I, who called the text of James the basis for a sacrament. This letter reveals that lay people as well as elders, bishops, or priests could carry consecrated oil to a sick person's bedside to anoint them. St. Augustine also mentions this ritual in one of his writings, and the way he mentions it suggests that he himself practiced it. Eastern and Western churches considered anointing as one of the seven sacraments, as they professed in conciliar documents from the Council of Lyons (1274) and the Council of Florence (1439).

In late medieval times, the sacrament in both interpretation and practice came to have a double focus: forgiveness of sin and comforting the distressed and discouraged person. Forgiveness of sin through the Holy Spirit was the dominant effect of the sacrament for the medievals. Fear of dying without forgiveness tended to cause a linkage of the rite with the final moments of life. Hence the title, "extreme unction" or "absolutely the last anointing." The reform Council of Trent tried to enhance the notion of the sacrament as one of faith-renewal for the sick, but their efforts were not as strong as they could have been. The council spoke of the oil blessed by the bishop and its application as "the most apt illustration of the grace of the Holy Spirit, with which the sick man's soul is invisibly anointed."

The council bishops saw the sacrament's goal as that of forgiving sin and "raising up and strengthening the sick man's soul, arousing in him great confidence in the divine mercy." This confidence, they said, was "to help him bear more easily the burden and pain of illness, and more resolutely resist the temptation of Satan, who is always at his heels." They added that bodily recovery might also be expected if it were, in God's eyes, for the good of the person.

After the Council of Trent, theologians tended to urge the use of the rite for those who were seriously ill, not just for those at the point of death, which had been the late medieval tendency. Because of the belief that the anointing and prayer could forgive sins, Catholic priests were trained to administer this anointing, one part of the "Last Rites," even when the person appeared to be dead. Medical science today disputes a good deal of the criteria which apply in order to pronounce someone dead. Catholics believed that mere appearances of death did not always tell the story. The rite of anointing and prayer could therefore be given even to someone who did not or could not respond. The faith of the People of God, of those administering the rite, supplied what the sick person was unable to articulate. Scripture does not tell us that the crippled beggar outside the temple believed anything at all about Jesus or Peter who cured him in Jesus' name. Jesus' own cure of the little girl who was thought to be dead or unconscious was in no way dependent on her faith; it was dependent on the faith of her parents.

The Shape of the Rite

As might be expected from the study of the sacrament of reconciliation, which showed variations over the centuries, the sacrament of anointing also has varied in style. St. James's text does not specify details about the prayer or the method of anointing. For a long time the ritual required, or at least allowed, multiple anointing of the five senses; eyelids, ears, hands, lips, and nose. One could also anoint that portion of the body in greatest pain.

Consistent with their plan to revise all the sacraments, the bishops of the Second Vatican Council ordered adaptations in the form of this ritual. They also prepared new guidelines for its use.

Those guidelines stress that the sacrament has two complementary aspects. The Church is supporting the sick in their struggles and pain, continuing Christ's messianic work of healing. Since we are all members of Christ's body, what happens to one has an effect on others. In this sacrament we express our share in the sufferings of the other. We also express our joint hope in the power of Christ.

A typical use of the ritual—whether at home or in a hospital, church, or nursing home—begins with the priest's greeting to the sick person and a prayer of blessing. Both the priest and the sick person are to realize that what is happening is an anointing in the name and power of Christ himself (see Mark 6:13). The priest, on behalf of the whole community, ministers to the suffering.

After the opening greeting and blessing, there is an acknowledgement of sin, similar to that used in Sunday worship. Scripture is read and if the patient's condition permits, it can be commented on briefly. Another prayer follows, then the biblical gesture of laying on of hands. This is a sign of blessing, as we pray that by the power of God's healing grace, the sick person may be restored or strengthened for a time. Imposition of hands is, of course, related to curing, as we see in Luke 4:40.

The priest then anoints the sick person's forehead and hands. Anointing with oil, preferably that made from a natural plant like the olive, is a sign of the healing and strengthening presence of the Holy Spirit. As the priest anoints, he says the following words:

> Through this anointing, May the Lord in his love and mercy help you with the grace of the Holy Spirit. May the Lord who frees you from sin save you and raise you up.

While this anointing could take place with only the priest and the sick person present, the revised ritual urges that family and friends, or at least some medical personnel, be present with the priest to join in the prayer. If a patient is sufficiently alert, he or she can participate also in the sacrament of reconciliation and receive the Eucharist, or "food for the journey" *Viaticum*, as it was often called. If a patient is not sufficiently alert or is unable to take food, anointing may be all that is called for.

One of the most moving experiences I had in this regard occurred when I was invited by a Catholic to anoint his brother dying of cancer in a Boston hospital. My friend led me through the hospital corridors as we joined other relatives and entered the dying man's semi-darkened room. His eyes were extremely sensitive to light. I greeted him and, together with relatives, we prayed and heard a passage of Scripture on which I commented briefly. I then anointed the dying man's head and hands. After another prayer specifically related to his needs, we all joined hands to recite the Lord's Prayer. In contrast to some other anointings I had performed prior to the Second Vatican Council, this was for me very moving. Doctors had stopped intravenous feeding, and the man died several days later. During the anointing our tears flowed, but there was comfort in the presence of a microcosm of the entire Christian community. Everyone, it is true, dies alone, but we who are baptized in Christ are never alone.

While anointing is often associated with relief of suffering, there is another aspect. It encourages those in pain to associate themselves as best as possible with the suffering and death of Christ. Here one thinks of Romans 8:17:

> But if we are children, we are heirs as well: heirs of God, heirs of Christ, if only we suffer with him so as to be glorified with him.

Also to the point is Colossians 1:24:

> Even now I find my joy in the suffering I endure for you. In my own flesh I fill up what is lacking in the sufferings of Christ for the sake of his body, the Church.

Conclusion

To conclude this chapter on reconciliation and anointing, it is useful to repeat that the way Catholics view these and administer them flows from their views on the nature of the Church, particularly from the biblical images of the people of God and the body of Christ. From the first moments of Christian life in baptism through the painful moments at the end of earthly life, individuals are seen as part of a network called the body of Christ. When one suffers, all suffer; when one rejoices, all rejoice. Christ is "bodied forth" in the pains, joys, sufferings, and triumphs of his brothers and sisters.

Both sacraments deal with a renewal of life. If we fall from grace we are invited to be reconciled, to return to the Father's house; if we suffer in illness or are at the approach of death, we are encouraged to associate ourselves with Christ's own sufferings. We are accompanied by the body of Christ in our "merciless solitude."

10

A Closer Look at HOLY ORDERS

Over twenty years ago, in May of 1964 to be precise, I was ordained to the Catholic priesthood in a historic New York City church. Eight of us seminarians who had shared seven years of life together—six of which were studies in philosophy and theology—were presented that spring morning to Cardinal Francis Spellman as tested candidates for priesthood. We had already been ordained to the lesser orders—acolyte, lector, exorcist, and subdeacon. We had been serving as deacons for the customary year, the diaconate being the first of the "major orders." Now, in the presence of family, seminary faculty, other priests, and friends, we eight were clad in white and lay prostrate on the marble-floored sanctuary, our heads cushioned by an arm. The choir, the cantor, Cardinal Spellman, and the people prayed relentlessly that God would assist us in the work of priesthood.

The rites were long and included an anointing of our hands and imposition of hands by others, wonderful biblical gestures. We in turn laid our hands on chalices presented to us and joined with the cardinal to officiate at a liturgy of the Eucharist. When it was over, we posed for pictures and went to pre-assigned places in the Church of St. Paul the Apostle to give "first blessings." In front of side chapels in that large New York church, our family and friends formed a line to receive from us a prayer of blessing made over their heads and ending with the sign of the cross. Tearfully we gave these blessings and tearfully people received. Some even kissed the hand that gave the blessing. It was as if we had been suddenly equipped with a new set of powers by the sacrament of ordination and adorned with a sacred aura. The first time someone reached for my hand to kiss it, I had to control the impulse to recoil. Kissing hands, as far as I knew, was done only in the movies, particularly the ones featuring counts and dukes at royal courts full of beautiful duchesses.

The respect and awe which Catholic people extended to me and my freshly-anointed seminary classmates was genuine; it also came from more than their personal connections with us. Their attentiveness arose from a long tradition and ancient belief about the nature of the Catholic priesthood. The great German theologian Karl Rahner wrote of this in one of his books. For him the priest's special status is linked to the celebration of the Lord's Supper.

> . . . we are not honoring any man. We are honoring the priesthood of Jesus Christ. We are honoring the Church, the entire Church of all those redeemed, made holy, and called to eternal life. We are honoring Her to whom we all belong, whether we are priests or "merely" believers and sanctified. . . .[7]

Rahner's perspective comes from the typical Catholic stress on our unity in the body of Christ. Any grace, dignity, or power that comes to one man is at the same time an enrichment of the whole.

Earlier I wrote about my own sense of awe and wonderment when I entered a confessional box to hear confessions for the first time as a priest. Total strangers were forming a line outside to reveal to me their weaknesses, their sorrows, their failings. They were coming to me to be pardoned in the name of Christ, but they were not coming to me as an individual so much as to a representative of the body of Christ. I as a person counted less than the function which the body of Christ had assigned to me.

This was emphasized for me again when, shortly after ordination, I visited St. Paul's College in Washington, D.C., where I had studied theology. I was greeted by the Mexican nuns who worked in that seminary as cooks, seamstresses, and diningroom helpers. They, like some of my relatives at the time of first blessings, kissed my hands. They wanted to honor what I represented more than they wanted to honor me. My personal weaknesses, well-known to family and friends, were for the moment quite secondary.

In the letter to the Hebrews we read that Jesus the High Priest was someone taken from among men, born of a woman, subject to the law. To stress that commonness, it is good for us to remember that after the bishop has laid hands on us, we remain flesh and blood. We, like our brothers and sisters, can get weary and are weak. We know discouragement, failures, and sinfulness.

My ordination to priesthood is only part of the sacrament of holy orders, since another step is the ordination or consecration to episcopacy. Yet the sacrament in general speaks of the question of Church authority. To understand holy orders it is necessary to review some of the history of Church authority.

Church Authority

I believe that it is accurate to say that Catholics and Protestants have, certainly since the Reformation, taken two divergent views of ordination and church authority. The prototypical Catholic approach began with Christ's own actions. He established various ministries in the church he founded. He sent the apostles to the world as his voice and his representatives. It was his will that these apostles would appoint successors. Catholics believe that in his special attention to Peter he laid the basis for the papal function. The apostles were to share in Jesus' authority and to shepherd the church, much like the Twelve Tribes of Israel.

Succeeding the apostles are leaders we call bishops. These had, from the earliest days, assistants called presbyters and elders. By the laying on of hands, the apostles shared with these successors the gift of the Holy Spirit which had anointed them at Pentecost. Down through the centuries into our day, the Spirit continues to be shared through the bishops. As Joseph Komonchak puts it, "the divinely established ecclesiastical ministry is exercised in different orders by those who from antiquity have been called bishops, presbyters, and deacons. . . .[2]

We support our view with certain New Testament texts and the writings of some of the earliest Christians. A typical Protestant-Catholic debate focuses on one of these texts, the famous passage beginning in Matthew 16:17, where we believe that Jesus confers special status on Peter. Catholics have often cited the text as part of their argument that Peter was the first pope. Protestants have interpreted that text differently, which throws a different light on the Catholic formulation.

In the Reformation debates between Catholics and Protestants, a polemical rigidity crept in. It is only in recent years, thanks again to newer research in history and biblical studies, that we Catholics can appreciate our tendency to be too dogmatic about some of our views. The title "apostle" was given to more persons than the Twelve. Books of the New Testament don't reveal a single or universally required form of church order. Further, because of the interchangeability in the New Testament of the words for "bishop," "elder," and "presbyter," it is not so clear that they meant to describe what we have later called a "monarchical episcopate."

If one wishes to be faithful literally to the system of church order found in the New Testament, there are grounds for seeing something less hierarchical than our triple model: bishop over priest over deacon. On the other hand, historical research shows a slow emergence of a three-fold office: bishop, priest, and deacon.

Although the Catholic view of church authority finds a partial justification in the New Testament, it is really the result of development, a growth which was not complete by the year 100. Our approach is only part of a wider movement from roughly the second to the fourth centuries. The wider movement produced what might be called the Catholic form of the Church with the following elements: a generally accepted list of writings to be used in public worship by all the churches, the canon of the Old and New Testaments, a common "apostolic" creed, a somewhat uniform liturgy, and an apostolic ministry.

It was as if the early churches, growing and testing their structures, were in a shakedown cruise. Challenges from heretics inside and from socio-political forces outside gave the Church a shape and tone which have proven to be long-lasting. Yet this shape and tone did not completely absorb or blot out other approaches to the authority issue.

Underneath the history of this development and interwoven with it is another model of church authority. This model sees evidence for and includes the notion that in the early church communities, the people saw certain needs, raised up appropriate ministers, and appointed worthy candidates for the resolution of problems. The local body of Christ, guided by the Holy Spirit, discerns the charisms needed, witnesses to a candidate's apostolic faith, takes part in the liturgical ordination, and receives this person as its now divinely established minister. The community of course feels free to pass judgment on his performance of the office.

The prototypical Catholic view of authority which stressed that Jesus appointed apostles, who in turn appointed bishops, who in turn chose helpers called priests and deacons, chose to underplay or ignore the other approach. We tended to see ordination not as a call from a local community, but as the conferral of sacred power and authority to be exercised wherever the authorities sent us.

In the alternate model, community call is an act of local self-determination and a response to what the community sees as their local ministerial needs. When a person is thus invited by the community, tested, and appointed, his authority is both from God and from the people. They recognize his or her charism, call him and receive him, but they receive him as at once chosen by God, endowed by God with the needed gifts, and blessed at ordination with the grace and power to minister in the church.

Current Catholic experience, particularly in regions where there is a shortage of priests, has led to a new development, or perhaps an old solution with new life—namely, the emergence of ministerial leadership among lay folk who can no longer rely on a steady supply of priests sent their way by the local bishop.

Latin America's "base communities"—smaller, more intensely communal and personal gatherings of believers for prayer, discussion, and action—have revealed men and women with sensitivity and skill in leading or shepherding. In some regions where there is no priest available for the traditional territorial parish, nuns or other laypersons serve as on-site pastoral agents, representatives of the bishops.

They organize prayer groups, Bible studies, marriage preparation programs for couples, funeral services, and other matters. Where these experiences are successful and positive, there are grounds for seeing in our time the re-emergence of the "community based" model for authority.

Both the hierarchical model and the community based model involve another element, that of "calling" or "vocation." Neither the community nor the bishop calls the person in the first instance. Rather, the individual is more apt to experience a call in the privacy of his or her own heart. The person who follows this leading could theoretically establish his or her own congregation, become a kind of ecclesiastical entrepreneur. In the Catholic tradition, however, the call must be validated by a community or the community's representative. Some have said that this notion of call, an individual's immediate sense of being given an assignment by God, is more typical of the Renaissance period and our own than of medieval or earlier times.

In the Catholic tradition, the Church tests the genuineness of the calling through its bishops and its seminary system. If the leadership believes the person to be worthy, he is ordained and then sent to some local community. In a small diocese, the young priest may in fact be known and eagerly accepted by his parish. But in many large dioceses, the priest assigned to a community may be a total stranger. The local community accepts him through faith in the bishop's judgment. By ordination the man has been "invested with personally possessed power to celebrate the Eucharist"; this is a portable gift to be used wherever one is sent. However even if ordination confers the power to forgive sin, preach, anoint, and celebrate the Eucharist, the bishop can restrict one's right to exercise these powers. Church law allows the bishop to control a given priest precisely to protect the local community from abuse or serious sin and error.

The community based model which historians have seen at work in the early centuries was not without its defects. For a time in some countries, local congregations did in fact nominate and elect their own pastors. One such election in the city of Rome became so bitter that rival factions actually fought in the streets, prompting the emperor to send out the imperial guards to restore order. Leading families or a city's major political powers often began to interfere too much in promoting their favorite son. In certain medieval situations, local dukes or counts had the power to name as their pastor someone of their choice. Some of these choices were of course unfortunate. A few bad results do not in themselves make the community based model wrong; it simply argues for balance in the matter of church authority.

Another factor in the Catholic approach to pastoral office was the requirement of celibacy. Very early in Church history, given Christ's own example, many Christians, male and female, chose to remain virgins for the sake of the kingdom. While at first it was an individual's choice and initiative, the practice soon arose of forming groups in homes, what later came to be called monasteries or convents. This style of life, a closer following of Christ, recommended itself to the churches and was gradually required of the clergy, bishops, and priests. Still, there seems to have been married Roman Catholic priests as late as the year 1000, A.D.

The Western Church gradually was able to ask celibacy of all its candidates, while the Eastern Church allowed its priests to be married. Celibacy for the sake of the kingdom, in a commitment to priesthood or pastoral office, can be a very freeing status. How we priests use this freedom varies of course. But beyond the actual historical records, there is a deep truth embodied in celibacy. It can serve as a pointer to the kingdom to come where there is no giving in marriage. It can free persons for intensive and mobile missionary work, and can promote an openness to the service and love of many.

When I was preparing to be a priest, I thought a good deal about the celibacy required, and I feel I undertook the commitment with as much understanding and generosity as I had. In different places and in different times of my life, this commitment has been difficult. Yet I feel that it has also proven to be a good challenge, and an invitation to purify my human affections from excessive self-interest and manipulation of others. I have been helped a great deal, I believe, by living in parish houses with other men similarly vowed who support each other in this particular call.

In a world where chastity is often ridiculed and where even church organizations sometimes give inadequate support to singles who want to stay that way, celibacy has a certain mystique. Millions of Americans a few years back watched the televised drama *Thornbirds*, the story of an Australian Catholic priest. Part of the drama had to do with his attraction to a beautiful young woman. The dramatic tension arose in part precisely because he was committed officially and publicly to celibacy, while struggling with his love of the woman. Priest-sociologist Andrew Greeley commented on the popularity of the television drama by saying that people are always fascinated by men and women who place a high ideal before themselves.

Those who try to live the celibate life–not for lack of opportunities for marriage or fear of the opposite sex, but out of their view of discipleship—may in fact fail at times in this project, but the effort itself serves as a pointer to the totality of giving which Christ asks of us all.

In light of the history of priesthood and its connection among Roman Catholics with celibacy's special status, it is hardly surprising that my friends and relatives had additional motives for forming a line to receive from my anointed hands a first blessing. They believed that I had become a "sacred person" through the power of the sacrament of holy orders. In accordance with Catholic teaching, theory, practice, and belief gave me an initial position above and beyond all other Christians. The qualifying adjective "initial" is crucial because once settled in a community of believers in a local parish, I could reveal myself to be less than acceptable, less than helpful to a community, no matter how fresh the oil was on my hands.

Perhaps it would be helpful here to clarify a matter of terminology. The sacrament of holy orders is the normal access to the formal offices of deacon, priest, and bishop. A cardinal is in current practice simply a bishop with special rank and authority attached to an administrative position. The pope is, at the heart of things, a bishop who has been selected by cardinals to be head of the Church.

The term "order," however, is also used in connection with another reality. The Jesuits are often called a "religious order," as are the Franciscans or Dominicans. The common language of Catholics here describes a sub-grouping of either men or women who agree to be full-time Church workers who often live together in convents or monasteries and are bound by certain customs and rules. They might include priests or they might not. The Franciscan "order" or the Jesuit "order" refers to such a grouping, established at a given period and place by a certain individual, St. Francis of Assisi or St. Ignatius of Loyola. There are many such groupings or families, and while male members of these may in fact be priests or bishops, other members of their family or order are not ordained. While these sub-groupings are under the supervision of individual local bishops, they may also have members at work across diocesan and even national boundaries. These families choose their own members, elect their own leaders, and manage many of their affairs without interference from local bishops or the pope. All officially recognized "orders" do, however, follow certain policies and procedural safeguards established in Church law.

The history of these orders is a story in itself, but this much can be said. When in a certain age, a gifted man or woman sees a new pastoral need not being attended to by the usual church agencies, it is possible for such people, on fire with a call, to begin to attend to this need. As they gather followers, they may have the nucleus of a new religious order or family. A modern example is Mother Teresa of India. While a member of another religious order, she was convicted of the need to attend to the poor in a new and direct fashion. She left her own order's traditional work in India and began to work among the dying. Young women, not only in India, were drawn to her and to her work. She is now in charge of a new religious order.

History reveals a waxing and waning of such groups. Some monastic orders, like the Benedictines, trace their origins to a distant past. Some orders were born, flourished, achieved their goals, and died. Others, like that of Mother Teresa, are of recent origin. Part of North American Catholicism's glory comes from courageous women, many of them born in Europe, who braved the stormy Atlantic, wrestled with a strange language, and traveled by riverboat, buggy, and Conestoga through Canada and the United States. They built the first hospitals, taught the first schools in log sheds, built high schools and colleges for women, comforted immigrants, and embraced orphans, the abandoned babies, and the elderly. Here is a rich field for feminist historians!

Conclusion

The history of the Catholic approach to ministerial leadership shows two models, the community based model and the "individual-as-called" model. The power of the community to choose its leadership was at times so great that a man could be forced against his inclinations and acclaimed as priest or bishop. There were also moments when a local community, by Church law, could reject a pastor whom they disliked or in whose selection they had no part. A vestige of this remains in the ordination ceremony today. At a given point, the ordaining bishop asks the people present if they approve the candidate. While it is possible for a loud demonstration to erupt, "Remove him" or "No, never," the usual response from a happy congregation is sustained applause, a form of assent.

The "individual-as-called" model has been most prominent in post-Reformation times, controlled however by bishops; there is a renewed interest today in the question of recognizing leadership which arises from within a community. No one in his right mind proposes the ordination of men and women who lack adequate training and the personal Christian maturity. Still, we find that at least in North America there are more and more generous persons willing to serve a local congregation in some way, full-time or part-time. Talents and generosity appear in our midst, full of promise for the local church.

For some of these people, there is no desire for ordination. For others, among them some women, there is a desire for access to holy orders. Some of these women have already shown both dedication and talent by serving in pastoral settings, visiting the sick, organizing retreats and Christian education programs, counseling and more. They feel that they have both proven their abilities and have received heartfelt support and recognition from the local churches in which they have worked. To be barred access to holy orders because of their sex seems to them discriminatory, and biblically unjustified. Since a person who feels the call is not automatically given holy orders, these women are frustrated. While the Catholic Church does struggle to reduce sexism within its own areas of control, we have not yet agreed to change the rule about ordaining women. The pain, controversy, and soul-searching continues as of this writing.

Contemporary Catholicism lives, not without tension, under the twin models, "leadership from the people" and the "individual calling," to be recognized by authority and sent. We also live under the tension between the "authority-first" and "power to the people" approaches. Thus we hear frequent appeals from Catholics to the pope for immediate disciplinary action against dissenters, be they bishops or Bible scholars. On the other hand we find local parishes or regional churches claiming that Roman officials are too ignorant, unaware, or insensitive to their needs. They feel that more local autonomy should be granted.

I view these tensions both normal and useful, provided they are handled with charity and a desire to help the whole Church. Can these different models and pressures be integrated? I like the suggestions given by Joseph Komonchak on this. We must keep in mind the following basic notion: Authority and community are in dialectical balance. The Spirit of Christ is surely at work in a special way in the ordained leaders, but not to the exclusion of the community. Community by its life, example, and challenge can minister to the leadership. Leaders, for their part, because they are responsible for the whole—a parish, diocese, region, nation, or a worldwide community of churches—must challenge the people as well.

Genuine authority is given to the ministers for the purpose of keeping the community faithful to Jesus' message and mission. Still, the exercise of this authority comes under the judgment of the same message and mission. Balance is also maintained by seeing that ordination to diaconate, priesthood, or episcopacy is an exercise of the Church's own responsibility, a commitment to the minister, and an act of worship. The bishop usually lays on hands in a worship service in which people are present to say *"Amen."*

Keeping in mind that the whole Church is a sacrament, the presence of Christ embodied in time and space, Catholics believe that ministry is the work of the whole. By baptism we are all called to be a priestly people, a royal people, a prophetic people. Yet there is within the unity of mission a diversity of gifts, and not all are called to the same task. Baptism focuses on the authority and mission of all; holy orders focus on the authority and mission of those few invited to a particular leadership.

11

A Closer Look at MATRIMONY

Given my youthful experience of Catholic schools, I naturally was taught that Jesus Christ had instituted seven sacraments, no more, no less. I learned in addition the traditional formula, that the sacrament was an outward sign, instituted by Christ to give grace. Whether this was taught to me by one of the many nuns who had an influence on me or by Jesuit priests in my first two years of high school, I cannot remember. I do remember, however, that the teachers sought to "prove" the Catholic view by pointing to a scriptural text or scriptural event which associated Jesus and a sacrament as we knew it.

We Catholics felt very comfortable with our scriptural texts for the Lord's Supper, baptism, anointing of the sick, and reconciliation. Our evidence that Christ instituted confirmation, holy orders, and matrimony was less impressive, even though a scriptural case can be made. Our case for matrimony could begin by quoting God's establishment of it in the Book of Genesis. My memory tells me that we spoke about Jesus blessing marriage, making it a sacrament by his presence at the wedding feast of Cana (John 2).

This sacrament, like the others, symbolizes and confers divine power to those who receive it with the proper disposition and faith. Matrimony as a sacrament was, in the words of an older and respected authority, "to sanctify the family, the cradle of society." The graces conferred by the sacrament were the graces to maintain an absolute and abiding fidelity, the grace of reverence for the sanctity of the marriage bed, and the ability to give devoted care to children. This care for them would of course include instruction in Christian faith.

Even if we couldn't point to Jesus' formal establishment of matrimony as a sacrament, we felt that matrimony qualified. Our method of proof was to heap up the texts which bear on the subject. God's blessing of Adam and Eve's initial relationship is an instance. Jesus' own firm stance on the value of monogamy is another. Emerging from these and other texts is the view that matrimony is another of the sensate manifestations of God's invisible plan for the human race. It is part of what Paul called the *mysterion* (1 Cor. 2:1, Col. 2:2), a broad term referring to the reality of God's plan revealed in the life, death, and resurrection of Jesus. Insofar as baptized persons enter into that life, death, and resurrection, their lives unfold in this mystery of grace and love.

One of the places where this sharing in the total mystery of God's self-giving in Jesus is most evident is in marital life. In the fifth chapter of Ephesians we read of Paul's high regard for matrimony. He compares the husband-wife relationship with the relationship which prevails between Christ and his bride, the Church. In Catholic circles, by the way, many translators followed the Vulgate's version of verse 32, "This is a great sacrament." This translation helped strengthen the Catholic case for seeing matrimony as one of the seven sacraments.

One Catholic scholar has recently translated verses 31 and 32 in another way. Theodore Mackin reads the text as follows:

> For this reason a man will leave his father and his mother and will cling to his wife, and the two of them will become one flesh. This mystery is a profound one; and I mean this about Christ and the Church.[7]

Just as anointing, washing, eating of food, and seeking God's pardon are the stuff of human existence and therefore capable of being expressions of God's total giving, so is matrimony capable of being an expression of God's total giving. Paul sees that marital giving and deference to one another as related to Christ and the Church.

I conclude from this that even if my parochial school teachers, and their teachers, had oversimplified the meaning of a sacrament and had even made only a weak case that Jesus had personally instituted matrimony as a sacrament, they were correct to hand on an insight about marriage that Paul has described in Ephesians. Matrimony is a mysterious and grace-filled opportunity for two baptized persons who have entered into a marital covenant. They are ministers to each other of the kind of agape love that Christ offers to the Church and the Church to him.

It is safe to say that for the early Christians, the reality of their new life in Christ was so powerfully felt and so very different from their state before baptism that they saw everything transformed. In Acts 2 we read of the idyllic sharing of goods and mutual assistance. Marriage, too, was to be transformed. Paul's view of marriage is in the context of "being imitators of God, walking in love as Christ loved us." There was to be a new reciprocal concern between master and slave, parent and child, husband and wife. In Ephesians 5:22 wives are supposed to be, as some translations put it, "submissive" to their husbands. Mackin prefers to translate this as to "defer" to their husbands. And husbands are to defer to their wives.

Mutual deference to one another was, in Paul's day, a rather revolutionary approach. Mutual consideration between master and slave, parents and children, husbands and wives was a drastic improvement over the lopsided treatment that was common in all these categories. The term "defer" has in it a sense of gentleness and mutual consideration which I like. It is the kind of things that true scholars do in their pursuit of truth, the kind of things that friends often do in order to show their concern and affection.

Paul, of course, is far from assuming that the cultural structures of his age are on the brink of extinction. He takes it for granted that slavery exists, as does the wives' status of obedience to husbands. Wifely submission to husbands, it could be argued, was the result of the first sin. Christ's victory over sin and death means that the Holy Spirit's own power is now available to help husbands and wives regain the mutuality of care, even if still in a society which has lopsided social conventions.

A Brief History of Christian Marriage

Any attempt to sketch a full history of Christian marriage will suffer from shortness of space. Yet it is important to recall that for some centuries, Christian church leaders did not offer any particular ceremony for weddings of baptized believers. Such ceremonies were not required for at least nine centuries. For most of this time couples entering matrimony simply went through the steps normal for their nation, tribe, or culture.

The germ for Christian ceremonies seems to be found in two situations, one being the invitation from the bride and groom to a local bishop or priest to be a guest at the feast or reception. A second situation which led to church involvement was the wedding of orphan girls. In some Christian communities it was the bishops who supervised the care of these girls and who functioned as their "fathers" at wedding rites. Historians seem to agree that early Christian believers entering marriage followed the customs of the day: in Jewish circles parents normally arranged the marriage of their children.

By the time of Christ, the ideal of monogamy among the Romans had fallen on bad times. Any sense of sacredness in marriage was weak. Men used prostitutes and slave women quite freely. In a society where wife-stealing or wife-swapping was common, the Christian insistence on fidelity was a rather stark challenge.

The priests and bishops of the Western Church became more and more involved in marriage issues, partly because a dying empire's civil authority was crumbling. The result was that cities and regions gradually looked to local bishops and their staff for administrative and legal decisions. Imperial authorities were either too distant or too disorganized to respond to the issues arising.

There was yet another major reason why Church leaders got involved with weddings. As the empire shuddered under continual assault and the migration and settlement of invading peoples—Franks, Lombards, and Germans—Roman Christians had to confront a very different view of marriage. These invaders did not believe in the need for partners to consent to marriage. Parents arranged marriages without the agreement of the children. By contrast, Roman law in the ninth century required that consent be given both by parents and legal guardians and by the people involved.

Part of the history of marriage in Western Europe is the struggle of Church leaders to soften tribal insistence that the fathers of the couple control the choices. These people saw marriage as a way of enlarging their social standing and as a means to increase their property holdings, with little concern for the desires of their offspring. Another part of this history is the tendency of many young people, both in the Western Empire and in the Byzantine, to frustrate their parents' plans by entering into a clandestine marriage with someone more to their liking. The marriage was clandestine in two senses: parents were not informed, and witnesses were not around.

We can well imagine the scenes when the star-crossed lovers surfaced after a short absence to present their parents with a situation of de facto marriage. Some of us might sympathize with the Romeos and Juliets. It sounds more romantic. Alas for romanticism! The reality was not always so rosy. A man who wanted to block a wedding of partners chosen by their parents could claim that he and the prospective bride had in fact been married in a secret commitment. Another tactic was for a man to enter a formal marriage and later claim that he had been previously married secretly to another person. Some men had of course paid witnesses to swear to this.

Church law, which had come to be more important in some places than other laws, had no protective clauses for secretly married partners. Thus, the Church struggled between tribal wishes to control marriage for materialistic reasons and young peoples' effort to frustrate parental projects.

When someone arose to claim a previous, informal marriage, the result was often a blocking of a planned marriage; it could also lead to abandoned partners and even children, embittered parents, and feuding families. All these problems provoked a reaction from Martin Luther, who argued that marriages attempted without the approval of both sets of parents, even marriages which had produced children, should be declared null. One result of Luther's criticism was a decision taken by Catholic bishops at the Council of Trent in 1563 to require a priest and witnesses for any marriage of Catholics.

To this day, Catholic priests who begin arrangements with a couple planning marriage fill out a document which asks the prospective bride and groom if they are entering freely into the marriage. In addition, the Church tries to make sure that neither partner was married before. In some Christian churches the marriage ceremony itself had a dramatic moment. It was the place where the pastor declared, "If anyone knows any reason why these two should not be joined in matrimony, let him come forward or forever hold his peace." How often someone popped up to denounce the proposed union, I don't know, but the aim was clear enough.

Catholic views of marriage in the recent past inherited this long tradition. We spoke of marriage as a contract entered into by two people who were free to do so, and who gave their complete consent. We insisted on the presence of a priest and two witnesses. We also stressed that the contract of marriage included partners' mutual giving to each other for the purpose of procreation. Both the biology and the Genesis command to "increase and multiply" seemed evident enough in their purpose.

To enter the twentieth century with such views was to have a distinct advantage in approaching marriage, but as the century was half-spent, it was clear that we needed a fresh view. As in so many areas, we are indebted to the bishops who gathered at the Second Vatican Council for a new look at matrimony. They confronted an era very unlike the age of Martin Luther and the bishops of the Council of Trent. Arranged marriages for the sake of property, land, or dowry considerations were less and less known. The romantic or modern sense of "love" between prospective partners had taken on a new importance. Despite the fact that many marriages in various parts of the world are still arranged by parents, European, North American, and South American customs today are different. One-sided stress on sexuality as primarily designed for continuing the human race had begun to lose ground, even though some governments worried about shrinking population still promote large families by the use of bonuses.

In the Second Vatican Council's *Gaudium et Spes*, "Pastoral Constitution on the Church in the Modern World," there is a more contemporary description of marriage, called there an "intimate partnership of life and love." It is established by God and endowed by him with its own proper laws. The council document focused on marriage as mutual sharing, using words like "surrender," "self-giving," "fidelity," "help," and "affection."

Yet the ideal description keeps in mind that the ability of couples to live this is beyond their own power. The sacrament of matrimony signifies the love of Christ for mankind and at the same time takes part in that love. Just as the love of Christ is made concrete in his willingness to give himself for others in self-sacrifice for the people of the new covenant, so matrimonial love is to be an uninterrupted "for-each-other" to the point of mutual self-sacrifice.

It is in this context of mutuality and self-giving that the bishops of the council speak of procreation of children; they are the freely accepted creative result of a responsible union of love. Christian families, as one Vatican II document puts it, are "what might be regarded as the domestic church" in which the "parents, by word and example, are the first heralds of the faith with regard to their children." As always, the challenge is to help men and women before and during marriage see the sacredness of what they do. To meet this challenge, the average parish priest is urged to take care in preparing couples for this sacrament.

My current experience of the North American Catholic Church is that bishops, priests, and laity are very concerned about the engaged couples who come to them. In his interviews with them, the priest tries to enlarge their vision as well as check on their emotional and legal freedom to commit themselves to a life-long covenant. Many parishes require couples to attend lectures, workshops, and weekend retreats designed to help them understand what they are doing.

One of the most famous of these programs is called "Engaged Couples' Encounter," a series of sessions held over a weekend designed to have the couple test its ability to communicate seriously on a wide range of issues. Couples in love are not always confronting issues about in-laws, finances, sexual activity, religious beliefs, or recreational patterns. Even couples who have been living together or known each other for a long time may never have considered such matters.

In some dioceses, bishops and their advisors have developed premarital questionnaires which each couple must complete. These questionnaires are then scored to see if would-be life partners have many divergent answers on basic issues. If the scores show wide divergences, the priest and the couple must meet for further discussion. In some cases, the couple's wedding may even be postponed or cancelled.

Naturally, some young men and women planning a marriage may at first be offended by these procedures and programs. They have known each other for a long time, their parents have approved, they have arranged for the reception and the groom's uncle is flying in from out of state. Why should there be any problem? The priest who is trying to prepare them may find that he is seen as a bureaucratic obstacle. Why the hassle?

Other couples, I hope the majority, attend the marriage preparation sessions with interest and often report back how helpful they were. Many wedding preparations become so clogged with concerns about invitations, suitable dress, and reception and travel arrangements that the couple forgets the substance of what they are intending.

Needless to say, when the honeymoon has ended, churches need to be present to married couples. While the churches do try to involve couples in church organizations or programs, Catholics in North America have placed particular emphasis and hope on the "Marriage Encounter" program. This is an effort to make a good marriage better. The dynamic is similar to that of the "Engaged Couples' Encounter." In fact, the "Engaged Couples' Encounter" is a spin-off of this.

"Marriage Encounter" is both a program and a movement begun in Spain through the combined efforts of three married couples and Father Gabriel Calvo. "Encounter" is a literal translation of the Spanish word *encuentro*, a meeting or rediscovery. The founders began to meet under the inspiration of a series of talks given about marriage by Pope Pius XII. From their meetings and Scripture study they developed core topics, which still form the basis of the program.

The program takes place on a weekend and the presentations are usually given by married couples and a priest. The methods help couples to search for and rediscover their vision of love. With this program, God's presence is essential, because the gift of love given by the couple becomes fruitful only in God's presence through the discovery of God's place within their lives.

While talks are given for the couples present, a key phase is that of dialogue between husband and wife. They are given an opportunity to discuss issues that have troubled their relationship, and they are invited to communicate and to offer mutual forgiveness.

The first "Encounter" program was held in Barcelona, Spain in 1962. It reached the United States in 1967 and has spread to Latin America, Europe, and Asia. Many couples have gone through the program and have been helped very much by it. Some of them return from the weekend with a new vision. Their own enthusiasm has helped the movement spread.

In North America, where the resources are available, the Catholic Church tries to provide more than the "Marriage Encounter" for its people. The local priest is often the first person to whom partners turn for help when marriage issues become troublesome. He in turn may have developed a network of counselors or psychologists to whom he may refer a couple. In some areas, the Church itself has a regional Marriage Counseling Office or Family Service Agency to which people may be directed.

For many years in North America, Catholics could look with some satisfaction at their marital success rate. Divorce among Catholics was a fairly rare phenomenon until the 1960s. In that shattering decade the rate of divorce among Catholics rose sharply. In 1977 more than one million American marriages ended in divorce. This was the third year in a row of divorces at that rate, and Catholics made up at least twenty percent of that total.[2]

While there had been some Catholic organizations providing spiritual support for divorced women prior to this time, a more active ministry to divorced persons began in the seventies. In early 1972 Father James Young of the Paulist Fathers began to work with laity of the Paulist Center in Boston, Massachusetts, on programs which would help people going through divorce. Priest and laity took the position that divorce is a great evil; they did not condone it. They simply tried to minister to persons experiencing the pain of separation and loss. For the divorced, there are agonizing questions about their own self-image; there is also a sense of shame and defeat. There is the brute fact of loneliness and the difficulty of being single.

Financial problems coupled with the trauma of child custody problems make for a painful period.

By 1975 a national organization, the North American Conference of Separated and Divorced Catholics, was formed. Among the results of this development can be counted a new sympathy for the plight of the divorced on the part of the average Catholic. Many divorced Catholics have been helped through a difficult time; some of these in turn have proven very helpful to others. More and more bishops and pastors have extended help to the divorced and separated Catholics in their areas. Many Catholics who had been divorced but not remarried had been led to believe that the very fact of divorce meant that they were excommunicated, unable to take communion. These were delighted to hear that the mere fact of having had a divorce did not mean that they were excommunicated.

Someone has estimated that of all the people getting a divorce, 50 percent will want to marry again. Since some of these fifty percent will be Catholics, it is evident that Jesus' teaching about marriage and divorce comes under intense scrutiny in these days. Did Jesus ever allow that a marriage could be set aside? Isn't the scriptural evidence contradictory?

Volumes have been written on the divorce clauses in the New Testament. For our purposes we can say that as the Church understood both Jesus and Paul on this subject, it wrestled with two realities. Jesus seemed to admit little or no excuse for divorce, while Paul (1 Cor. 7:15) allowed the break-up of a marriage in given circumstances. These two realities led to different practices in the churches.

Eastern Orthodox Christians have allowed a member a second church wedding under certain circumstances, since Jesus himself seemed to admit that a marriage might be dissolved in the case of *porneia,* often translated as adultery (Matt. 5:32). The Western Latin Church has not allowed a second wedding as such, but has allowed annulment of a marriage. Technically speaking, annulment declares that a marriage bond, despite appearances, never existed.

Because of the Christian insistence on a person's consent to marry, a consent freely given, it was possible to annul a marriage if lack of freedom could be proven. Assume that a young woman, under extreme pressure from her parents or in-laws to marry, does in fact go through with the marriage. Assume that later she can prove that, had it not been for that pressure, she would not have married. A church tribunal might grant her an annulment on the basis of the fact that from the very beginning she did not consent to this fully and freely.

In the years since the Second Vatican Council, Church law and the Church courts have broadened their definition of marriage to include as essential a community of life, a mutual covenant. Here the focus shifts from a person's technical freedom to marry (no previous marriages, no fraud or psychological pressure) to their capacity to give themselves in a responsible way. A tribunal, following this more nuanced view, might declare a marriage null when it can be proven that one of the partners, even though of "sound mind," lacked at the beginning the capacity to enter with the other into a lifelong union which would be one of sharing and caring.

Whatever one may think of this approach, it is clear that Latin Catholics and Orthodox Christians have upheld the sacredness and permanence of marriage. They have also tried, respecting the biblical cues, to provide reasonable assistance to men and women who entered marriage in questionable circumstances, or whose marriages unravelled in tragic ways. Some see these measures as necessary but partial answers to the wider question. Are there pressures on marriages which should be faced by the churches?

In a newspaper I read every day there is a business section which has tragically familiar headlines, "Plant Closing Forces Lay-Offs," or "Foreign Competition Means a Cutback." Marriages in which neither husband nor wife can earn enough money for basic needs seem programmed for trouble. The fact that so many mothers need to work, not just because they are liberated feminists or frustrated careerists, is a sad commentary on modern economic realities. We have somehow constructed a society in which home-management and childcare by the parents seems unacceptable economically or culturally. The Church's ministry to married people must take into account every nation's global interdependency in economic matters. Housing, schools and jobs have as much to do with marital stability perhaps as sexual malfunction or communication difficulties between the spouses.

Conclusion

The Catholic Church sees the sacrament of matrimony as one not to be entered into lightly. To prepare young couples for this sacrament, and to provide aid and encouragement for those already married, we sponsor the "Engaged Couples' Encounter" and "Marriage Encounter" programs. Because marriage is a serious sacrament, the Church encourages young people to counsel with a priest or bishop to make certain that they are compatible before they are pronounced "man and wife." And, since tradition shows that some marriages began lacking full awareness, full commitment, or full capacity to give of self, the Church can declare a marriage null if essentials are lacking.

From the teachings of Paul and Jesus, we find some hints about divorce and remarriage. The Church has two views on this, the Eastern Orthodox view allowing a divorced Catholic to remarry under certain circumstances and the Western Latin view allowing an annulment of a failed marriage given certain circumstances. In any case, a divorce does not indicate excommunication from the Church.

Some years ago television preacher Bishop Fulton J. Sheen wrote a book called *Three to Get Married,* the third person being Christ. This title says it all. Matrimony is a sacrament, the partners' graced participation in and embodiment of the *mysterion,* God's giving of himself in Jesus and in Jesus' members, the Church.

12

A Closer Look at SOCIAL JUSTICE

One of the most frightening prayers in the Christian collection is also the most common: the Lord's Prayer. Whenever I say this prayer, whether leading a congregation in worship or at home with my fellow priests, I find it hard to say, especially the phrases "thy kingdom come, thy will be done." It seems wrong to me to say these without being committed to action, without being part of a people engaged in making God's kingdom come on earth in some basic form. Yet, the "how" of that prayer remains elusive, or at least tantalizingly varied. One incident comes to mind.

I was stationed for a time at the University of California, Santa Barbara, as the 1960s drew to a close and the seventies dawned on a people in turmoil over civil rights, university reform, and the Vietnam War. The campus where I was studying is a beautiful one situated by the Pacific Ocean. One day there was a demonstration, initially peaceful yet increasingly passionate, against the university's administration. While students and others chanted rhythmically at the doors of a modernistic university administrative office, police arrived in numbers. Under a brilliant sun slanting off the building's steel and glass, some protesters sought to block the entrance. Inside, nervous university officials and secretaries tried to go on with their work.

All around the building, California Highway Patrolmen stood with their backs to the building at intervals of perhaps fifty to a hundred feet, facing onlookers and passersby. If one chose, one could join the demonstration by walking unopposed between the policemen. The loosely laid police line seemed menacing in a quiet way, like a rope that could be tightened to shape a noose.

I saw all this as I left one of my classes to walk toward the student ghetto on the edge of campus. Drawing near to one of the highway patrolmen, I was stunned to see that he had carefully applied masking tape to cover his police badge. He was, this action told me, prepared for violence and he was prepared to act with brutality. Anyone mistreated by use of undue force would have no chance to tell any court or review board the man's number or name.

Looking at the taped badge I thought immediately of the charges which had appeared in Southern California underground newspapers about police brutality at demonstrations. As I turned all this over in my head, a student from among the demonstrators approached me and other bystanders. Young and well-groomed, he called to us from his side of the police cordon, "Come, join us in this demonstration! It is your chance to make history!"

After some thought I turned away from the young man and the entire scene, either from cowardice or lack of conviction that this demonstration, any more than others this campus had seen, could affect real changes in government or university policy. As I walked back to the parish house where I lived, I realized that the young man's invitation to make history was haunting me. It also dawned on me that my very decision not to walk through police lines to join the demonstration was itself a way of shaping history. Demonstrating or not demonstrating—either way is making and shaping history on a small scale. As I walked and reflected I also realized that I may have decided to shape history in the wrong way.

We pray so easily, "Thy kingdom come, thy will be done," and we seem very rarely to tremble about it, weigh its demands, or follow through with courage. The Lord's Prayer is a prayer of hope and a heartfelt desire for the kind of society which would not have to bow its head in shame when Jesus returns to ask what we have done for him through the hungry, homeless, and imprisoned.

The prayer is also a judgment, an observation that God's kingdom is superior to the blood-stained kingdoms which countless men have designed, launched, and imposed, be it pre-Hispanic Incan civilization, Hitler's Third Reich, or any contemporary versions. In this prayer we declare that a kingdom built by God will be better. We also pray that God will be in our midst shaping, nurturing, and guiding our activities for the fuller realization of this kingdom.

What is Social Justice?

Social justice means speaking about God's kingdom and the ways in which we think about it, act on its behalf, and yearn for its completion. The Catholic view of social justice flows from our understanding of the kingdom. And this understanding is linked inextricably to our belief that God wishes to empower us, and can empower us for the fulfillment of the prayer, "Thy kingdom come, thy will be done." Fruitful, free collaboration between God and the believer is the key to this issue.

My nervousness in reciting the phrases about the coming of the kingdom stems from my own sense of inertia and cowardice, my sense that before I can begin to enact grand plans for God's kingdom elsewhere, I must allow God's will to be more than a tiny outpost in my own heart. During the Vietnam War when thousands of peace demonstrators thronged into Washington, D.C., they encamped as close as possible to the White House. President Nixon made confident statements to the press to the effect that the government was not about to be swayed by "mob" rule. But the demonstrators, with more courage and hope than I had, may have "made history" by creating the momentum which led to a rapid settlement of that war.

It is excruciatingly difficult to know with total clarity when one is working for the kingdom or against it, and good Christians disagree. Some of the devout, with their eyes on Soviet arms build-up, worry that the American shield over freedom and democracy will be paper-thin. Equally devout Christians pour blood on a missile nosecone to protest the foolishness of relying on them for a security which seems also paper-thin.

Should Catholics and Protestants be divided about the meaning of the prayer taught them by Jesus? Chances are good that, in these days, our divisions run across the Protestant-Catholic dividing line. In many denominations, "liberals" will feel more at home with other "liberals" regardless of denomination, and "conservatives" will be finding a sympathetic hearing from other "conservatives" not of their denomination.

The History of Social Justice

It may be helpful to sketch in broad outlines this Catholic's understanding of the history of our efforts to establish God's kingdom. A sense of history can be very helpful toward an understanding of our views of social justice, and I was made aware of this by something that happened to me twenty or more years ago.

While stationed in Toronto, Canada, in the years just following the Second Vatican Council, I was asked on occasion to speak to non-Catholic audiences about the Church. One day I was invited to speak on the changes in the Church to an audience of Jewish men who had gathered in their temple for a breakfast and lecture. After I had concluded my remarks, someone rose to ask if it were not true that the Catholic stress on eternal life, after-life, had not swamped our commitment to improving the quality of human life on earth? He was particularly impressed with medieval concern about heaven and hell.

I answered that medieval Christianity had indeed stressed the heavenly kingdom more than the earthly, but that my forebears in the faith had not forgotten the struggles for peace or justice on earth. His question nonetheless had made the point. Doesn't a belief in eternal life drain energy from the battle to humanize earthly life? History may help answer the question.

It must be said that from the earliest days of Christianity, followers of Jesus found a new vision of life as well as a new pattern for their life together. The Scriptures provide us with pictures of these new ideas and relationships. However brief it was, there was the glorious time when "the community of believers were of one heart and one mind. None of them ever claimed anything as his own; rather, everything was held in common." And further, "Nor was there anyone needy among them . . ." (Acts 4:32,34).

The Gospels provided indicators for a new approach to all of life such as the Beatitudes or the great last judgment scene from Matthew 25. Jesus' repudiation of violence, his compassion for the poor, his repeated pleas for forgiveness, and his insistence on the eternal values of the commandments all inspired Christian men and women to a never-ending, fertile, and varied outpouring of energy on behalf of a better world. From the Palestinian villages the flame of hope and the vision of a new life passed quickly to other Middle Eastern lands, to Upper Egypt, modern Iran, Armenia, India and the remote western islands of Ireland, Scotland, and Britain. What a magnificent tribute this is to the vitality and zeal of the Christian believers! What an unparalleled opportunity they had! In less than three centuries Christians would be seen in the ruling classes of both the Eastern and the Western Empires, as well as among the slaves.

Was this rapid spread of Christianity a triumph for God's kingdom? Did the respective empires become, for all the official Christianization, more humane and compassionate? Some analysts have seen this official status and recognition as the sale of birthrights for a mess of politically suspect pottage. Some see the "arrival" of Christianity as an acceptable religion to be a deathblow, the dying pulse of pure energies radiating from Jesus and the first believers.

Other historians and analysts see it in a very different light. The penetration of the Roman Empire by Christianity enabled the instruction, consolation, upbuilding, and salvation of millions. Conversions to Jesus created in both Eastern and Western Europe an immensely creative and culturally productive civilization. When the great migrations of nations occurred, east and west experienced the culture shock of waves of "barbarians." While this invasion caused the demise of much that was civilization, much resurfaced among the barely-converted immigrants and invaders. Seeds of faith, sparks of true light, and a softening of the worst savagery can be credited to Christianity.

Who then, "made history" for Jesus' sake? It is not easy to decide, but from this distance what seems true is that both the newly-converted and the more mature Christians saw the value of societies, tribes, or nations in which Christian values found expression. These conglomerations of peoples, languages, and laws—sometimes at war, sometimes in nervous alliances—were to receive the name "Holy Roman Empire."

The Roman Empire of the Caesars had disappeared, but the nostalgic vision of a time of peace and culture remained. The adjective "holy" spoke for the desire that this new empire embody Christ's teachings better than the old. And the so-called Dark Ages were astonishingly alive because of this vision. While it is true that the kingdom prayed for by the Christians was not always what Jesus would have blessed, it is also true that the Spirit of God again and again found collaborators who argued for it, worked for it, prayed for it, and suffered for it.

Some of the people whom Christian history honors for fidelity to the kingdom vision were women of remarkable calibre. In the fourteenth century, we find a woman known as Catherine of Siena, a woman mighty in prayer, a mystic and visionary who waded deep into peace-making in the local politics of Italy. We don't understand her campaign for a crusade against the Turks, but we can applaud her fearless speech and actions to bring peace to the factions fighting the papacy. She was an absolutely devastating critic of the clergy of her day and at the same time a diplomat for civil peace.

Another woman of the same century was St. Bridget of Sweden. She was a daring critic of the abuses of power by bishops or abbots. She was also an advisor to princes and kings on political policies and a tireless advocate of the papacy's return from Avignon, France, to Rome. These two women combined a deeply developed spirituality with intense activity for a better realization of God's kingdom in their time and their society.

Among the men who had the kingdom vision are St. Benedict and St. Francis. Benedict, the son of a well-placed Roman noble, felt the need to live his faith at a more intense and more single-minded pitch. In the fifth century he began a life which became over the years one of the most powerful models for Christian monasticism. He became the theoretician and founder of a socio-religious institution which had a powerful impact on the shape of Western Europe. Benedictine monasticism to this day contributes to the building up of the kingdom throughout the world. Francis of Assisi, the twelfth century son of a wealthy cloth merchant, also felt the need to live the Christian life in a purified form. His simple and literal following of Jesus, his contact with the poorest, his famous friendship with the animal world, his establishment of a religious order bearing his name—all of this is perhaps well known. His spirit led thousands and thousands of men and women to a more faithful following of Christ. The Franciscan vision, still calling the Church to attend to Christ among the poorest, remains one of Francis's greatest legacies.

Perhaps not as well known as Francis's love of Lady Poverty is his evangelizing zeal. He made three mission trips out of Italy to carry the gospel of Christ beyond his own country. He set out once for Syria but was shipwrecked and had to return. He tried on another occasion to convert non-believers in Morocco, but he fell ill and had to end the journey. He tried once more, this time having Egypt as his destination, but like the other ventures, this one also failed. Utterly dependent on Christ, this giant of prayer and activism so radiated Christ that he started a worldwide movement which is still alive today.

When Western Europe began to experience the excitement, challenge, and disruption associated with the Renaissance, other men and women saw the opportunity to bring God's kingdom to completion or partial fulfilment in their day. Just as Martin Luther and John Calvin saw the connection between religious reform and societal problems, so did the heroes and heroines of the Catholic "counter reform." Here I think of warrior-turned-priest Ignatius of Loyola, the founder of the Jesuit order. His commitment to Christ and his personal vision led to the establishment of an immensely talented corps of men who tried over the centuries in countries as far apart as Canada and India to make the kingdom of God known and vital. This sixteenth century Spanish gentleman left his mark; the Jesuits today continue in his spirit to be workers for the kingdom.

History reveals with painful impact how the kingdom of God became confused with the religious, political, and economic status quo. History also shows that despite cycles of reform and lapse, Jesus' vision continued to haunt the Christian heart. Yet the ways of making the kingdom real varied. Francis of Assisi made it alive by his literal-minded obedience to the gospel command, "go sell what you have and give to the poor." Is it just an accident that one of today's leading exponents of liberation theology is Rev. Leonardo Boff, a Franciscan priest from Brazil?

Millions of Christians lived the kingdom vision and made a difference in their town, village, occupation, and family. They, too, made history, inspired by the Holy Spirit, empowered from on high. The kingdom of God came into being, although partially, temporarily, and with imperfections, through the day to day relationships, cultural pursuits, and economic transactions of their age. Historians, even those who pursue the tiniest details left in chronicles and manuscripts, may never retrieve for our eyes and ears the energies, sacrifices, and glories of the nameless millions who made their history under Jesus' inspiration.

If it were a matter of simply blessing any and every vision of God's kingdom, my task here would be simpler. The truth is, not everyone's vision of the kingdom is equal. If some armed rabble, led by a prince-bishop, takes it into its head that God is asking for the slaughter of some Jews by the roadside, we cannot pretend that it is the correct vision. If deeply-believing Christians today set up armed camps in Lebanon or in South America, waving a Bible to justify their cause, we need to take a long look. In order to convince someone that my vision is correct or at least reliable, I have to find some authority for what I propose to do or arrange.

While early Christians relied clearly on Jesus' teaching, which they recalled and preserved in the Scriptures, they also tried to supplement their vision of the kingdom with what they knew about politics, culture, economics, and war. Their "secular" knowledge was part of their approach to embodying the kingdom of God. In the Catholic tradition, this has meant that over the centuries we have been willing to learn from the world, from writers, and from books other than the Bible to help us implement the vision that Jesus gave.

Even when Catholics try very hard to develop personal and societal ethics from the Bible, they continually discover that the Bible seems inadequate to the technical challenges arising in our age. In medical ethics, we wonder about terminating life-support, deciding who gets a transplant, and the care of defective newborns. In business ethics we struggle to judge the morality of banking practices and farm foreclosures. In technology and science we wonder if the peaceful uses of some new device justify the expenses involved in research and development.

Above and beyond issues which the Bible does not directly discuss, there is for Catholics the issue of building the kingdom here on earth, through society or through government. Beyond stereotypes Catholics and Protestants have of each other, or beyond those which the "liberal Catholic" and "liberal Protestant" have of the "conservative" Catholics and "conservative" Protestants, there is a common religious past and a common religious heritage. By this I mean the ancient, ever-threatened, ever-imperfect, ever-desired vision of a society in which law, economics, education, politics, and popular culture were shot through with Christian principles and oriented toward a full realization of the kingdom begun in Jesus. Was the title "Holy" Roman Empire a cynical use of words to justify imperial lust, or was it a genuine effort to build a new international order based on peace? When in later centuries people spoke of the "divine right of kings" or of "most Christian rulers," did it not reflect the hope that Jesus' will would be concrete and visible?

When European Christians crossed the great oceans, they retained and re-invigorated their ideas about the kingdom in its earthly aspects. In the vast stretches of South America, Spaniards and Portuguese established a union of church and crown. In the new American colonies, like Virginia or Massachusetts, the pioneers linked church and state. Theirs was a classic, total vision.

John Calvin, Martin Luther, and St. Ignatius of Loyola could not have conceived of a society which did not have religious and Christian principles embedded in it. They would see it as quite natural for Christ's values to find expression in societal matters. Social justice means the partial enactment of the kingdom of God on earth. This vision and program is still at work today. Not long ago thousands of church people rallied to demonstrate publicly in West Germany against nuclear war. Church people are lobbying intensely in the United States, some in favor of more aid to El Salvador, others against it, some opposed to MX missiles, others in favor of a "strong defense against communism." What separates us from Calvin, Luther, and Ignatius is a new system of governments and vastly more complex economic systems.

In Luther's day it was very important to have the protection and sympathy of a certain duke or count. It is more useful today to have the votes of legislators. Let the French Revolution mark the place where it changed. Queens and kings, no matter how hard they counter-attacked, were on the defensive from 1799 onward. Culture, economics, politics, and social policies were increasingly out of the rulers' control. Religiously concerned Christians, on fire with the kingdom vision, took their pleas, petitions, and pesterings to the senate, the parliament, the congress, or the assembly. American abolitionists used every conceivable technique, in face of bitter opposition, to persuade legislators and the public that the slavery issue was an economic, cultural, political, and religious evil. In one sense it could be said that they wanted to legislate their morality for the whole nation.

Among the hordes of Catholic immigrants to the United States in the nineteenth century, there were few who had experienced democracy in Europe. There were many, however, who saw it as a better climate for the growth of the gospel than any they had ever seen. There were Catholics on fire with the notion that democratic values provided a better base than European royal houses for the triumph of Catholic truth. They had a vision of the United States as a Catholic nation, a vision echoed by Protestant preachers, who called for a crusade to make America Protestant.

While American believers were engaged in the great democratic experiment, traditional Catholic textbook writers in Europe continued to say that the best possible way for a society to flourish was by a close unity of religion and the state. In Latin America, where real democracy was in many countries a facade for oligarchy or dictatorship, the Catholic reflex of support for the Spanish or Portuguese crown continued in support of the ruling powers.

Entering the twentieth century, sensitive consciences screamed at the price people were paying for industrialization, scientific and technological progress, and urban growth. Churches had to face in a new way not so much the problem of the beggar or the battered wife; they now had to face what we today call "structural unemployment" and poverty as a phenomenon in itself. City slums festered with disease, violence, high infant mortality rates, abandoned children, and impoverished women. The captains of industry who fought unions, legislators whose votes had been purchased, the promoters of government agencies designed to favor an already powerful sector of society—these seemed like poor choices in the army of those trying to establish the kingdom of God.

Small wonder that devout evangelicals, among them Walter Rauschenbusch, who learned about urban horror first hand from his New York City congregation, grew restive and began to see that the Jewish prophets spoke to American problems in the so-called Gay Nineties. For reasons too complex to mention here, a gap opened up between Protestants concerning the weight to be given to societal reform and the importance of direct evangelism and defense of orthodoxy. The social activists seemed too often tainted by the blight of liberal theology and Germanic Bible studies.

A Challenge to Contemporary Christians

Entering the space age with its nuclear, electronic, laser, and satellite dimensions, we Christians find it harder and harder to come to grips with our minority position in an increasingly non-Christian world. We also find ourselves, more than ever, challenged to understand modernity in the light of the gospel principles. If Christianity's ancient desire of enactment of the kingdom is to take place, intelligent and committed laypersons are required. The Church can be a positive, light-bearing and moderating influence at the service of the modern world, but the challenge is enormous.

We need to proceed with care and courage. On one hand we must have repeated recourse to the Bible, studied faithfully, mediated prayerfully, without expecting it to have clear, direct applications for weapons in outer space, genetic engineering, or even more government aid for research and development. On the other hand, we must train ourselves as well as possible in the relevant modern sciences and professions. We cannot hope to proclaim a kingdom that is meaningful if we fail to understand both the promise of modernity and its shortcomings. It is a time when proclaiming the kingdom, living the kingdom ethic, and preparing the ground for its fulfilment require of all Christians a high degree of knowledge about societal forces and a capacity for long-term commitment to institutional change.

I believe that Catholics and Protestants share the historic quest for God's kind of world, a vision which many of other faiths share as well. I believe that we all share, too, the opportunity to "make history" in however powerful or modest our fashion. I also believe that it is the power of Christ's Spirit which can lead us to pray and work together on many issues of vital concern.

Am I deluding myself with false ecumenism? Do I misperceive as a converging river what are really only isolated runlets? I hope not, and I am encouraged in my hope by two major developments. One development is a rising tide of fine writing among Protestants on the issue of social justice. Some of these writings have helped contemporary readers see the social justice commitments of some of the great preachers and teachers of the Protestant past, such as Jonathan Edwards, William Wilberforce, John Wesley, and Charles Finney.

Another development is the Catholic move to revitalize its ethical teaching through a fresh reading of Holy Scripture. Since the forties and fifties in modest beginnings, then in the sixties and seventies like a rising tide, Catholic biblical scholarship has produced high quality translations, commentaries, and study guides. Catholic biblical scholars have increasingly challenged our bishops, priests, theologians, and laity to rethink their approaches to the Bible and its use.

One example of the Catholic retrieval of biblical concepts for social justice teaching is that of the kingdom of God. The United States Catholic Bishops in their 1983 statement *The Challenge of Peace: God's Promise and our Response,* offer pastoral guidance on war and peace. This is a thoughtful and prayerful statement based squarely on the biblical notion of kingdom. As the bishops put it, the "distinctive contribution of the Church flows from her religious nature and ministry . . . to be in a unique way, the instrument of the kingdom of God in history."[1]

After reviewing some traditional Catholic principles about war and peace, the bishops note that peace, like the kingdom, is both a divine gift and a human work. They bring forward scriptural perspectives from both the Old and New Testaments to illuminate their remarks.

We read in Mark's Gospel that after the arrest of John the Baptist, Jesus proclaimed the good news that the reign of God was at hand. He made this present in his actions, and made it central to his call for followers. In Matthew's Gospel we read that after his successful victory over temptations in the desert, he began to proclaim this theme, "Reform your lives, the kingdom of God is at hand."

What is even more striking is that Jesus went beyond merely repeating the calls for reform typical of Old Testament prophets. The call to conversion was an invitation to enter God's reign through adherence to Jesus. Jesus declared that in him, the reign of God had begun and was in fact among the people.

I think that Protestants could agree with Catholics about the type of kingdom Jesus introduced, a new reality in which God's power is manifested and the people's longing for justice is fulfilled. We are called by Jesus to a new way of life characterized by forgiveness and a type of love which is active, life-giving, reaching out beyond family and friends to embrace even our enemies.

As the bishops' document makes clear, Jesus' words constitute an awesomely high ideal for us all. In his own life he shows us new possibilities and he shares with us his own Spirit and gift of peace. His refusal to defend himself with violence, his forgiveness of his persecutors, his prayer for them at the moment of his death—all this astonishes us and moves us to awe.

The early Christian communities, gifted with Jesus' own Spirit, struggled to live his vision, as we read in Acts 4:32–35. They looked forward, with God's help, to the time when the fullness of God's reign would make itself known in the world. To quote the bishops:

> To follow Jesus Christ implies continual conversion in one's own life as one seeks to act in ways which are consonant with the justice, forgiveness, and love of God's reign.[2]

The entire thrust of the bishops' statement is an invitation to Catholics and others to rethink fundamental directions in United States policy. It is a challenge, too, of overcoming the false dichotomy between evangelization and social action. They are asking their fellow Catholics to reorient their thinking and to engage in courageous action on behalf of the kingdom, on behalf of the transformation of history.

If some worry that social activism, whether by Catholics or Protestants, will lead to unthinking cooperation with Marxists or secularists, they should be aware that the American bishops do not expect social action to be uncritical or utopian. Catholics cannot agree with a philosophy which says that we humans on our own can establish a perfect world. Nor do we believe that efforts to improve the world which include violence, hatred, or destruction of population centers are worthy of our support.

The bishops reminded us in their pastoral letter that we are called to live very practically and concretely a tension between our vision of the kingdom of God and the embodiment of the kingdom in our own lifetime or in our own society. We live already in the grace of the kingdom, but it is far from being completed, whether we look at our own hearts or at the world around us. We have to keep in mind both truths, "Jesus' life, death and rising have inaugurated God's kingdom on earth," and the belief that he will come again, at the end of time, to judge the living and the dead, establishing the kingdom in perfection. We are therefore a *pilgrim* people in a world boiling with conflict and injustice.

This tension between the hoped-for kingdom and what we can accomplish in our lives is illustrated by a story circulating about Mother Teresa of Bombay. Someone supposedly criticized this devoted servant of the dying poor for not turning her efforts to the Indian government. Why didn't she lobby the government for changes in its food and employment policies? Why didn't she concentrate on the causes of the problem, rather than on the dying who were the tragic result? Her answer to the critics implies that the questioners were impatient to have the kingdom of God on earth in its fullness now. She said, "I have not been called to be successful, only faithful."

Catholics profess when they recite the Nicene Creed that Jesus will come again in glory to judge the living and the dead and that his kingdom will have no end. God alone knows the day and the hour of the world's consummation, and God alone, in Jesus, will reestablish the kingdom of perfect peace and justice. In the interim, we continue to live in the vision that haunts us and impels us, and in the pain of our defeats, failures, and partial victories.

Bishops at a meeting, however, do not constitute the mass of the Catholic Church. It is to the laity that we look for a revitalized understanding of their calling and the kingdom imperative. We are able to agree with Howard Snyder's call to the laity in his challenge:

> By grace and the power of God, all Christian men and women are free to minister, free to be servants of Christ in the work of the Kingdom.[3]

Kingdom work or ministry is "any service carried out in the name of Jesus that serves people or nature and shows forth God's rule in the world."[4]

Because sin permeates all the structures of society—economic, political, legal, and religious—kingdom ministry or kingdom-building can and should be carried out on behalf of Christ in all these areas. The mystery of Christ's incarnation teaches that there is interaction between God's history and human history; it also teaches that Jesus wants us to see him in particular in the poor, the oppressed, the refugee, and the alien.

Yet there is no area of human life that can be overlooked. People who work in the arts, environmental sciences, theoretical research, in agriculture and management of natural resources also deserve our encouragement. The management of the earth for the benefit of all is a key focus for kingdom ministry. Howard Snyder's call to the laity has a parallel in the advice of the Catholic bishops to the laity in the Second Vatican Council. The laity,

> . . . by their special vocation, seek the kingdom of God by engaging in temporal affairs and by ordering them according to the plan of God.[5]

By contrast, we find that Pope John Paul II in his many talks and travels, particularly in Central and South America, has urged priests to reduce their direct involvement in political parties and government posts. One of his reasons is the fear that the laity may be overshadowed or hindered in what should be their own field of work, their calling in professional, administrative, and social work.

It was this fear of "clergy dominance" which prompted some Catholics a few years back to make a statement about this. As they saw it, the good news calling for peace, justice, and freedom needs to be announced through the prism of lay experience. Priests and bishops, unlike days of old, are no longer the only educated folks, nor even the best educated in their areas. Technical expertise, political wisdom, and sensitivity to civic problems can be found among the laity. Between the gospel on one hand and day-to-day decisions, Christian social thought is at work. Committed believers at work in the world can and should be prime movers in kingdom building. If one stands in a downtown area of most major North American cities around five o'clock some evening, one can see a massive stream of humanity converging at bus stops, subway stations, and underground parking lots. This river of life gushes from a countless number of commercial, financial, industrial, and governmental offices. These men and women daily lend themselves to decisions, policies, and implementation. Some of it is for the kingdom; some is not. Priests, bishops, and theologians in theological colleges or seminaries can help these people, but the laity must take primary responsibility.

Conclusion

"Thy kingdom come" puts before all Christians the never-ending task of building, in modest ways, for our time, some realizations and concrete examples of the kingdom inaugurated by God in Jesus Christ. Kingdom hopes, kingdom visions lead Christians to construct an ethical response to the evils of their age. The ethical response varies in details but arises from three sources: Holy Scriptures devoutly studied within the community's living faith and experience, wisdom and inspiration passed from one generation of believers to the next, and state-of-the-art expertise in philosophy, biology, computers, or whatever else is required.

I have emphasized the variety of ethical response because Catholics are not now, nor have they always been, united in their approach to kingdom building. I had the chance recently to spend some time in Peru and Chile where the problems of poverty, longstanding injustice and violence, both governmental and anti-governmental, give a color and tone to the situation that we in North America have difficulty understanding.

However the great debates about liberation theology are resolved, one of their contributions to North American Christians will be the challenge to our perspective on social justice. The virtue of Father

Gustavo Gutierrez's version of liberation theology is the call to respect the way our impoverished, oppressed brothers and sisters in the faith see basic Christian truths—salvation, sin, and the kingdom.

Becoming a new creation in Christ, we as a people, a "royal priesthood," as Peter would have it, mesh with society. Whether we live in the cardboard shanties around Lima and Mexico City or the sleek highrises of North America, we must care enough to revitalize as much as we can of our society. Because Christ entered human history and took it seriously enough to confront a set of limited local authorities and problems, we must do as much.

Conversion of one individual means that one more agent of the kingdom is added to the task of obedient response to the prayer we utter so often. Catholics and Protestants, I feel sure, agree that obedience or the faith that issues in works is possible only through the presence of him who reigns in the Spirit and with the Father. I also feel sure that Catholics and Protestants agree that God alone can bring to completion, to full flowering and realization that kingdom for which we work, hunger, and pray.

Finally, the issues which divide us these days are less likely to be the traditional ones of post-Reformation polemic. We are more likely to be split on ways of establishing the kingdom. Both Howard Snyder and the pacifist Catholic Worker Movement personnel would ask all of us to simplify our life style in clothing, food, and recreation. Massive public demonstrations of a non-violent kind bring out Christians of many denominations to bring to governmental attention the evils of war, factory closings, and hunger. Many Christian denominations have in their midst men and women committed to raising social and political consciousness, to forming community groups, bombarding elected representatives with petitions. Even in Latin America where frightened governments and police and security forces are violating human rights, divisions among Christians are less likely to be Catholic-Protestant than non-violent versus drastic action.

I never questioned the bravery of the middle-class university students at Santa Barbara's history changing demonstrations against war. If we cannot all agree on who or what is serving the kingdom, we can at least praise the courage and sensitivity of all who seek to live, with God's help, that most disturbing prayer, "thy kingdom come."

13

A Closer Look at MARY AND THE SAINTS

While working in Boston, Massachusetts, a few years back, I was asked to call on a patient in a local hospital. He was a man in his early sixties, a retired truck driver, burly in arm and shoulder; he was also diagnosed as having terminal cancer. On my first visit we sat in the sunny patients' lounge and got acquainted. One of his major concerns was his wife. She, it appears, was suffering from some emotional problems. As we spoke she was receiving treatment in the psychiatric department of another hospital.

On another visit to see the man, I met his daughter and his wife. While he slept in his room I chatted with them, and when I asked the wife whether she prayed to God about this tragedy, she said that she did. She prayed, she said, that her husband might suffer as little as possible. She prayed particularly for this to St. Jude, known in Catholic lore as the Saint of the Impossible. The woman was a long-time "fan" of St. Jude, and had even made a pilgrimage one year from Boston to New Jersey where there is a large church erected in St. Jude's honor. Special prayers are offered there to the apostle.

"Did St. Jude," I asked, "answer your prayers over the years?"

She said, "Oh, yes, usually." I felt that I was in the presence of a legendary Catholic type, a woman of modest education, an immigrant to the United States from Eastern Europe, possessing more faith in St. Jude than in Jesus. As my stereotype was taking shape, she made a remark which stopped the process in an instant. Speaking of her friendship with the Saint of the Impossible, she remarked, "Whenever he doesn't answer my prayer, I always learn later that there was a good reason why." She added, with a knowing nod to her daughter who smiled, that she had a better understanding of these things than a friend who was a fan of St. Anthony. When St. Anthony didn't answer her friend's prayers, the disappointed petitioner got very angry and took it out on the statue of St. Anthony. Apparently she was often in the market for a new statue for her home prayer shrine!

By contrast, the woman devoted to St. Jude had a sense of contentment about her relationship with the saint. If favors were not granted, she would be able to understand that God in his mercy does not grant requests which are not timely or for our good. I felt within myself a new respect and affection for this woman. She had, despite all her afflictions, a beautifully personal and familial kind of faith.

This woman stands for much that non-Catholics and some modern Catholics find hard to understand. It may help here at the beginning to hint at a view of the world which underlies devotion to Mary and the saints, a world view that some moderns do not have. The world view in question is that which includes a vivid sense of companionship with the deceased. A story about a nun who is also a native American Indian will illustrate.

Her name is Sister Jose Hobday and she was raised on an Indian Reservation. I heard her give a talk a few summers ago in Colorado. She began her talk that night with a gesture. In front of her on a table there was a shallow ceramic bowl. In it she had placed a wick-like strip of prairie grass, sweet grass from the Great Plains' own bounty. With a match she lit the prairie grass and waited for the slow curl of smoke to rise. A pleasant odor reached us. She then spoke movingly of the contributions native Americans could make to the Christian churches if the "White Man" could only accept it. She explored in particular the subject of the dead.

Nearness to one's deceased ancestors is crucial for the native American's spirituality. Among many North Americans, by contrast, spirits of the deceased have become childish in Halloween costume or vicious in an unending series of ghoul or monster movies. Sister Jose revealed her own sense of closeness to her deceased mother. Often when she faced a problem or difficult decision, she prayed for help from "spirit friends," including, of course, her mother.

For this native American nun it was normal to live each day in the presence, usually kindly, of her ancestors. She also remarked that native Americans had trouble understanding why the "White Man" hired total strangers to bury their relatives in places which they rarely visited. For Sister Jose, this was most peculiar behavior.

The chances are that not only native Americans but even the "White Man" has felt from time to time that a deceased relative, spouse, or parent, is present and anxious to help or comfort. Chances are also good that we white Americans don't talk about this much to each other for fear of being called crazy. Greater heads than mine can account for the fact that millions of men and women all over the world, past and present, have a sense of reverence and companionship with the spirits of the deceased—as well as fear, which Western Europeans and North Americans tend to dismiss as superstitious.

The Catholic approach to the holy men and women who have died arises from a worldview that shares something of that described by Sister Jose. Some of these holy men and women whom we honor were so reknowned in their little village or city that people called them "saints" before they died. Some of their names or their life histories have never gotten official Catholic, universal approval in our international calendar. Nonetheless they reportedly hover around a certain village or shrine. Other men and women of well-attested holiness of life have gained official Catholic recognition, and we Catholics can feel about them as Sister Jose feels about her mother's spirit-presence.

We believe that these holy ones are alive in and with the Lord. They are enjoying the reward promised with the Father. Having overcome the temptations and trials of life, they are the Church triumphant. Grown to their full stature in the Lord, they are able to communicate with the Lord; they pray for their friends and enemies now as they did in their lifetime. On earth, they saw only darkly, "through a glass"; in heaven they pray with full vision.

Besides appreciating the powerful companionship of these holy ones, Catholics have been inspired by their examples of discipleship on earth. Not so strange then that at baptism a person receives a new name, becoming a new person in Christ. That name is usually that of some already established saint. A newly-baptized person has a new status and lives a new reality in a new family, the family of Christ. Fittingly, they take the names of proven performers who have in the past graced that family, and who, by their prayers, can grace it still.

It is the sense of accompaniment, presence, and powerful prayer which has led so many Catholics to name towns, rivers, hospitals, and streets after saints. Major cities in California bear the names of saints conferred by the Spanish explorers, the Midwest has places named after saints by French explorers, and the great inland waterway between Canada and the United States bears the name of St. Lawrence.

This sense of accompaniment, presence and power leads the Catholic Church to call on these mighty heroines and heroes on their feast days, usually the day of their death. We remember them in prayer, we ask for their prayers to the Lord, and we recount the glory they have, God's gift to them.

In the official Catholic service book there is a prayer of praise which we offer to God on the feast of a saint. Before the Eucharist, the priest reads or chants the following address to God:

> You are glorified in your saints,
>   for their glory is the crowning of your gifts.
> In their lives on earth you give us an example.
> In our communion with them, you give us
>   their friendship.
> In their prayer for the Church you give us
>   strength and protection.
> This great company of witnesses spurs us on to
>   victory, to share their prize of everlasting glory,
>   through Jesus Christ our Lord. . . .[1]

The restraint of the official liturgical prayer on the feast of saints is one thing; quite another is the way some saints are remembered and celebrated. In the Catholicism of my youth, nuns in full habit figured strongly. Day after day, year after year in the stuffy, overcrowded classrooms, they gave their all for my classmates and me. While these nuns had official catechism books from which they taught, they often varied the diet by telling stories of the saints or of Old Testament figures. Some of these saints' stories had been embroidered by centuries of telling, and occasionally prettified by a piety that is no longer appealing.

Some saints had crept into the Church's round of observances from popular enthusiasm, and some of the tales told about them lacked historical basis. Sometimes, too, a saint who in his or her lifetime was very frank about sins, faults, or failures was badly served by a later admirer who "cleaned up" the shadow side. One of the modest reforms of the Second Vatican Council was to shift some of the saints out of the official, worldwide calendar. A reason for this shifting was a conviction that some saints had not been historically as well-founded or well-known as we had thought. Some Catholics, on learning that St. Philomena (my mother's middle name) or St. Christopher had lost rank, were disgusted. Others, realizing that a shift from the calendar doesn't stop anyone from praying to a favorite, simply kept on with their devotion.

Relics

While less emphasized in North America today than in the past, knowledgable observers of Roman Catholicism know that there was a remarkable interest in and use of saints' relics. Much has been written about the ludicrous or fraudulent trade in items of clothing, pieces of bodies, bits of bone, hanks of hair, and the rest. Some of the great cathedrals of Europe house great collections of relics, enshrined in cases decorated with precious stones and gold settings. Villages, towns, and royalty competed to see who could accumulate the best collection. These cathedrals sometimes were built at places where some saint had lived, visited, or was buried, as is the case of St. James's shrine in Santiago de Compostela, Spain.

Much of the interest, if not all of it, in these things stemmed from the conviction that these relics, used with faith, had healing power. Instances of this healing power through prayer are frequent, and not just in medieval times. The Protestant Reformation took a dim view of these non-biblical extravagances, as well as of devotion to the saints. They seemed to dethrone Christ as sole redeemer; they tended to make people think that salvation, health, success in marriage, or good crops came through magical incantations, relics kissed, or pilgrimages accomplished.

Here I think it is helpful to look at two aspects of this practice. First, there is among all of us a natural inclination to keep souvenirs of places or persons who mean something deep to us. When my father came back from World War I, he had as relics a French military canteen, a battered bronze candlestick from a bombed-out home, and an American army canteen in which he had inscribed many of the principal battles of the war. Each piece had its story and each piece brought back to him some moments of those days when he worked with the ambulance corps in France. Most nations have preserved places, homes, or battlefields which have particular power for their history. We enshrine mementos, photos, objects of clothing and manufacture in hundreds of ways, from the Smithsonian Museum in Washington to a tiny cottage in New Hampshire which was once the home of President Franklin Pierce.

The erection of shrines and the collection of relics is simply a part of this, and in many cases a nobler part. If we save a saint's hand, it was usually a hand that blessed or sustained the poor; it was not an instrument of violence. I remember once seeing the little room where Montreal's beloved Brother André lived and worked for many years. It was small and simple and helped me grasp why he was so beloved. He was a humble man who answered the door of a large residence of priests. He was also the first contact many people had with a church figure. His advice, patience, and practical help endeared him to thousands.

The harder question is the "power" aspect of relics. Can a relic in itself, the bit of bone, the bloodstained garment which took the bullet killing Bishop Oscar Romero in El Salvador, achieve any miracles? I am not aware of any Catholic teaching that attributes power to this or that object. My understanding is that this or that object can be a vehicle of grace when used with faith. I have noted elsewhere how "fleshly" or "earthly" Catholicism is, revealing surely its Jewish ancestry. Since God has entered creation and especially humanity through Jesus, and since all of creation is destined for renewal, then bread, water, wine, oil, and embraces can be rich with the divine. If a given relic has proven to be part of an effective transformation in someone's life, we assume that God's power was at work in answer to someone's prayer.

I mentioned earlier Sister Jose Hobday's plea for understanding of the native American culture. The first Americans had and retain to some degree a lively sense of their ancestors' presence. I offer another example, this time from the native culture of Mexico. A few years ago, while serving as a university chaplain in Boston, I got to know a graduate student from Mexico who opened to me a door about the native Mexican. This student was himself of Indian descent, short, swarthy, and a fascinating teller of the Indian story. He spoke to me one afternoon with affection of the small Indian village in which he had been raised. As a student of architecture, he spoke in particular of the older colonial church where he and other villagers worshiped. It was a church that dated to Spanish conquistador days. It had in front of it a large open space enclosed by a low wall. He told me that the Spanish priests used to oblige the Indians to assemble in the walled space for lessons in religion.

Inside the church, architectural features reflected native culture. Men sat on one side, women on the other, showing, my friend said, the complementarity of men and women in that village. His Indian father had the responsibility for wresting a living from the Mexican soil; his Indian mother was supposed to attend to things of the spirit. It was the mother who supervised education and spiritual development.

Within the open, walled enclosure outside the church, the priests had erected a small bell tower. My friend remembers that, as a child, he watched some of his friends go into the enclosure to pull vigorously at the bell one day. They urged him to do the same and when he seemed hesitant, they asked, "Don't you want to remember your ancestors?"

Catholicism, imported from Spain and laid over the pre-Christian Mexican Indian culture, brought with it a feeling for the companionship of the dead. The imported religion found among the natives a common ground. Bell-ringing in that village could mean a call to worship, feast, or fast; it could also mean that Indians were reaching out to their deceased.

It is this same sense of connection with our deceased which undergirds our teaching about Purgatory. To speak of saints praying for us is to speak of men and women whose lives exhibited as much holiness and grace of Jesus as one can attain. We know, however, that many Christian men and women die at a distance from God. Death finds them unprepared, not at peace with themselves, and far from peaceful with family or associates. Though believers, they die with a large agenda of unfinished business. What happens to them at death?

One approach says that all who die lie in sleep until the trumpet's call. All will then awake for the judgment. Another approach says that through death itself one enters immediately either into God's embrace or into the fearsome absence of God called "hell." A third approach is possible and Catholics have found some hint or support for it, beginning with the apocryphal text of 2 Maccabees 39–46. The text shows that at least some Jews before Jesus believed that their prayers and sacrifices could help the deceased who had sinned.

Paul in one place speaks of our final testing by fire, to see whether our works are of gold, brass, iron, or straw. His imagery in 1 Cor. 3:13–15 is quite vivid:

> . . . the work of each will be made clear. The Day will disclose it. That day will make its appearance with fire, and fire will test the quality of each man's work. If the building a man has raised on this foundation still stands, he will receive his recompense; if a man's building burns, he will suffer loss. He himself will be saved, but only as one fleeing through fire.

"Testing," even "fire" awaits all who die. In that testing the dead cannot help themselves. Catholics have followed the Jewish instinct found in 2 Maccabees that we on earth can ask the Lord to be merciful. Their sins have of course been forgiven, but their works—that which was the fabric of their daily existence, fruits bitter or sweet, legacy of pain or service—shall all be assessed and purified.

Cemetery markers bearing the initials RIP show a family's prayer that the deceased may rest in peace, may be helped by prayer to achieve a peace which they had only imperfectly in life. Who of us can say that when our hour comes we will be emptied of self and ready to be filled with God's presence and love? A book review of a new study of the Dutch Reformation preacher Arminius tells us that on his deathbed the controversial man prayed the following prayer:

> O thou great Shepherd who . . . brought again from the dead, Jesus, my Lord and Savior, be present with me, a sheep of thine that is weak and afflicted. O thou God of my salvation, render my soul fit for the heavenly kingdom and prepare my body for the resurrection.[2]

Arminius, good Protestant Reformer that he was, was not likely to be asking for a quick passage through Purgatory. But his feeling that his soul had to be made fit for the kingdom and his body ready for the resurrection expresses the Catholic sentiment.

We believe that before the general resurrection, there is a trajectory of purification at God's hands. It surely begins with death itself, but we think it continues for a time after death. We believe that we can help those in this process by our prayers. All are invited to the Lord's banquet, but some need appropriate clothing if they are to stay. Official Catholic teaching about Purgatory is very modest; speculation and imagination about it is sometimes wild and foolish.

Devotion to saints, venerating the holy men and women, asking for their prayers, feeling the presence, whether triumphant and glorious or in suffering and anguish of the departed—all of these practices may be pre-Christian. But the question is whether it is anti-Christian. The sensibilities and feelings of millions cannot be overlooked. We who launch satellites to the moon and spend our days in air-conditioned temples of the computer may be more numbed than we should be to some profound truths. We may be forgetting the great company of witnesses spurring us on to the victory.

The Blessed Virgin Mary

Raised as I was in a Catholic home, attending Catholic elementary school and high schools, I found it normal to pray to Mary, to see her statue in church or classroom, to sing hymns praising her, even to march in a procession honoring her. I still have the rosary which I used. At one point in my early high school years, my older sister tried to convince the whole family that we should gather nightly as a family to recite the rosary together. We were able to manage it about three nights in succession when our enthusiasm collapsed. I daresay that none of us felt that Mary was a goddess. She was simply a powerful friend and protector, an intimate of Jesus.

Despite this background, I found in later years a drastic drop-off of interest in Mary. In my first year in seminary I became sufficiently concerned about it to ask for advice from a seminary professor. He loaned me a book about Mary by a well-known Catholic writer. It turned out to be so full of miracles and weeping statues that I set it aside after only a chapter or two. I decided that I would not worry about this anymore and turned the matter over to God. If in his good time and way he wanted me to understand Mary better, I would welcome it. For the moment I decided not to try to force myself in this area.

In matters of Mary, like those of the saints, we have yet another topic which has produced problems in the field of ecumenism. While Mary is surely a more prominent figure than the saints, and surely given a greater dignity by God, the "cult" of Mary seems to many Christians unpalatable or, worse, unpardonable. Certain exaggerations relating to Mary's power and privileges have driven some right-minded folks away from her. "Why not," as the critics say, "go straight to Jesus, instead of praying to Mary?" Doesn't the cult of Mary draw attention away from Jesus, our sole mediator? Worst of all, where is the biblical evidence for those infamous Catholic doctrines, the Assumption of Mary and her Immaculate Conception?

The best place to begin is with Scripture. Keeping in mind what I have written earlier in this book about the Catholic use of Scripture, I suggest that we look to the texts, not so much for "evidence" as for portraits. The word "evidence" has a factual, cold, data-like sound; Christian Scriptures contain facts to be sure, but they also tell stories and paint portraits. When looking at an oil painting, one can ask, "Is this a good likeness?" meaning, "Would I recognize the person in the painting if I bumped into her outside the gallery?"

One can look at portraits in another way, however. One can say, "This is a picture which has captured the depth and spirit of the person represented." Before a good portrait one can sit for hours, learning more, being stirred, entering into its depth. It is in this sense that Catholics have meditated the portraits of Mary in Scripture.

One priest, Rev. Patrick Bearsley, has taken a long, loving look at two scriptural portraits of Mary and as a result calls her the "perfect disciple."[3] His thoughtful study impressed me, and it covers two significant events in Jesus' life: the wedding feast at Cana (John: 2), and the Crucifixion (John 19:25–27).

Over the years when the story of Jesus and Mary at the wedding feast has been read and explained, I can recall how the priest in the pulpit tried to convey its meaning. Particularly difficult was Jesus' abrupt reply to Mary's remarks about the shortage of wine. "What would you have me do, woman?" seems in contemporary English somewhat gruff. Why didn't he call her "Mother"?

I like the idea that Jesus' use of "woman" is at the same time both respectful and a sign that she and her Son are no longer relating as blood relatives. They are now disciple and teacher. The closeness and intimacy of mother and son fades before a new, deeper intimacy as Mary becomes a disciple.

The usual translation of John 2:4 is "My hour has not yet come." In John's Gospel, Jesus' "hour" is the hour of glorification, the hour of revelation of power. Reputable scholars say that John 2:4 could just as well be translated, "Has not my hour come?" Mary serenely tells the waiters to be ready for Jesus' orders. Here Mary is putting into practice what Jesus taught: "Whatever you ask for in my name, I will do" (John 14:13).

A second powerful gospel portrait is that which climaxes Jesus' ministry, the Crucifixion scene in John 19:25–27. At the foot of the cross we find "the beloved disciple," John, with Mary. Dying, Jesus commends John to Mary, calling her now "John's mother"; John in turn now becomes Mary's "son." Even as Jesus was dying he has presence of mind enough to provide for his mother. John's courage, which keeps him at Jesus' side, is proof of his ability to take care of Mary.

But there is more here than this. At Cana, Mary becomes a disciple of Jesus, a deeper relationship than flesh and blood. At Calvary John and Mary enter into a new relationship; it is not based merely on Jesus' affection and trust in John. We believe that it is based on their new union in Jesus through the gift of the Holy Spirit.

John's Gospel, one of the richest theologically and one of the most symbolic, says that in dying, Jesus "gave up his spirit" (Confraternity of Christian Doctrine translation, 1961). This signals both the end of Jesus' earthly, natural life and the beginning of a new creation. Matthew, Mark, and Luke say that in dying, Jesus "gave up his spirit" or "expired." Similarity of the language in the English should not make us overlook the fact that the Greek in John's version is unusual. It should be likened to the Pentecost scene of Acts 1:14 where Mary and the apostles, waiting in the Upper Room, experience the outpouring of the Holy Spirit. John's Gospel portrait of the Crucifixion has at the same time a hint of Pentecost and a new relationship between believers and disciples through the sharing of Jesus' Spirit.

Mary is the perfect disciple, beginning with her act of faith in her request of Jesus at the wedding in Cana. She is also the faithful disciple to the end. A meditative look at the portrait of Mary in John's Gospel is not the same as "proof" of what Catholics teach about Mary. It is rather an invitation to see her as a follower and disciple, someone who ranks with Paul and Peter and the rest.

An ancient tradition says that St. Luke was a painter, and it is fitting to look at his "portraits" of Mary as well. His first two chapters are of special importance. He stitches together Old Testament material to evoke the great heroes and heroines of Judaism. Mary emerges as the fullest expression of Jewish longing and obedience. Abraham and Sarah both asked, "Shall Sarah who is ninety bear a child?" (Gen. 17:17 and 18:22). Sarah has her doubts.

In Luke 1:32–34 Mary also asks, "How shall this be done?" The angel's announcement to Mary is a paraphrase of 2 Samuel 7:8–16, where David is promised a great name, a throne and kingdom, and a dynasty that will be blessed by God. Jesus will be the greater fulfillment of the promise, Son of the Most High. We see Mary, as Luke portrays her, as the end-product of a long history and the turning point for a new history. Her trusting response to the angel, "I am the servant of the Lord. Let it be done to me as you say," speaks to Catholics once more of her discipleship, her trust, and her commitment to God. She is one of the New Testament's "poor in spirit" who are to delight in the promised Messiah.

Gospel portraits aside, it must be stated that the Catholic view of Mary has also been enriched by other literature. The New Testament is a collection of books or writings, a mini-library. In the first two or three centuries of the Christian era, churches read and circulated pieces of literature about Jesus, Mary, and the apostles other than those which were later judged best for official public use. Some of those "apocryphal" gospels of were taken by Catholic leaders to be reliable, or at least helpful in the transmission of faith from one generation to another.

Today one can find Catholic statuary, devotional literature, and popular preaching marked by the extra-canonical material. One example is the story that Mary's parents took her while she was still a child to the temple in Jerusalem, where she was presented to God for his service. She made a vow of dedication and remained there for a number of years, being educated in Jewish Scriptures and history. Another tradition says Mary's parents were named Joachim and Anna. None of the four biblical Gospels gives this information. It is information from extra-canonical sources. While we might hesitate to call this information inspired, it is no reason to rename all the women called Ann or all the towns, valleys, and rivers called San Joaquin.

I mentioned earlier that every generation tends to bring its own filter through which it interprets Jesus and the gospel events to itself and its age. A hundred or a thousand years later, the interpretation may seem forced or dissatisfying, even to those who share the same faith and venerate the same gospel texts.

Some have interpreted Jesus in recent years as a charismatic reformer and critic of the Jewish establishment, winning a following from the rural Jews suffering from Roman taxation and military occupation. Others have seen in Jesus the ultimate psychologist who reads and cures persons' hearts with tremendous skill. One can interpret Jesus in many ways and combinations, especially if one sits before the gospel portraits and meditates prayerfully. There is a "plasticity" which we viewers and readers bring to the Scriptures. That Jesus can be read differently in many different eras and cultures is perhaps a helpful sign that he is from God.

This same "plasticity" applies to Mary. In the early centuries, she became for some the Christian expression and counterpart of the pagan fertility goddesses. In the Middle Ages, she was benevolent intermediary between God and man, the protector of cities and of town guilds. As the Benedictine John Main puts it,

> The importance of Mary and of Marian devotion is that her life has taken on an important symbolic significance in the Christian tradition and, by grasping this significance, we can experience ourselves as being real participants in the mystery of existence.[4]

The shrine of the Blessed Mother of Guadalupe in Mexico City illustrates yet another type of symbolic value. Catholicism was the religion of the Spanish invaders. It may have been quite a shock for the Spanish clergy to deal with an alleged appearance of Mary to an Indian named Juan Diego. The woman who appeared spoke the Indian dialect and showed herself in a place where Indians had venerated an Indian goddess. For Spaniards, it was perhaps a lesson that the person we refer to as "God's Mother" and the Lord himself highly esteemed these Indians. For the Indians, it was a sign that the conqueror's religion contained a new and richer symbol of mercy for them.

For contemporary North American Catholic women, Mary has become a challenge. Some writers and thinkers have recoiled from traditional pictures of Mary—meekness, obedience, mildness, downcast eyes, and the like. Earlier Christian writers and preachers not only described Mary but put her forward as a model. To say that Mary was holy was to say that she mirrored the "state of original justice" that Eve had lost in the Garden. Different visions of how God had intended men and women to be before the Fall affected the features of Mary's life to be held up for admiration.

One Catholic woman who speaks of her own earlier disenchantment with Mary, yielding to a new respect is Doris Donnelly, who was pregnant with her son Christopher during the Vietnam War. The young man scheduled to be the baptismal sponsor was a medic in Vietnam. For some reason the medic, who was working in a "safe" area, came under "friendly fire." When Doris got the telephone call with the news of his death, Christopher, still in the womb, kicked her in the stomach. That triggered for her a new understanding of the Blessed Virgin. All the representations of Mary which can be found in statues and holy cards, even in glorious Renaissance masterpieces, vanished. All those sermons preached about Mary's obedience, humility, and acceptance exploded. Doris needed a vigorous and courageous woman who could help her sort through her outrage and grief, who could help her exchange pain for enlightenment. She found this woman in Mary.[5]

Doris Donnelly began to reread the gospel portraits of Mary and began to see new things from her own context of pain. In Bethlehem, she sees a woman enduring poverty and squalor, rejection by those who control city housing. She sees a woman who will hope for the time when the rich will be sent away with empty hands, and the poor will have all good things (Luke 1:53).

When Doris looks again, with her new set of eyes, at Michelangelo's stunning statue of the Pieta, the bereaved mother holding the dead Jesus on her lap, she sees in that pose and stance a whole crowd of mothers in grief—the Hiroshima mother kneeling with her dead child in her arms and her eyes raised to heaven, the bereft Lebanese mother running through destroyed streets carrying the charred body of her son, the Salvadoran mother gently washing the fiberless ribs of her twelve-year-old daughter who had been raped and murdered. As Doris Donnelly writes,

> Like Mary, these women want their grief to be public; they refuse to shield the atrocities from us or to render the victims anonymous.[6]

Having said all this, do we Catholics nonetheless still hold to unscriptural doctrines, not taught in the first centuries, about Mary? In particular, how can Catholics justify their belief in the Immaculate Conception and the Assumption, for which there is surely less scriptural "evidence" than there is for the sacrament of confirmation?

Each of these teachings could occupy an entire book, but in what follows I will try to clarify them. First, in the Immaculate Conception we are speaking of a doctrine that says nothing about the physicalness or naturalness of Mary's own beginnings. The doctrine does not concern the marital life of her parents. Nor, as some Catholics mistakenly think, does the doctrine speak of Jesus, as in *his* conception.

Positively put, the doctrine says that Mary from her birth onward, was the kind of person that God intended her to be. In technical language, we say that she was from the first preserved from the effects of original sin. It is due to original sin that, as Paul put it, we have at war within us two laws, the struggle between good and evil. Because of the fall of Adam and Eve, the world's original balance, harmony, and trajectory has been disrupted. Each of us knows from experience how flighty our minds are, how fickle our willpower, how careless we are with the great gift of our imagination. We believe that Mary entered life with an advanced share of the balance, harmony, and character which Jesus wins for all of us through redemption. Mary, like all of us, had to be redeemed. She, who summed up all the best of the Old Testament, marks the turning point of human history. She is the new Eve, having the holiness and integrity which the new Adam gives to every baptized person and which is destined to grow to completion in eternity.

This teaching of course raises a question: How could Mary benefit from Jesus' redemption before it had taken place? Brilliant French theologian Louis Bouyer reminds us that this is the same problem we have with heroes and heroines of the Old Testament. Ever since the breakup of the harmony described in Genesis, ever since the alienation from God and each other that has plagued the human race, God never stopped chasing us with his grace. That grace, that love, that enhancement had already sanctified many of the just in the Old Testament, like Jeremiah. In Jeremiah's case, the sanctification came while in his mother's womb. So it was for John the Baptist. In Mary's case, Catholics believe that God's enhancing love and holiness produced their effect more promptly and more completely.[7]

The teaching of the Immaculate Conception arose according to one writer from a very early and well-attested Christian belief in the holiness and sinlessness of Mary. When the fifth century Council of Ephesus, declaring firmly the divinity of Jesus, gave Mary the reflex title "Mother of God," attention was focused on her sinlessness and status. In both Eastern and Western Churches, a belief in her sinlessness came to full expression in the eighth century. There is additional evidence that some Christians observed a feast, Mary's Conception, before the year 700.

Keeping in mind that the exercise of papal teaching power is relational to the faith of the whole Church, it is important to know that Pope Pius IX had addressed questionnaires to Catholic bishops and theologians around the world prior to declaring as formal dogma the Immaculate Conception in the year 1858. He wanted to be sure that there was already among the people a positive feeling and sense of this truth before he gave it official expression.

Let us turn now to the Assumption of Mary. A good modern source for Catholic teaching, The New Catholic Encyclopedia, gives the heart of this teaching as follows:

> The Immaculate Mother of God, the ever-Virgin Mary, having completed the course of her earthly life, was assumed body and soul into heavenly glory.[8]

It is clear to all that there are no New Testament texts which give evidence for this teaching. Pope Pius XII, who made the formal declaration of this doctrine in the year 1950, reminded Catholics that resurrection from the dead is the natural outcome of Christ's victory over Satan. Resurrection from the dead is the promise given to all who are faithful disciples of Jesus. Scripture, said the pope, shows Mary intimately united with her son, sharing his fate from Cana to Calvary.

St. Paul assures the Romans (6:4–13) that through baptism they are joined to Christ and share his victory over death. There is some evidence that Christians as early as the third century believed that Mary had already been raised to heaven. We might do well to pause for a brief reflection on this teaching.

As we have said before, in Christianity and particularly in the Catholic tradition, there is a reverence for the bodily, the earthly. God's Son was formed from the flesh of the Virgin, and his earthly death led to bodily resurrection. Death and corruption are seen as consequences of sin. Though sinless, Jesus went through the door of death for our sake. Rising to new life is the sign of the victory and the completion of God's plan for us.

Catholic tradition considers that the only other person ever created who was sinless was the Virgin Mary. Just as the grace won by Jesus for humanity touched her in advance at the Immaculate Conception, so we believe the grace of resurrection won by Jesus for us all comes to her before the general resurrection. I hope that it is clear that these teachings about Mary are theological *implications* of teachings about Christ. If Christ is not divine, Mary, while perhaps a remarkable lady, could not have been called Mother of God by the council of church leaders in Ephesus in 431, A.D. If Christ were not Redeemer, source of all graces, no one could say that Mary was conceived without sin, nor could they infer her resurrection in Assumption terms.

Catholics have to admit that even in the presence of carefully worded official teaching designed to keep clear that Jesus is Redeemer and that Mary's status flows from him, there are still exaggerations in preaching, art, song, and popular piety. There is often a tendency for careful teaching to have develop around it a kind of luxuriant undergrowth which can be dangerous or misleading.

Some Protestants have been particularly disturbed by another title heard in connection with Mary, that of "Co-Redemptrix." On the surface it seems to give Mary a partnership, almost equal partnership, in the salvation of the human race by Christ. This strikes many as profoundly unscriptural and very shocking. When Catholics use this title, they seem to testify to their failure to see Jesus as the "sole mediator."

At least since the fifteenth century, Catholics, especially theologians, have been fascinated by the question of Mary's involvement in the work of redemption. Some writers have used the title "Co-Redemptrix," a title which the Second Vatican Council Bishops avoided as being too open to misunderstanding and too unecumenical. One modern writer has suggested the title "Associate of the Redeemer." Since the Second Vatican Council, scholars and theologians have shifted their interest away from Mary's role in redemption as "associate" to that of a symbol of the Church as a whole and prototype of the perfected Christian.

When Mary says her famous "yes" to the angel in Luke 1:38, she gives a faith response to the gift of redemption offered in her Son. It was the kind of answer that showed a readiness and a receptivity to God's will. It is mind-boggling to think that so much of later history depended on this obscure teen-ager's cooperation with God's eternal plan. The fate of humanity was linked to her in a way that few of us can claim.

In the general Protestant reaction to medieval errors, there was a strong reluctance to attribute to Mary any greater role in redemption beyond being the bearer of the Son. Once Jesus is born, on his own, so to speak, Mary's part in redemption ends. For this reason, Catholic hankering for more titles like "Co-Redemptrix" or even the blander "Associate of the Redeemer" seems misguided.

In the chapter on social justice, I observed that Catholics believe they, by Christ's grace and presence, can in modest ways help to build on earth some foreshadowings of the kingdom of peace and justice. The fullness and completion of these qualities can only come through God when he wills it. In a limited sense we could say that all serious Christians, baptized in Christ, trying to build the kingdom, are *mediating* Christ's blessings to the world. If this would be an acceptable formulation for us ordinary followers of Christ, then the idea of Mary as mediator, as associate of Christ, might be acceptable too.

Her association with Christ begins, if the Immaculate Conception logic be allowed, at her first moment of existence, since it is his redeeming grace that gives her holiness. Association continues through the Nativity, Jesus' childhood, at the first of his public works, and at Calvary. Luke also makes her part of the community of believers at Pentecost. The Catholic perspective here has drawn out the implications to associate her with the risen Savior gloriously reigning as "Queen of Heaven."

Devotional Practices

It could well be that for some Catholics, like the one I described in connection with St. Jude, a certain saint or the Blessed Virgin may in fact occupy the center stage in their religious life and understanding. Just as Catholics have arranged outdoor public processions in honor of the Blessed Sacrament or for their favorite saints, so they have done to honor the Blessed Virgin. Religious orders have taken her name as theirs, artists have painted her in a thousand different ways, medals bearing her image have been distributed widely, and song writers have given us airs to sing—some appalling, others profound.

In contemporary North America where people are familiar with the shopping mall concept, a comparison may help. We see the Catholic Church like a good shopping center. It is well-stocked with essentials but has lots of other things for peoples' wide variety of tastes. On a trip to South America recently, I had difficulty feeling much attraction for the large supply of statues of the Virgin, but I could see very quickly from the attitude of the people in those churches that Mary speaks to them of divine grace and redemption in a way that my American Catholicism might not. The key thing to recall is that abuses of devotion to Mary and the saints do not necessarily destroy the validity of the insights. It was an awareness of abuses and appreciation for the insights which led the bishops at the Second Vatican Council to make a statement about Mary. They also urged care in preaching, reform of some devotions, and an effort to make a closer link of these things to biblical themes and Christ.

Alongside many prayers to Mary, hymns and images in painting and sculpture, the most typical Catholic devotion is that of the rosary. There is an old tradition which says that the Blessed Virgin appeared to a medieval saint and handed him the rosary, urging him to use it to pray and to explain the faith by teaching with this visual aid. There is no need, however, to make this prayer-aid strictly Catholic. Saying prayers with a counter, knots on a string, or beads on a chain is a practice found in other religions.

In its Catholic form, the rosary usually consists of five groups of ten small beads, each group interrupted or divided from the other by a space on a chain or string and marked with a larger bead. A small chain or string addition is attached to the larger and has a cross and a few beads also. To say the rosary is to recite a memorized prayer, the Hail Mary, at each small bead, and the Lord's Prayer at the larger beads, keeping track by counting on the beads.

The "Hail Mary" prayer is taken in part from Luke 1:28. Older translations have the angel saying, "Hail Mary, full of grace, The Lord is with thee. Blessed art thou among women." Catholics added the phrase, "Blessed is the fruit of thy womb, Jesus. Holy Mary, Mother of God (the title given her by the Council of Ephesus in 431, A.D.), pray for us sinners now and at the hour of our death."

We are encouraged to say this rosary prayer while keeping our imagination occupied with some event in the life of Christ or Mary, the "mysteries" like Christmas or Easter or Good Friday. At the large bead we say a short doxology, "Glory be to the Father and to the Son and to the Holy Spirit, as it was in the beginning, is now and ever shall be, world without end. Amen." We then say the Lord's Prayer and return to the Hail Mary and the small beads.

With some instruction and an average memory, Catholics have had a handy, portable, all-weather review of the major events of Christianity. Since this prayer is linked to fingering beads, the blind can use it. Since it doesn't require any reading, it is useful among the illiterate. Memorized prayers are helpful anywhere, anytime, even without fingering knots or beads.

No one says that saying the rosary is obligatory; it is simply a way of prayer that has proven helpful to millions. Rhythmically and repeatedly we join the angel in saluting the mother of the Redeemer, and we think of him and his work for us. We ask her to help us be as faithful in our discipleship as she was in hers. We recite the Lord's Prayer and, when we start with the crucifix, another powerful Christian symbol, we are encouraged to recite the Apostle's Creed, a mini-textbook on Christian doctrine.

Conclusion

Catholic devotion to Mary as well as Catholic teaching about Mary arise directly from what we believe about Jesus. His identity, origin, and work are the controlling factors in what is said about Mary. She is always the lesser star moving in the orbit of the greater light. In the New Testament we find portraits of Jesus and Mary which support our views of Mary's holiness, her motherhood, and her virginity. Teachings like those of the Immaculate Conception and the Assumption emerge in the first place from what we believe about the power of Christ to renew creation, and in the second place from a meditative reading of the whole Scriptures, including the Old Testament.

Catholics believe that Mary is the greatest of the saints, and, like them, she is vitally present and interested in us, despite the fact that she went long ago to her eternal reward. She and the saints share the new life in Christ. We believe that they are all as interested in us as they were in the welfare of their own contemporaries. So we ask them to pray for us as they prayed for their own in their lifetime.

There is a delightful speaker and author, Helen Roseveare, who spent heroic years in the Belgian Congo as a medical missionary. She tells with relish the miracle accomplished by a prayer group organized by her mother in Belfast, Ireland, thousands of miles from Dr. Roseveare's Congo hospital. The hospital's staff and patients experienced absolutely astonishing gifts "out of the blue" because her mother and friends in Northern Ireland were fervently at prayer.

Catholics believe that their prayers can help their recently deceased friends, relatives, and enemies. We believe that the saints, among them the greatest, Mary, can pray for us from their places before God's throne. In them we have quite a powerful prayer chain.

14

A Closer Look at THE PAPACY

In the summer of 1950, between my freshman and sophomore years of college, my parents provided me with the money for a summer of travel in Europe. One of the vivid memories of that summer was a visit to St. Peter's Basilica in Rome for a public audience with Pope Pius XII. I arrived early to beat the crowds, and I secured a place to stand, a two foot open section at the railing of a low barricade erected by the ushers. As the hour of the pope's appearance approached, more and more people pressed in behind me and squeezed into what was left of the open space. At the scheduled hour, this immense basilica was jammed with people. As the pope entered on schedule from the rear, this vast group exploded with the sound of applause and cheers.

Unable to see to the rear of the church from my vantage spot, I realized that I could follow the chairborne pope's stately progress up the main aisle by the moving waves of sound. Brought finally to the front, he was carried in a slow circular movement around St. Peter's main altar. As pilgrims from different countries massed around the barricade and groups squeezed into the balconies, I got a closer look at his pale thin face and gold-rimmed glasses. Each group seemed eager to outdo the other in applauding or shouting, "Viva Il Papa." In the course of his remarks he inserted words of greeting or blessing in as many languages as he could muster. I was only a speck in a sea of joyous, tumultuous emotion and praise, and I felt oddly unmoved.

My lack of emotion puzzled me. Was it because we Americans are less demonstrative than Italians or Spaniards? Certainly not at basketball play-offs! Was it because the entire scene seemed unreal, as if I were at a film of the event? Was it because all the pomp and praise focused on a mere mortal?

About twenty-five years later, while working as a university chaplain in Boston, I had a chance to test whether my emotional capacities had enlarged. The city once famous for its "Irish Need Not Apply" signs went slightly crazy as it welcomed Pope John Paul II. As is his custom when visiting, the pope set aside some time for a short prayer moment with the clergy. He went directly from Boston's Logan Airport in a motorcade through some neighborhood to the cathedral where hundreds of clergy and a few nuns had gathered. Someone had brought a portable television and was monitoring the papal motorcade. As it drew near, the Secret Service men became somewhat more edgy. When the pope entered at last through the rear doors, this restive, chatty, clerical assembly began to applaud and cheer.

A priest of my acquaintance was determined to get a good look at the pope as he walked up the cathedral's main aisle. Since the view was blocked by priests, my friend stood up on the back of a pew for a look. From his height, clapping, he looked down at me and asked me why I wasn't cheering. I looked up at him and said, spoilsport that I am, "Let's wait first to see what he says!" Again, as was the case in 1950, I felt unmoved.

Whatever the reasons are for my personal reserve at such events, it is useful to remember that John Paul II, during his visit to the World Council of Churches in Geneva, Switzerland, acknowledged that the office of the papacy is one of the important barriers to church unity. In the stormy days of the Reformation, as well as in the present, the office of papacy and its incumbent have aroused very strong emotions of opposing kinds.

In this chapter I want to describe something of the Church's understanding of papacy, its authority, and its infallibility. To begin with, some correctives are in order. First, it is not Catholic teaching that anything the pope says is infallible. Occasionally one finds Catholics who sound as if they believe this. They are mistaken. Second, it is not Catholic teaching to say that the pope can make new teaching on his own, the isolated prophet pulling a brand new idea out of his own intense personal meditation and confrontation with the Holy Spirit. Popes have made some lonely pronouncements but Catholics do not have to believe that these are free of error.

Having cleared the ground of two possible misunderstandings, let us move forward to more positive statements. One of the best approaches comes from Father Richard McBrien's two volume work on Catholicism. He grounds his treatment of papal infallibility in that of the Church. In an earlier chapter I discussed the topic briefly. I will add to it here.

Infallibility of the Church

What exactly is infallibility? It is immunity from error, a charism which we believe has been given to the Church. It is a negative charism—that is, it prevents the Church from falling into serious error in its teaching of faith or morals. It does not, however, prevent church members, the pope, or others from sinning. The charism is negative in two additional ways. It does not guarantee that the Church's formulation of some truth will be the best possible, nor does it guarantee that the presentation of the teaching will be done in the most perfect way. An image may be helpful.

Many of us have had perhaps the fun of swimming in a lake or pond where there is a lifeguard on duty and an area of water roped off by buoys or floats. The guard and the roped-off area, marking rocks, or sharp drop-offs of the lake bottom function as restraints, negative controls on what we do in the area allowed for swimming. Within the secure area we can dive, splash, dog-paddle, or float. Such is the Church's charism of infallibility—over the centuries marking the danger zones and asserting its truth, even if the manner of doing it or the words chosen to assert it may be clumsy.

What assurances do we have that the Church has such a gift of infallibility? The Catholic view of this rests on the following points, listed by McBrien. In the first place, we acknowledge the authority of Jesus in proclaiming the kingdom of God. Here there is plenty of scriptural grounding. We notice in addition that in the Scriptures, Jesus' own authority to teach, preach, and cure is transmitted or conferred in some measure on the apostles or the seventy others he appointed. One example is found in Luke 10:16:

> He who hears you, hears me; and he who rejects you rejects me; and he who rejects me, rejects him who sent me.

The "Pastoral Epistles," Titus and 1 and 2 Timothy, show the early Church's concern for sound doctrine. Further, we take seriously the teaching that the Spirit has been given to the Church as a guide to all truth. John 16:13 says:

> But when he, the Spirit of truth, has come, he will teach you all the truth. For he will not speak on his own authority, but whatever he will hear he will speak, and the things that are to come he will declare to you" (Confraternity of Christian Doctrine, version).

As early as the first and second centuries, struggles erupted around Gnostic heresies and others. Thus, early Christian authorities and writers linked the reliable handing on, literally *tradition-ing,* of the apostolic teaching with the faith of the churches established by the apostles themselves. It was felt even then that the best place to see and hear correct teaching was to see and hear it in places which had been shaped by the apostles, Jesus' specially chosen witnesses.

By the middle of the third century, a special importance was being given to the faith taught by the Church at Rome. The death in Rome of both Peter and Paul, sturdy pillars of faith, helped that city gain some prominence in matters of authoritative teaching. From these modest beginnings it is, however, a long distance to current Catholic understanding of papal infallibility. We can only sketch some of this development, but before doing so, we must ask a preliminary question. *How can one observe the functioning of the Church's charism of immunity from error in matters of faith and morals?*

The best way to observe this immunity from error in matters of faith and morals is the faith and moral standards of the Church at large. "At large" means not only as extended around the world; it also means over the centuries. If we take a very negative view, checking off all the sin, war, violence, greed, and lust of millions of Christians, we might be tempted to say, "This crowd certainly has failed to grasp what Jesus taught; they have also failed to follow him." The question is not whether they have sinned. The question is whether or not this crowd understood what Jesus was asking and teaching even though they wouldn't or couldn't live it.

It can be argued as well that from time to time, in various places, sometimes by bishops and popes, at other times by priests, deacons and laity, errors were taught. Could one go further to argue that, because of this, the world lost the truth that Jesus wanted us to have? We Catholics would prefer to say that even though in various places and times erroneous ideas were taught as if they were the gospel, we believe that there were always many more places, persons, and eras when the main truths that Jesus taught were being taught. If space allowed, we would point to some of the great men and women in every age who, either by their lives or by their writings, witnessed to the truths that Jesus taught.

A well-known scholar and convert to Catholicism of the nineteenth century, John Henry Newman, did an historical study of an early heresy in the Church—Arianism. As I understand him, his research led him to the conclusion that for a time and in many places what the official leaders, namely the bishops, were teaching about Jesus was "Arianist" or heretical. Newman also discovered that in many places for many years, the orthodox understanding of Jesus was held by the laity. A prominent part of the Church was in error for a while, but the Catholic truth was cherished in the hearts, minds, and practice of the men and women at large.

John Henry Newman was not suggesting that biblical truths be decided by Sunday opinion polls among the worshipers. He was, however, pointing to a reality that deserves some attention. It was possibly that reality which the bishops of the Second Vatican Council had in mind when they spoke of a certain infallibility among the laity.

In the document *Lumen Gentium*, "Dogmatic Constitution on the Church," the bishops reminded us that the whole body of the faithful has been anointed in truth by the Holy Spirit (see 1 John 2:20, 27) and cannot go wrong in matters of belief. All of us somehow collectively embody a more than natural sense of the faith. This capacity to detect and savor the truth comes to the surface and can be relied on when "from the bishops down to the last member of the laity, there is universal agreement in matters of faith and morals."

If it can be said that there is some immunity from error, infallibility, among the members of the Church as a whole, it must also be said that there is some special character to meetings of Church leaders, especially in ecumenical councils.

The prototypical example for Catholics is found in the fifteenth chapter of Acts, which reports decisions made by an assembly of Christians debating controversial points. While the text does not say that all the believers were present, it does highlight the role of Peter and James. What is particularly striking is Acts 15:28:

> It is the decision of the Holy Spirit, and ours too, not to lay on you any burden beyond that which is strictly necessary.

This remarkable text claims the Holy Spirit's authority and approval of the decisions they are sending to Antioch, decisions shaped and debated by an assembly of prominent Churchmen (and women?). The decision taken was epoch-making, and it had repercussions over the centuries. In later centuries it is hardly a surprise that meetings of bishops, imperial diplomats, theologians, abbots, and others claimed the Holy Spirit's guidance for Church councils which shaped major doctrinal statements. Eastern Orthodox churches continue to stress the view that bishops meeting in council can give special expression to the infallibility which Jesus wanted the Church to have in teaching and transmitting the faith.

The meeting described in Acts 15 had the particular advantage that apostles and eye-witnesses of Jesus' life were present. Trying to meet a new problem that Jesus had not explicitly addressed, they were nonetheless men and women closer to understanding him and his ideas than we are. Subsequent Church councils held after the death of the eye-witnesses knew the importance of making decisions based on Scriptures. Key criteria for deciding against heretics were fidelity to the apostles' teachings which had been handed down and to the Scriptures, that teaching written down and collected over a period of 250 to 300 years. Both Catholic and Orthodox today agree on the importance of councils for giving authentic expression to the teachings of Christ.

What is not shared by Orthodox and Roman Catholics is a conviction that the papacy has a special role in the Church's exercise of the charism of infallibility. The Western Catholic feeling for this grew slowly over the centuries but came to full view and formal declaration only in 1870, at the First Vatican Council. A little background may help.

Vatican I, a short council from the fall of 1869 to the summer of 1870, had for its agenda a large body of topics—among them the role of priests, bishops, and papacy. The bishops who assembled in Rome for that council felt a special burden for their work. They were witnesses to one of the most remarkable centuries of the modern era. It was a century that saw new geographical discoveries, the invention of telegraph, steam power, railroads, and astonishing breakthroughs in chemistry and other sciences. It was also a century of new philosophical and social thought. Nationalism, democracy, and freedom of speech, press, and thought were battle slogans. Catholics of the day found themselves lining up on opposite sides of issues, especially on the importance of democracy. Some democratic movements often seemed to be anti-religious.

The council's meeting was at a crucial time in particular for the Italian peninsula. North of the papal states, political pressures were exerting an influence to annex territory long considered belonging to the papacy. South of Rome, Italian revolutionaries led by Garibaldi were organized in military units, advancing gradually toward Rome. The avowed aim was a united Italy, a modern nation instead of a peninsula owned by three major kingdoms, semi-independent city-states, and a portion ruled by the Austro-Hungarian empire.

While the bishops were meeting, a modest papal army was trying to slow the advancing liberation armies. In Rome itself, French troops on loan served as the hard-core protection of the city. Political, philosophical, social, and scientific developments which had often assaulted religion and the Bible were uppermost in the minds of the bishops. They wanted to give some stress to the authority of the papacy to teach correct doctrine in a confusing age. Many of them felt that the moment had come to give formal expression to the Catholic view of papal infallibility.

Sensing perhaps that the council might be shortened, considering the depressing news from the front lines, some of the bishops, possibly encouraged by Pius IX himself, pushed the papal infallibility topic to the head of the agenda. As discussion began, the assembly sent the matter to committee; that committee was charged with preparing a statement which the full meeting could support. The members of the committee were of one mind that there was such a thing as papal infallibility. What they were unprepared to agree on was the extent of this and its relationship to other types of infallibility. There was also the problem of timing. Was it appropriate to make such a declaration? Was it inopportune?

One historian has noted that many American bishops resisted a declaration; they were worried about the impact such a definition would have across the sea, where Protestant critics of the papacy were alive and well. The Americans were often "inopportunists," agreeing with the concept but opposed to its being proclaimed or defined at this moment. They were outnumbered by the "opportune" camp. Yet there was another struggle about the content of the declaration.

There were maximalists who sounded as if they could use a new papacy-generated infallible doctrine every decade. Opposed were minimalists, who wanted papal infallibility to be described in as limited a fashion as possible. These minimalists by and large won the day both in committee and in the whole council. Thus, the final document affirmed that the pope himself, under certain conditions, exercises "that infallibility with which the divine Redeemer willed his Church to be equipped in defining the teaching of faith and morals." The key phrase is "that infallibility which the Lord himself wanted his Church to have." Papal infallibility is thereby grounded in the Church's infallibility.

This solemn declaration was one of the council's major proclamations, but there was one more. These same bishops debated and approved another solemn decision, one that concerned papal authority to govern. As theologian Avery Dulles put it, the bishops declared that the pope "enjoys primacy of jurisdiction over all particular churches, pastors, and believers." This meant that the pope's ability to ask for obedience in appointments, supervision of the churches, and the enforcement of Church discipline was augmented. While the declaration did not demolish the governing authority of bishops, it certainly did not boost them.

Due to European political and military developments, the council's projected discussion of the role of bishops and priests never took place. Garibaldi's patriotic unification army was apparently unstoppable, and drew nearer to Rome with each passing day, and war broke out between France and Prussia in the summer of 1870. After the disastrous French defeat at the battle of Sedan, the French government could no longer afford to keep troops in Rome and they were recalled. The city was in effect wide open with only a token papal army in place. The bishops, concerned about their own people at war and unwilling to be made prisoners by Garibaldi's advancing army, began to leave the proceedings. The council slowed to a stop.

It was to be almost one hundred years before Catholic bishops from around the world could meet again to finish Vatican I's business. In the meantime, to the delight of some and the horror of others, Pope Pius IX ordered his little army to surrender to Garibaldi in order to avoid bloodshed. His troops fired one cannon shot as a token protest. Papal flags were lowered, and the pope lodged official diplomatic complaints with other governments. He then confined his movements to the restricted area of Vatican City. Without leaving Italy, he in effect went into exile.

Among Catholics, the pope's new situation aroused mainly sympathy. He was a genial man who had helped promote major evangelization and missionary work in many parts of the globe. Having been pope for an unusually long time, he knew many of the bishops then in place. He had encouraged pilgrimages and visitors to his offices in Rome, and he had provided facilities for seminarians from many countries to study in Rome.

It is perhaps in part for these reasons that Catholicism of the late nineteenth and much of the twentieth century placed such a high value on loyalty to papal authority. The council, by making the declaration on infallibility and by enhancing his governing authority, set the stage for the way subsequent Catholics came to understand the papacy. Italian patriots who annexed or "liberated" papal territory unwittingly caused others to sympathize with the pontiff. Furthermore, the manner of teaching the declaration on papal infallibility sometimes distorted the idea, often in the maximalist vein. Not every preacher, writer or seminary professor was as careful as they could have been about this. Some of the bishops who had debated and approved the document lived to witness later, unbalanced interpretations.

A legitimate exercise of papal infallibility had to be done under certain conditions. Here are the five conditions:

1. A pope must be acting in union with the faith of the Church and he must be acting as the expressor of that faith.
2. He must be acting in his capacity as chief shepherd and teacher of all the faithful, not just as bishop of Rome or in some lesser capacity.
3. He must be invoking or utilizing his supreme apostolic authority inherent in his position.
4. He must be teaching a revealed doctrine of faith or morals.
5. He must be binding definitively all the faithful.

Popular preaching, journalists, seminary professors, and writers of books, tracts, and pamphlets did not always convey as well as they should have these limiting conditions. The "maximalist" mentality which had been evident in the council surfaced afterward. As a result, some teaching amounted to what one writer has called "creeping infallibility." It was an effort to widen the umbrella after the council had narrowed it.

Papal Jurisdiction

Pope Pius IX died in his self-imposed exile. Succeeding popes continued to negotiate with the Italian government for return of property and recognition of the Catholic Church's special status in Italian society. A satisfactory settlement was not reached until the 1920s. Europe and the rest of the world would endure two major wars and some minor ones before Catholic bishops could meet again. When they did, they could not simply dust off Vatican I's forgotten agenda items. They would have to take an entirely new look at the old agenda and deal with a new one. Yet, even in a renewed church, the papacy looms as a controversial topic.

One reason is that according to our polity, the pope has universal jurisdiction over all of us. He is the chief executive officer, with the last word on many things. While he is often very content to let local or lower authorities shape actions and policies, he can theoretically overrule these either personally or through the Vatican agencies established to assist him in worldwide supervision.

Second, he is considered the chief theologian for the whole Church. Some popes are more theologically able than others, and the very position gives his views a certain natural advantage over the views of others. If these other theologians and bishops find him in agreement on some teaching or policy, they are happy to claim him as an ally. If they find him in disagreement, there is a chance for tension.

Third, although stripped of ancient territorial rights, popes retain a few acres of land which constitute an independent nation, Vatican City. Along with Luxembourg, Monaco, and other small states, the Vatican can send and receive diplomatic officers, attend international gatherings such as the United Nations or conferences on world hunger or disarmament, and can make allies or declare itself neutral. Like sovereign nations, the Vatican can issue coins, print money and postage stamps, raise an army, and have a flag. The pope is, of course, the head of Vatican State.

It is not Catholic doctrine that the pope must have territory. He is Bishop of Rome but need not have more land to supervise than the archdiocese or Rome. Catholics differ about the value of having international law status for the papacy's acreage. In my view, lacking an army, navy, air force, and missiles, the Vatican State is no threat to anybody. However, its diplomatic service has often proven very helpful in easing world tensions and in giving useful information on occasion when circumstances warrant. And it is the only spokesman at times for views which flow from the gospel.

The pope's position as chief executive officer can be a source of strain, in part because he is geographically very distant from far-flung churches under his jurisdiction. In recent years, alongside annual visits from bishops, there are regular meetings of a synod, bishops from all over the world, to help him learn of local conditions and understand what needs are becoming evident. While local churches do and must present him with their points of view, as well as their preferences in the nomination of bishops, it remains the case that major Vatican office heads, all bishops, and major policies have at least to be approved by him.

This jurisdictional authority, like any authority, can be abused. But it is also true that it can help rescue local churches from some of their own errors or narrow perspective. Where there are factions within a national or regional church, the papacy can serve to challenge people to rise above their problems, or can mediate between parties in an effort to restore harmony. We must also recognize that in various places people have suffered from abusive use of church power by local priests or bishops. Having a higher level of authority, the pope at Rome, can be a useful check on ecclesiastical arrogance.

As the Church's chief executive officer, the pope is assisted by priests, bishops, cardinals, lay folk, and nuns in various administrative positions. The administrative offices, together called "Curia," function somewhat the way any government bureau functions. Heads of the offices constitute a kind of cabinet. As Head of State, the pope appoints a Secretary of State to supervise diplomatic missions. As a teacher and theologian, he relies on experts in various fields. He has a kind of "brain-trust" to help him articulate the Church's teaching and defend it. John Paul II, the present pontiff, has also enjoyed give and take from his volunteer advisors in the Pontifical Academy of Science.

Wearing these hats, not to mention being Bishop of Rome, is a big task for anyone. Thus, the papacy can be both criticized and praised. Sometimes the heads of various Vatican agencies, relaying papal decisions or performing administrative duties, overplay their authority. Sometimes papal diplomats, like those who helped Argentina and Chile work out a recent border dispute, are praised. One of the most powerful criticisms directed against the pope as a teacher in the last twenty-five years was that arising from a papal document on birth control.

Pope Paul VI issued a document entitled *Humanae Vitae* in July of 1968, which provoked a storm of protest. I want to give some of the history of this controversy in order to help clarify papal authority in teaching and papal exercise of infallibility. During the Second

Vatican Council, the bishops were aware that, along with many other things, modern approaches to marriage were needed. What is marriage today? What are its chief purposes? Was procreation so much at the heart of marriage that artificial birth control would be an attack on its very essence?

In the course of the council, Pope Paul VI asked the bishops not to discuss marriage; instead he wanted them to allow a papal commission, established in 1963 by Pope John XXIII, to debate the teaching on marriage and to present to him their findings at a later date. Pope Paul VI enlarged the commission, which consisted of bishops, priests, and laity. Various fields of expertise were also represented on the commission—moral theology, medicine, and demography. The council ended before the commission had come to its conclusions. A journalist, Robert Hoyt, wrote that the commission had by 1966 prepared a series of documents about the nature of marriage, particularly concerning artificial birth control. The French newspaper *Le Monde* and the American Catholic weekly, *The National Catholic Reporter,* succeeded in publishing these.[2] The impression given was that a majority of the commission favored a change in the Church's position on artificial contraception.

When Pope Paul VI's formal assessment appeared in 1968, it looked as if he had gone against his own commission's recommendations: he found no reasons which were compelling enough to change the Church's teaching. There was immediately a widespread negative reaction to the papal document, partly because it appeared in the midst of a decade of rising expectations and turmoil.

It was 1968 when massive, often violent, and frequent student demonstrations took place in France, Germany, and the United States. These demonstrations demanded varying degrees of university and societal reform. It was in 1968 that James Earl Ray gunned down Martin Luther King, Jr., as he stood on the balcony of a Memphis motel. In the summer of 1968 many American cities braced for the worst and got it. It was a summer of riots, killing, looting, and arson. It was also the summer when another assassin was able to kill United States Attorney General Robert Kennedy in Los Angeles.

Three years had passed since the Second Vatican Council's dramatic opening of windows, and Catholic circles saw both enthusiasm and resistance for the changes. Some parishes seemed hopelessly mired in the past; others plunged headlong into passionate experimentation. Some congregations found themselves at odds over nuns marching in civil rights protests; others waxed indignant over the use of guitars and Broadway show tunes made Christian. This was not the kind of reflective environment in which a long-awaited and ultimately frustrating papal document could settle quietly.

The encyclical's approach to family planning, which it encouraged when done in a responsible way, outraged many men and women who had studied the work of demographers predicting global famine unless soaring birth rates were curbed. Within the Catholic community, the encyclical came as bad news for many younger, well-educated Catholics who had applauded the step into modernity made by the Vatican Council.

Yet for many other Catholics raised in the atmosphere of the earlier twentieth century, part of their faith was unquestioning loyalty to the papacy and its directives. These, laymen as well as clergy, were astonished and pained by the dissent. For these loyalists, the encyclical was near to infallible or at least the very highest church authority giving direction to a confused world.

It was bad enough that the average Catholic following these events relied mainly on forty seconds or a minute on the nightly television news or brief articles in local papers; it was bad enough that married couples struggled to absorb the news. Worse still was the reality that not too many actually studied the papal document. And worst of all, from one perspective, was the loud, public, and prominent dissent issued by a group of theology professors at the Catholic University of America in Washington, D.C. While their disagreement expressed respect for the pope's teaching authority, they criticized the way this had been exercised. No one could accuse them of not having read the encyclical! To their protest there were joined eventually more than six hundred fellow professionals.[3]

These professional teachers of theology were not alone in their dissent. Here and there there were priests who expressed their disagreement publicly, and in some places had to deal with their bishops' rebuke or punishment. A Gallup poll of those days reported that "of every hundred adult Catholics in a representative sample, fifty-four opposed the pope; only twenty-eight supported him." Laity who consulted their local priest-confessors for advice often found divided counsel. Some said that "since Rome has spoken, the issue is no longer debatable." Others reminded people that Catholic moral teaching had for many centuries insisted on the rights of consciences over all laws, civil or religious. This kind of advice left the door open for serious-minded dissidents to remain in the Church.

In the immediate shock of dissent and protest, the focus of attention was bi-polar, the pope versus the people. Unheard from were the groups of bishops in various countries. For many Catholics, bishops were seen as middlemen in the organizational chart, surely "above" the laity and dependable echoes of papal teaching. Hoyt quotes a somewhat cynical assessment by John Cogley, an American Catholic historian and journalist of the day.

> The bishops are in one hell of a spot. On the one hand, they are hung up on their loyalty to the Pope and the traditional teaching about authority that they endorsed during the council; on the other, they have a dissident laity and rebellious clergy on their hands—too numerous to purge, too independent to cow, too convinced to persuade.[4]

The bishops were soon to make their voices heard. Individual bishops, especially in areas where dissent was most explosive, had often spoken their minds, but as groups, it took time. When they did respond, some national bishops' groupings gave the impression that, while loyal to papal teaching, they had their own point of view. Four examples come to mind.

Belgian bishops mentioned that non-infallible teaching, which the papal document on birth control was, did not require absolute and unconditional adherence. Swiss bishops, while acknowledging that a papal encyclical has more theological weight than an individual opinion, reminded their people that even "papal declarations in an encyclical are not of equal weight and application." They were perhaps thinking of the difference between general moral teachings which carry great weight and the varieties of application which may not be as binding on the conscience.

Canadian bishops noted the problems raised by the encyclical and reminded people of their task of forming their consciences in light of it. In a section of their response, called "Preliminary Pastoral Considerations," designed to help priests advise the laity, they said that counselors will meet people who are basically respectful of the Church's ability to teach Jesus' doctrine, yet who feel a conflict of duties between responsible parenthood and conjugal love. If, as a result, these people feel incapable of observing the teaching on artificial contraception, they can have the certitude that they are not cut off from God.

American bishops as a group, not known for their rebelliousness, responded in November of 1968 with their own document, entitled *Human Life in Our Day.* Commending Paul VI for his teaching, they saw the pope's document as a positive statement about marital love and responsible parenthood. They liked the pope's broad Christian vision of human destiny, his holistic view of marriage, and his statement of the first principles for a sound sexuality.

They said that the encyclical was authoritative, obligatory, and authentic teaching, especially concerning contraception. They did not say that everyone or anyone practicing contraception is personally guilty of serious sin. They agreed with the pope, however, that there is objective evil in deliberately closing the marital act to the transmission of life.

To help American Catholics understand the bearing of the encyclical, the bishops pointed out that the papal statement is not making harsh or condemnatory statements about individual couples. It is rather trying to carve out a moral standard, seeing in artificial contraception an evil. In traditional Catholic moral teaching, it is one thing to say that stealing, lying, or cheating another of goods due them is an evil; it is another to say that every person who engages in these activities has a sinful intent. A person whose children are dying of starvation, according to traditional Catholic ethics, can steal bread to feed them. Killing another is a great evil, but in self-defense against an aggressor, the victim who kills would not be as accountable as a cold-blooded murderer would be. The bishops are saying that the pope is challenging Catholics to see contraception as an evil.

While the American bishops' statement was unsatisfying for many of the laity and clergy, their document made a commendable linkage between the question of transmission of life in marriage and the preservation of life in society. They spoke as a group in favor of government policies which would assist American family life. They repeated their objection to abortion, and they raised the issue of international threats to peace.

In language which would become more familiar with passing years, the bishops wrote:

> We seriously question whether the present policy of maintaining nuclear superiority is meaningful for security. There is no advantage to be gained by nuclear superiority, however it is computed, when each side is admittedly capable of inflicting overwhelming damage on the other, even after being attacked first. . . . Any effort to achieve superiority only leads to ever-higher levels of armaments as it forces the side with the lesser capability to seek to maintain its superiority. In the wake of this action-reaction phenomenon comes a decrease in both stability and security (*Human Life in Our Day*).

In short, we also view the nuclear arms race as a threat to modern life.

Recent Gallup polls and subjective evidence from Catholic laity and priests in the United States at least suggest that while more and more couples are turning to methods of natural family planning, many more have not been convinced by the papal teaching. Pope John Paul II has addressed the issue on various occasions, making it the subject of a series of talks he has given in Rome. It remains to be seen whether his continuing challenge to take an unpopular view of the matter will be effective.

I believe that the strength of Pope Paul VI's encyclical is in his effort to retain a philosophical and theological closeness for sexual activity and procreation. Contemporary, popular morality has become very tolerant of sexual activity involving marrieds or unmarrieds, between partners of the same sex or the opposite. There is even a bizarre attempt made to justify sexual activity between older persons and minors as "recreational" or "healthy." Pope Paul's encyclical does not condemn sexuality as evil, nor does it attack the pleasurable or recreational capacity of sexual intercourse. It does, however, try to keep in focus the main orientation of sexual conduct.

When Pope Paul VI's encyclical first burst on the scene, there was early speculation by some that it was an infallible teaching. A papal spokesman at the Vatican took pains to deny this, as did theologians. It was, however, an exercise in the papal role of chief teacher. Clearly, Pope Paul was not inventing any new doctrine. He tried to restate as best he could, keeping in mind some of the Second Vatican Council's new attitudes, what he saw as a line of teaching about a serious moral issue that arose to prominence in modern times.

Generations of married couples have struggled with the problems of family. There are parts of the modern world where large families are in fact the only possible way to insure financial security for aging parents. Even in American colonial times, the infant mortality rate was so high that parents in a sense "had" to have a large family if they hoped to reproduce two children who would survive until adulthood.

Better medical assistance and improved nutrition have been joined, at least in developing nations, to the technological break-throughs. There are now several reliable, cheap birth control devices. Older methods of avoiding too many mouths to feed—abortion, abandonment, and infanticide, particularly of female babies—could be abandoned.

The papal teaching on this issue, especially in Western Europe and North America, is a great challenge because so much of public opinion about sexuality, career, and family runs in a different direction. Underneath the precise issue of artificial contraception lies the deeper attitudes we have about marriage and sex. Even if Christian couples are able to appreciate and live their marriages out of the depth of their faith, it is not at all the case that they will come to the same conclusion about a specific aspect of their marriage.

It is perhaps for our grandchildren to decide whether the pope was simply prolonging a dying point of view or acting as a prophet. I know Catholics on both sides of that question. I believe that the papacy has an important role for the rest of us; it is that of balancing our views, helping us rise from some of our own narrowness. We can be enriched by an "outsider," even if we don't always agree. If we wish to call Pope John Paul II a conservative on sexual ethics, we should read him on other matters. In his encyclical on labor I find him a raving liberal.

Perhaps it is my interest in balance that leads me to take delight in a certain visual aid to describe the Church. Apart from the "Vine and Branches" imagery, I love the geodesic dome, popularized by the scientist and designer Buckminster Fuller. For anyone not familiar with it, it is both intricate and simple, a balanced, airy, and sturdy figure composed of triangles and pentagons beautifully interspersed. Some architects have used the geodesic dome for houses. The United States erected one large example in Montreal, Canada, for that city's 1967 Exposition.

Once in the doldrums of a gray New England winter, I purchased a model builder's kit of the geodesic dome for my own entertainment. I love the way its multiple sides and angles both support and are in dynamic tension with each other. A look at this little wood replica tells me that every part needs every other part, and I think of the Catholic Church in this respect.

Once I had built my model geodesic dome, I suspended it from the ceiling outside my office and noticed that over the months it began to sag here and there, due mainly to my clumsy construction methods. If one angle began to jut out too much, it pulled away from adjacent angles, and they in turn tended to sag. I couldn't help thinking of the history of the Church.

At times in its history, it seems as if the jutting angles called "church councils" controlled the life of the whole. At other times, it seems as if the protruding thrust of papacy dominated. Yet each of these points could never exist in isolation. Let the remaining angles and struts be saints and sinners, bus drivers and supermarket check-out clerks. All of us need to be together; all of us also help balance, by counter-vailing pull, those places where someone is trying to burst upward into isolation or sag downward to our mutual loss.

My image of the balanced, airy interplay of angles, the tensions of the lines and forces, helps me remember the complex interrelationships which exist in the Church. The beauty of the geodesic dome, this airy sphere suspended, is that it speaks also of a group of believers moving through history and time. My personal view is that there is currently a slow movement away from papal prominence to a phase in which bishops and laity are more active, more independent, and less passive. Would this mean a new profile for the papacy?

You may recall that the First Vatican Council had intended to discuss the role of bishops but could not. The Second Vatican Council did have the chance to restate for modern times how the bishops viewed their own role, as well as the role of priests and laity. Yet, there are areas left undefined. Of new prominence are the regional groupings of bishops—Australian, South Pacific, Peruvian, and Ugandan. What weight do their pronouncements have? Can they teach with authority?

Since the Second Vatican Council, the pope has convened synods of bishops at three year intervals or more often. This is a smaller gathering than the Second Vatican Council, as each nation sends only delegates selected by the national bishops themselves. What will the authority of this body be? Can it function as an informal "cabinet"? Beyond these questions there is the relationship between the papacy and all the bishops, as well as that between papacy and ecumenical councils (which are not necessarily meetings of bishops).

The papacy of the future, and it is possible that this future is already being shaped under our noses, may look less and less like a king or emperor over all, and more and more like a visible symbol of our union in Christ. The style of leadership and governance can and probably will become more and more collaborative.

As a teacher, the pope cannot be a mere mouthpiece for what has been previously agreed to by the whole Church. We believe the papacy has been gifted with more than that. The charism of the papal office is to express the faith committed to the whole Church, rather than the pope's personal conviction. At times, therefore, controversial or challenging papal teaching may in the passage of time find an echo in the ranks of the faithful. In this way it might win the agreement of the whole, at least eventually.

Again, I can't help thinking of the geodesic dome with its interconnected angles, sides and struts. Papal teaching is inexorably connected to the rest of us. In order to teach infallibly, the pope must align himself with the faith of the whole Church. This faith has already come to expression in Scripture and the documents of tradition. If the pope were to separate himself from this faith, which is alive in the whole body, he could become a heretic.

A new look at the papacy, precisely because it is an obstacle to ecumenical union, is producing stimulating questions and formulations in the theological discussions taking place between Anglicans and Catholics, Lutherans and Catholics, and others. "Could there be," some Protestants ask, "a permanent value to the continued existence of the office of Peter?" Could Catholics restate their view of the papacy in such a way that it would be convincing for others? Does the papacy have to function as a kind of one-man production?

Perhaps the papacy could be shaped less as a monarch and more as a prime minister or elected president. In Western governments these have real power, real authority, but it is exercised with a clearer awareness of the limits of leadership. Some critics would like the pope to rely less on his *Curia*, the heads of the major Vatican departments, and more on bishops in countries around the world. It would take more vision than I have to predict how it will be in the future. History tells me, however, that papacy has changed over the centuries, and that there is no reason to think that this institution will stop evolving in the future. Some of us clearly wish for a more rapid pace.

Conclusion

As discussed in an earlier chapter, Catholics believe in the infallibility of the Scriptures. Along with the Orthodox Catholics of the East we also believe in the infallibility of the Church, especially as articulated in certain of its great assemblies or ecumenical councils. In addition, we see a particular aspect of the Church's immunity from error articulated in the life and thought of the whole People of God. This flows from Jesus' promise to send the Holy Spirit to the Church, remaining with it in successive generations, and producing an unerring quality when there is universal agreement on faith and morals throughout the body. We also believe that definitive judgments about faith and morals are, as Francis A. Sullivan once put it:

> . . . normally the fruit of the deliberations of the whole episcopate with the pope.[5]

Catholics also believe that the pope's special call is to service on behalf of the faith and the communion of the whole People of God. This call to service, which can be one of encouragement, challenge, material assistance, or other things, includes the burden, when circumstances require, of pronouncing definitive judgments on matters of faith. These pronouncements can be as binding as are decisions of ecumenical councils.

An entire chapter on Church infallibility and papal prerogatives within this book can give the impression that our teaching about the papacy is on a par with our teaching about Jesus' divinity or resurrection. While there is an obvious connection between teaching about Jesus and the view that the Church has been given a certain immunity from error, an immunity that comes to the surface in papal declarations, it would be misleading to place papal prerogatives, papal power, or papal politics on the same plane.

It is our view that, out of love for the Church, Jesus gave himself over to death and provided as our chief shepherds successors to Peter and the apostles (1 Peter 5:4). These successors are to help and guide, but we must be careful in our thinking. Our rock-bottom convictions of faith are possible only through the grace of God. Faith is his gift. And absolute assurance about faith cannot depend on the infallibility of the pope. Nor should we think that our hope of salvation rests in the capacity to tell someone what we believe is the correct doctrine. Since the charism of papal infallibility within that of the Church has been exercised relatively infrequently, it is surely the case that our understanding of correct doctrine has come from the broader stream of Church teaching, catechism, preaching, and tradition.

With God's help, we cling without fail to the faith once delivered to the saints, and our hope for salvation lies, as it does with everyone, in the mercy of God.

NOTES

Chapter 2

1. Donald Bloesch, *Essentials of Evangelical Theology, Vol. 1: God, Authority, Salvation* (New York: Harper & Row Pubs., Inc., 1982).
2. Richard McBrien, *Catholicism, Vol. 1* (Minneapolis: Winston Press, 1980).
3. John Shea, *The Challenge of Jesus* (New York: Doubleday & Co., 1977), 11.
4. John A. O'Grady, *Models of Jesus* (New York: Doubleday & Co., 1982), 114.
5. John Paul II, "Sources of Renewal," *The Implementation of Vatican II*. P.S. Falla, transl. (San Francisco: Harper & Row Pubs., Inc., 1979), 66.
6. Ibid., 67.
7. *Maryknoll* Magazine, July 1984, 29.
8. Morris Inch, *The Evangelical Challenge* (Philadelphia: Westminster Press, 1978), 87–88.

Chapter 3

1. Monsignor J. D. Conway, *What Do They Ask about the Church?* (Chicago: Fides Press, 1958), 10.
2. Avery Dulles, S. J., *Models of the Church* (New York: Doubleday & Co., 1978), 39.
3. Leslie Rumble and Charles M. Carty, *That Catholic Church: A Radio Analysis* (St. Paul, MN: Radio Replies Press, 1954), 19.
4. Monika Hellwig, *Understanding Catholicism* (New York: Paulist Press, 1981), 116.
5. Ibid.
6. Catherine of Siena, *The Dialogue* (New York: Paulist Press, 1980), 232.
7. Walter Abbott, ed., "The Dogmatic Constitution on the Church" (*Lumen Gentium*), *The Documents of Vatican II* (New York: Guild Press, 1966), paragraph 16.
8. Ibid., paragraph 10.

9. *Rite for the Christian Initiation of Adults*, Provisional Text, United States Catholic Council, 1974.
10. Abbott, *Lumen Gentium*, paragraph 13.
11. Vatican Council Two, *Decree on the Missionary Activity of the Church* (1965), chapter 1.
12. Conway, *What Do They Ask?* 152.

Chapter 4

1. Gerald P. Fogarty, S. J., "The Quest for a Catholic Vernacular Bible in America," *The Bible in America: Essays in Cultural History*, Nathan O. Hatch and Mark A. Noll, eds. (Oxford: Oxford University Press, 1982), 163.
2. George H. Tavard, commentary and trans., *Dogmatic Constitution on Divine Revelation of Vatican II* (New York: Paulist Press, 1966), 28.
3. Abbott, *Lumen Gentium*, paragraph 7.
4. Tavard, *Dogmatic Constitution*, 65.
5. Clark Pinnock, "How I Use Tradition in Doing Theology," *TSF Bulletin, Vol. 6*, (Sept./Oct. 1982).
6. Monika Hellwig, *Tradition: The Catholic Story Today* (Dayton, OH: Pflaum Press, 1974), 41.
7. Avery Dulles, *Models of Revelation* (New York: Doubleday & Co., 1983), 44.

Chapter 5

1. John Stott, "The Biblical Basis of Evangelism," *Let the Earth Hear His Voice* (Minneapolis: Worldwide Publications, 1975), 75.
2. Pheme Perkins, "Reconciliation in the New Testament," *New Catholic World, Vol 227*, (Jan./Feb. 1984), 25–27.
3. John Paul II, *Redemptor Hominis* (Daughters of St. Paul Edition, 4 March 1979), paragraph 9.
4. Ibid., paragraph 11.

Chapter 6

1. Alexandre Ganoczy, *An Introduction to Catholic Sacramental Theology* (Ramsey, NJ: Paulist Press, 1984), 19.
2. Ibid., 24.
3. McBrien, *Catholicism*.
4. Hellwig, *Understanding Catholicism*, 136.
5. Ganoczy, *An Introduction*, 37.
6. Brian McDermott, S. J., *What Are They Saying about the Grace of Christ?* (Ramsey, NJ: Paulist Press, 1984).
7. Ibid., 22.

8. Ibid., 23.
9. McBrien, *Catholicism,* 746.
10. Charles Davis, *Sacraments of Initiation, Baptism, and Confirmation* (New York: Sheed and Ward, 1964), 92.
11. Ibid., 95.
12. Marge Alcala Isidro, "Christian Education for Evangelization in the Local Church," *Let the Earth Hear His Voice,* International Congress on World Evangelization (Minneapolis: Worldwide Publications, 1975), 596.
13. William Bausch, *A New Look at the Sacraments* (Mystic, CT: Twenty-Third Publications, 1983), 73.
14. McBrien, *Catholicism,* 753.
15. Abbott, *Lumen Gentium,* paragraph 16.
16. Ibid.
17. Davis, *Sacraments,* 106.
18. Ganoczy, *An Introduction,* 83.
19. McBrien, *Catholicism,* 756.
20. Ibid., 757.
21. Robert Imbelli, "Theological Achievements of the Second Vatican Council."

Chapter 8

1. McBrien, *Catholicism,* 1057–58.
2. Donald Bloesch, "A Call to Spirituality," *The Orthodox Evangelicals* (Nashville: Thomas Nelson Pubs., 1978).

Chapter 9

1. Ladislas Orsy, *The Evolving Church and the Sacrament of Penance* (Danville, NJ: Dimension Books, 1978).
2. Richard Gula, *To Walk Together Again: The Sacrament of Penance* (New York: Paulist Press, 1984), 203.
3. Kate Dooley, O. P., "Reconciliation in the Early Church: Lessons from History," *The New Catholic World,* (Jan./Feb. 1984), 16–21.
4. Jay Dolan, *Catholic Revivalism: The American Experience, 1830–1900* (Notre Dame, IN: Notre Dame Press, 1978), 146.

Chapter 10

1. Karl Rahner, S. J., *Meditations on the Sacraments* (New York: Seabury Press, 1977), 61.
2. Joseph Komonchak, "Church and Ministry," *The Jurist, Vol. XLIII* (Washington, D.C.: Catholic University of America, 1983), 273–288.

Chapter 11

1. Theodore Mackin, S. J., *What Is Marriage?* (New York: Paulist Press, 1982), 63.
2. J. J. Young, "Divorced and Separated Catholics," *Change in the Church, New Catholic Encyclopedia, Vol. XVII Supplement* (Washington, D.C.: Catholic University of America, 1979), 191–2.

Chapter 12

1. *The Challenge of Peace: God's Promise and Our Response* (Washington, D.C.: United States Catholic Conference Office of Publishing Services, 1983), 8.
2. Ibid., 17.
3. Howard Snyder, *Liberating the Church* (Downers Grove, IL: InterVarsity Press, 1983), 223.
4. Ibid., 222.
5. Abbott, *Lumen Gentium,* paragraph 31.

Chapter 13

1. "Preface for Holy Men and Women," *The Sacramentary* (New York: Catholic Book Publishing Co., 1974), 511.
2. "Get to Know Arminius," *The Banner* (The Reformed Church, 14 October 1985), 7.
3. Patrick J. Bearsley, S. M., "Mary: The Perfect Disciple," *Theological Studies, Vol. 41* (Sept. 1980), 461–504.
4. Dom John Main, A. S. B., *The Other-Centredness of Mary* (Montreal: The Benedictine Priory of Montreal, 1983), 5.
5. Doris Donnelly, "Maternity's Raw Faith," *Sojourners* (Nov. 1983), 23–24.
6. Ibid., 24.
7. Louis Bouyer, *Seat of Wisdom* (Chicago: Henry Regnery and Co., 1965), 104.
8. J. W. Langlinais, "Assumption of Mary," *The New Catholic Encyclopedia, Vol. 1* (Washington, D.C.: Catholic University of America, 1967).

Chapter 14

1. Avery Dulles, "Toward a Renewed Papacy," *The Resilient Church* (New York: Doubleday & Co., 1977).
2. Robert C. Hoyt, *The Birth Control Debate* (Kansas City, MO: National Catholic Reporter, 1968).
3. Ibid., 7.
4. Ibid., 147.
5. Francis A. Sullivan, S. J., *Magisterium: Teaching Authority in the Catholic Church* (Ramsey, NJ: Paulist Press, 1983), 96.